TEMPERAMENT

Astrology's Forgotten Key

by
Dorian Gieseler Greenbaum M.A.

The Wessex Astrologer

Published in 2005 by
The Wessex Astrologer Ltd
4A Woodside Road
Bournemouth
BH5 2AZ
England

www.wessexastrologer.com

Copyright © Dorian Gieseler Greenbaum

Dorian Gieseler Greenbaum asserts the moral right to be recognised as the author of this work.

ISBN 190240517X

A catalogue record of this book is available at The British Library

No part of this work may be reproduced or used in any form or by any means without the express permission of the publisher. Reviewers may quote short sections.

Acknowledgments

A strange thing happened in the writing of this book. During every part of my research, writing and revisions, I was mysteriously led to people who came to offer help at just the right moment; and they in turn led me to others who were equally helpful and supportive. This round robin of benefactors includes the following:

Joseph Crane, who read the first and subsequent drafts and lent an ear on numerous occasions as I worked through problems.
Robert Hand, whose work on temperament inspired me to do my own research, and who gave Garry Phillipson my email address.
Garry Phillipson, whose interest in temperament led him to me, and whose suggestions, ideas and all-around good sense made this book better. Garry also showed my manuscript to Patrick Curry.
Patrick Curry, who used my manuscript in the readings for his course "Astrology as Ancient Psychology" at Bath Spa University College, and who was kind enough to write the preface for this book.
Bernadette Brady, who found me a publisher and also contributed valuable suggestions to improve the scope of the book.
John Frawley, whose work with temperament helped me to sharpen my own.
Nadine Harris, who contributed an eagle editorial eye and rearranged some of my tables.
Graeme Tobyn, who went out of his way to meet with me one evening, whose book on Culpeper is an inspiration, and who alerted me to the existence of Kant's temperament theories and to the book *Saturn and Melancholy*.
Tom Callanan, who gave excellent advice on the third part of the book.
Peter Standaart who, out of the goodness of his heart, created a software program using my temperament formula, and was my own personal cheerleader.
Anne Lathrop, who created a temperament scoring table for me.
Michael Fagan, who lent me the unpublished Marc Edmund Jones material on temperament.
Chantal Allison, who helped me negotiate with the Bibliothèque Nationale de France.
Margaret Cahill, who saw something good in my original manuscript.
The Waldorf students, parents and teachers, who gave me something to study.
My astrology students, whose insightful questions improved my own thinking and writing.
And finally, always, to Don, who provides constant love and support.

Permissions

I am grateful for permission to use material from the following:

Bibliothèque Nationale de France, for permission to use the cover and frontispiece art, taken from their manuscript of Bartholomaeus Anglicus, *On the Properties of Things*.

Shepheard-Walwyn, London, for permission to quote from *The Letters of Marsilio Ficino*, vol. 2, p. 33, 1978.

Inner Traditions International, Rochester, VT 05767, www.InnerTraditions.com, for permission to quote from *Meditations on the Soul: Selected Letters of Marsilio Ficino*, 1997.

Penguin Books Ltd., London, for permission to quote from Jonathan Barnes, translator, *Early Greek Philosophy* (Penguin Classics, 1987).

Quotations from the following are reprinted by permission of the publishers and the Trustees of the Loeb Classical Library, Cambridge, Mass.: Harvard University Press. The Loeb Classical Library ® is a registered trademark of the President and Fellows of Harvard College.

> Ptolemy: *Tetrabiblos*, Loeb Classical Library Vol. 435, translated by F.E. Robbins, 1940.
> Hippocrates: *Vol. IV*, Loeb Classical Library Vol. 150, translated by W.H.S. Jones, 1931.
> Aristotle: *Vol. III*, Loeb Classical Library Vol. 400, translated by E.S. Forster, 1955.
> Manilius: *Astronomica*, Loeb Classical Library Vol. 469, translated by G.P. Goold, 1977, rev. 1992.

Floris Books, Edinburgh, Scotland, for permission to use the chart on p. 55 from Marieke Anschütz, *Children and their Temperaments*, 1995.

Rudolf Steiner Press, London, for permission to use the charts on pp. 54-55 and quote from Gilbert Childs, *Understand Your Temperament!*, 1995, 1998.

Anthroposophic Press, Herndon, VA and Great Barrington, MA, for permission to use the chart on p. 52 and quote from *Discussions with Teachers* and *Anthroposophy in Everyday Life*.

Robert Hand, for permission to reproduce the diagrams on pp. 4 and 19; and to quote from his translations of Bonatti, *Liber Astronomiae Book III*; Montulmo, *On the Judgment of Nativities*, Part 2; and an unpublished translation of Garcaeus, *Astrologiae Methodus in qua secundum doctrinum Ptolemaei...*, 1574.

Kristina Shapar, for permission to quote from her translation of *Ramon Lull: Treatise on Astronomy*, published by The Golden Hind Press, Berkeley Springs, WV, 1994.

Robert Zoller, for permission to quote from his translation of Bonatti, *Liber Astronomiae Books I and II*, published by The Golden Hind Press, Berkeley Springs, WV, 1994.

Nicholas Goodrick-Clarke, for permission to quote from *Paracelsus: Essential Readings*, published by North Atlantic Books, Berkeley, CA, 1999.

Rudolf Steiner College Press, Fair Oaks, CA, for permission to use the charts in Appendix G and quote from *The Temperaments in Education* by Roy Wilkinson, 1977, 1994.

Table of Contents

List of Figures and Tables

Preface

Introduction

Part 1 - Theory and History of Temperament	1
Part 2 - Temperament Theory Applied: The Waldorf Study	57
Part 3 - Using Temperament in Modern Astrological Practice	73
Appendix A - Determining Temperament Etc. Through the Ages	141
Appendix B - Robert Burton and *The Anatomy of Melancholy*	150
Appendix C - Ramon Lull's Descriptions of Temperament	154
Appendix D - Nicholas Culpeper's Descriptions of Temperament	157
Appendix E - Poems on Temperament	159
Appendix F - Culpeper's Compound Temperaments	160
Appendix G - Roy Wilkinson's Temperament Charts	163
Appendix H - Birthcharts of the Children used in the Waldorf Study	165
Appendix I - Names, Temperaments and Temperament Factors	201

List of Figures and Tables

Figures

		Page
1.	Seasons correlated with qualities and elements	4
2.	Schoener's Qualities, Elements, Seasons, Planets, Humors	4
3.	One example of how Aristotle's theory of the elements works	11
4.	Ramon Lull's System of Elements and Qualities	29
5.	Jungian Functions	47
6.	Functions Correlated with Qualities	48
7.	Steiner's Circle of Temperaments	52
8.	Childs' Temperament Diagram	55
9.	Anschütz's Greek Humors Diagram	55
10.	Qualities of the Planets (A Possible Schema)	78
11.	Ptolemy's Moon Phases	81
12.	Lilly's Moon Phases	82
13.	Lilly's Worked Temperament Example	90

Tables

1.	Ptolemy's Assignment of Qualities (*Tetrabiblos*, Book I)	19
2.	The Nature of Signs According to Abu Mashar	24
3.	The Nature of Planets According to Abu Mashar	24
4.	The Qualities of the Signs According to Al Biruni	25
5.	The Nature of the Planets According to Al Biruni	26
6.	Qualities of the Planets, by phase (Garcaeus)	37
7.	Qualities of the Moon, by phase (Garcaeus)	37
8.	Qualities of the Sun, by phase (Garcaeus)	37
9.	Marc Edmund Jones' Temperament System	49
10.	Steiner's correlation of body and temperament.	51
11.	Childs' Mottoes, Theme Tunes and Temperaments	54
12.	Temperament Matches by Individual Factors (counting compound temperaments equally)	65
13.	Temperament Matches by ASC sign, Moon sign, ASC ruler, ASC almuten, Moon ruler, Season	66
14.	Temperament Matches by ASC sign, Moon sign and Season	66
15.	Qualities of the Sun by Season and Sign	80
16.	Analysis of Temperament in the Natal Chart	88

How to Recognize the Temperaments	Appendix G	163
Reactions of Children to various situations according to Temperament	Appendix G	164
The Golden Rules for treating Children according to Temperament	Appendix G	164
Names, Temperaments and Temperament Factors	Appendix I	201

Notable Charts	Page
Allen, Woody	119
Astaire, Fred	112
Blair, Tony	96
Branagh, Kenneth	128
Burton, Robert	153
Bush, George W.	92
Christie, Agatha	121
Cleese, John	107
Da Vinci, Leonardo	124
Ficino, Marsilio	34
Frank, Anne	110
Harrison, George	102
Jung, Carl Gustav	45
Limbaugh, Rush	126
Lindbergh, Charles	117
Margaret, Princess of England	115
McCartney, Paul	136
de Saint-Exupéry, Antoine	105
Schopenhauer, Arthur	131
Simon, Paul (singer)	99
Steiner, Rudolf	50

Preface

This is a wonderful book. Not only deeply researched and carefully written but thoroughly enjoyable, it enriches our collective cultural and intellectual life. The primary context for this contribution is astrology, that tradition which in its millennia-long history has survived so many 'deaths' and rebirths to flourish anew. But Greenbaum's book also reaches out beyond astrology and enables new connections.

Fittingly for such an ancient subject, its starting-point is some very old connections between astrology, philosophy and medicine. They are also appropriate, however, because this is a time when the fundamental pieties of modernity are coming into serious question. That universal quantitative stuff is real whereas multiple particular qualities and forms are not; that true knowledge is 'objective' not 'subjective'; that a sharp division between world and self, matter and mind, outer and inner, can be sustained: all this not only can but must now be doubted. So it is not surprising that part of this process involves returning to premodern insights with deep roots. Actually, as Bruno Latour points out in *We Have Never Been Modern*, we never stopped *living* as if sensuous particularities were real and qualities were shared by objects and subjects alike; rather we learned to pretend it was not so. Greenbaum's book invites us to re-cognize a lived and living world.

Of course, that world – including temperament – ultimately resists complete understanding (which is why modernist analysis, which refuses to acknowledge any limits, turns it into a dead world in which life is a tiny and meaningless accident). But discussing and thinking about experience is part of being human, so think about it we will; and concerning temperament, Greenbaum shows us a subtle, elegant and rich way in which to do so, and perhaps go as far as we can. I also welcome her return to a deeper, wider and more humane understanding of 'research' – one which, instead of fruitlessly trying to eliminate human participation, welcomes it.

In another perspective, this book is one of the fruits of a renaissance within astrology, sometimes called the traditional revival, that began in the 1980s. Increasing dissatisfaction with modern psychological astrology, marked by a smugly insular emphasis on the supposedly new and progressive, coincided with astrologers' rediscovery of their ancient Greek, medieval and early modern roots. This book adds greatly to making that material available, of course, but it also reflects a new maturity. Greenbaum doesn't reject modern astrology so much as skilfully enriches it, making available to astrologers a fertile new synthesis. (Actually, again, the best psychological astrologers were always aware of working within a tradition with premodern Hermetic and neoPlatonic origins, as indeed was Jung himself.)

Finally, *Temperament and Astrology* also contributes to another kind of cultural conversation: the increasing dialogues between practising astrologers and scholars studying astrology, to their mutual enrichment, that has been taking place in the last two decades or so. The rediscovery I just mentioned abounds with instances of this process, and it is increasingly taking place within as well as outside university departments: for example, the Sophia Centre at Bath Spa University College, the Study of

Religions Department at the University of Kent, the Warburg Institute in London, the Humanities Department of the University of Amsterdam, and Kepler College. This development is greatly to be welcomed, and as both practitioner and scholar of astrology, Dorian Greenbaum is perfectly placed to add to it. With this book she already has, but I suspect (and hope) it is only the beginning!

Patrick Curry November 2004

Man as Affected by the Humors

From Bartholomaeus Anglicus, *On the Properties of Things*
15th Century, France, Le Mans
Held by the Bibliothèque Nationale de France

Introduction

> His life was gentle, and the elements
> So mix'd in him that Nature might stand up
> And say to all the world, "This was a man!"
> — Shakespeare, *Julius Caesar*, Act V, Scene 5

It is human nature to want to put things into categories, whether they be as broad as animal, vegetable and mineral or as narrow as Delicious versus Macintosh apples. We are no different in our urge to categorize human beings in every way possible. Jung says it is because we want to "bring order into the chaos,"[1] and he may very well be right. We have been classifying humans physically, mentally and psychologically for thousands of years. One kind of classification, temperament, has been used by scientists, doctors, philosophers and astrologers for over 2000 years. What is the relationship between temperament and astrology? What is temperament, and how did the theories about it evolve? What is the history of temperament in western civilization? How has it been used in modern times? How can we use it to better understand ourselves today? All these questions will be explored in the following pages.

The first part of this book will be devoted to a definition of temperament, discussion of the four qualities and the elements, and a look at the theory and history of temperament in the west. The second part will describe a study I did correlating Rudolf Steiner's theories of temperament in Waldorf education to the astrological birthchart. The third part will provide some ideas for using temperament in modern astrological practice, along with examples. All three parts will be useful in giving a complete picture of the nature of the relationship between temperament and astrology.

---

1. C.G. Jung, trans. Baynes, *Psychological Types, Collected Works Volume 6* (Princeton, N.J.:Princeton University Press, 1971), p. 531.

Part 1
Theory and History of Temperament

The temperament theory and analysis which have come down to us in the modern western world began with the Greeks. From Empedocles' first hypotheses about the components of the cosmos, to the latest websites devoted to "modern" temperamental analysis, temperament has been a subject of continual fascination. Astrologers were early to join the bandwagon, and from classical to modern times they have studied temperament as a component of chart analysis, often using complex formulae. Given astrology's strong roots in Greek culture and philosophy, this is not surprising. The doctrine of temperament alluded to by Hippocrates, developed by Galen and used by Ptolemy persisted through medieval astrology and into William Lilly's time. What is temperament, and what are its components? Before we explore the history and theory of temperament, these are the questions that must be answered.

What is Temperament?

It might be easier to define temperament by what it is not. In the first place, it is not the same as personality, although personality can incorporate parts of someone's temperament in its expression. Personality is shaped by both internal and external factors, whereas temperament is entirely innate. Temperament is not character, though in some ways the two concepts have a commonality. Character can refer to the distinctive features or qualities that distinguish one form from another, and so is innate like temperament; but it also refers, at least in modern English connotation, to the moral nature of a person. The original Greek meaning of the word χαρακτήρ (*charaktēr*) is "stamp," as in something used to make an impression in wax or metal. So character is an impression on the person which, in that connotation, implies something from without (parental or societal) rather than within.

Temperament, by contrast, is *inherent*. We are born with our temperaments, and while there may be overlays of one temperamental style or another during our lives, what we get is what we keep. A card-carrying phlegmatic does not suddenly become a raging choleric. Any mother of more than one child can see temperamental differences in her offspring almost from the moment of birth, qualities which only become more pronounced as her children age. Such differences have even been the subject of books on child development.[2] So temperament really has to do with a person's nature or disposition.

---

2. Dr. T. Berry Brazelton, *Infants and Mothers: Differences in Development* (New York: Dell Publishing Co., revised edition, 1989) is one of those who talks about the temperamental styles of infants, though he doesn't use that word.

As a primary phlegmatic, I can admire the innate social skills of my daughter the sanguine. I might acquire some of those social skills through my interactions with the outside world, but I have to learn them; they are not a part of my nature. Our inborn temperament is also what we fall back on when faced with a new situation: are we the take-charge, choleric type who rushes in to meet every new experience with gusto? Or the quiet melancholic, who hangs back and analyzes and would rather die than be the life of the party? Are we sanguine, looking to make new friends and social contacts, or phlegmatic and just want to be left alone?

That I can even use these words today and know that many people will know what I mean is a testimony to the enduring ideas behind temperament theory. Even though we now tend to think of choleric as angry, melancholic as depressed, sanguine as happy-go-lucky and phlegmatic as lethargic, these words are still very much in our vocabulary.

If we go back into the past, we can discover the origins behind our modern use of these temperamental words. The word temperament comes from the Latin *temperamentum*, which means "mixture." But a mixture of what? A "temperament," according to the Greeks who evolved the theory, is a mixture of qualities that combine to form elements in physics and humors in medicine. There are four qualities: hot, cold, wet and dry. There are also four elements: fire, earth, air and water; and four humors – choler or yellow bile, melancholer or black bile, blood and phlegm. The Greeks looked for a state of equilibrium or balance among these four elements and humors: such a person was said to be well-mixed, or well-tempered. (Such a phrase even comes into modern English when we speak of someone with a "good temper.") It was important to know a person's temperament so that imbalances could be treated.

The ideas about temperament evolved from ideas about the nature of the world, and the original building blocks of the world. The Greek philosophers and physicists (the word "nature" is φύσις, *phusis*, in Greek) of the second half of the first millennium BCE developed the theories out of which temperament arose, using the qualities and the elements. It will be useful now to take a look at what the qualities and elements are, what they represent and how they act.

Hot, Cold, Wet and Dry

Hot and cold are active principles – that is, capable of initiating change. Hot, by heating, can also bring about dryness; cold, by cooling, can bring about moisture. In Greek thought, they are very much on a continuum; Galen, for instance, was always very aware that these states were relative, so "hotter than" and "colder than," based on each quality's proportion in the mixture.[3] Robert Hand says that hot increases the energy level of a system, while cold decreases it.[4] Thus hot tends to speed things up while cold tends to slow things down. Wet and dry are considered passive, in that they are initiated by the actions of hot and cold. Wet has no specific form, and can take on the form of whatever it is in; it tends to connect things. It is fluid, soft and flexible. Dry can be easily confined within its limits, and

---

3. Claudius Galen, *De temperamentis (Περὶ κράσεων) Libri III* (Stuttgart: B.G. Teubner, 1969), p. 1 ff.
4. Lecture March 25, 1995, Lexington, MA. Acknowledgement is due to Rob for many of the ideas expressed in this section.

tends to separate things. It is structured, brittle and rigid. Wetness is associated with growing, dryness with manifesting. Heat and moisture are energy building and life affirming; just think of the explosive growth in the late spring when rain and warming temperatures combine in a riot of fertility. Cold and dryness are energy decreasing, where connections are being slowed and broken, just as autumn's cooling combines with the lack of rain to begin the slowing down of the life cycle.

English is full of expressions that we use, without even thinking about them, to characterize people as hot, cold, wet or dry. A person who gets things going and has a lot of vitality is a "hot ticket." Someone who seems to have no emotion is a "cold fish." When we're "hot under the collar" we need to take some time and "cool off." The opening act at a show "warms up" the crowd and "breaks the ice." A person who's "all wet" has probably made connections where none exist, while a "dry wit" has made precise correlations that are funny because of their precision. Completely dry is "dry as a bone." A "dry stick" might be told to "go jump in a lake," that is, loosen up and get more wet. A "hot streak" has a lot of activity that increases; a "cold streak" doesn't. Alcoholics go to rehab to "dry out."

It should be pointed out that there are gradations in these qualities. Thus, a pillow is wet because of its squishyness, and a chair dry because of its hardness; but a wooden chair will be wetter than a metal chair. A pool can feel cold when we first go into it, but after a few minutes can feel warm, even though it is still relatively cold. Walkers heat themselves less than runners, but both are engaging in energy-increasing, thus hot activity. Qualities can also be applied to things that are not necessarily physically hot, cold, wet or dry. Salsa music is hot and wet; Philip Glass is cold and dry. "New age" thinking tends to be wet; Kant is definitely dry!

Fire, Earth, Air and Water
How do the four elements fit with the qualities? In Aristotle's system (about which more later), the qualities generate the elements, and when we put them together we can see definite correlations with the seasons. Hot and wet combined make air, hot and dry make fire, dry and cold make earth and cold and wet make water.[5] Thus, using a circle with the qualities dividing it into quadrants, air becomes the midpoint between hot and wet, fire the midpoint between hot and dry, earth the midpoint between cold and dry, and water the midpoint between cold and wet. The diagram[6] on the next page shows how this works. Drawn like this, we can also immediately see that, in correlating this to the seasons and to the signs, the air point is 15 Taurus or Beltane, the fire point is 15 Leo or Lammas, the earth point is 15 Scorpio or Samhain and the water point is 15 Aquarius or Imbolc (Candlemas).

---

5. The Stoic system is different; we will discuss it later in this book.
6. Diagram after Robert Hand.

4   Temperament: Astrology's Forgotten Key

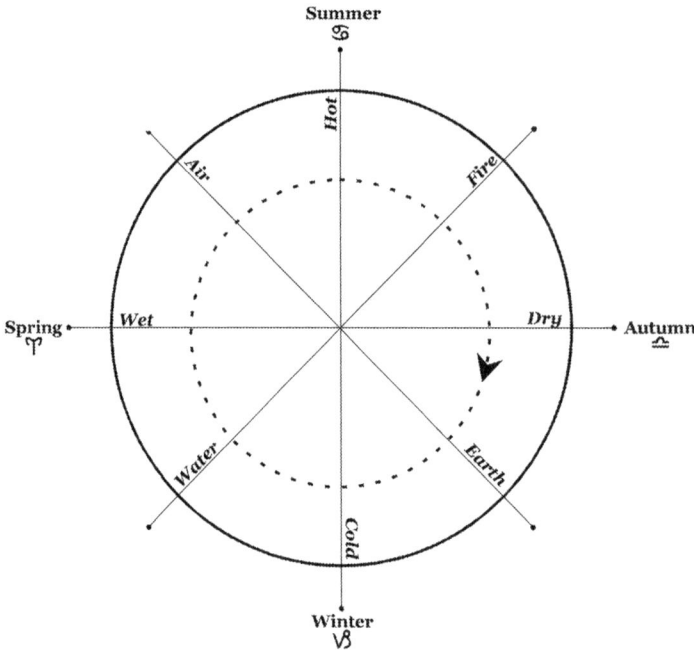

Figure 1. Seasons correlated with Qualities, Elements, Seasons, Planets

The following diagram from Schoener's *Opusculum Astrologicum*[7] arranges the diagram somewhat differently, assigning qualities to the seasons and planets, and also their associated humor. The humors

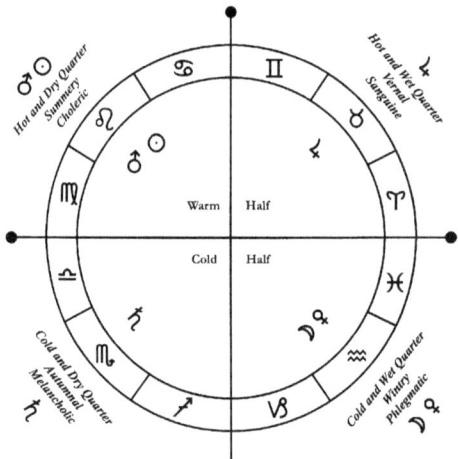

Figure 2. Schoener's Qualities, Elements, Seasons, Planets, Humors

---

7.   Schoener, Johannes, *Opusculum Astrologicum* trans. Robert Hand (Berkeley Springs, W.Va.: The Golden Hind Press, 1994), p. 13.

physically correlate with the qualities assigned to them: blood is hot and wet, yellow bile hot and drying, black bile cold and drying and phlegm cold and wet.

Now that we can see how temperaments were assigned to planets, seasons and qualities, we can also assign them to the elements: sanguine to air, choleric to fire, melancholic to earth and phlegmatic to water. So the sanguine, as an air type, combines the active and connecting qualities of hot and wet, and is sociable and friendly, but not tending to remain with one thing for too long. Cholerics, the fire types, mix hot and dry. They have a strong will, ambition, and even some of the irascibility for which their temperament is known (they don't care if they are the most popular, like the sanguines, as long as they can be in charge). The melancholic, earthy, cold and dry, is the detail person, deliberate, logical but also with depressive tendencies. Phlegmatics, watery and mixing cold and wet, are stolid and emotionally contained but with a strong feeling nature. Physically, sanguines tend to be fairly well-proportioned (the typical mesomorph), cholerics stocky and well-defined, melancholics on the tall side and somewhat bony and phlegmatics well-padded. Aging usually accentuates these physical characteristics.

The above discussion has been just a brief overview of the components of temperament, to provide a beginning familiarity with the concepts to be discussed and analyzed in the rest of the book. Now, we shall explore the history and theory of temperament, from its roots in Greek philosophy to its offshoots in modern temperament typers like Jung.

The Roots of Temperament: Science, Philosophy, Medicine

Greeks before Empedocles

John Burnet[8] asserts that Greek cosmology, and later physics and philosophy, were strongly influenced by the changes of the seasons as a cycle of growth and decay, leading to the observation of pairs of opposites at war with each other: hot against cold, wet against dry.[9] Recognition of these qualities appears very early in the minds of the Greek thinkers. The search for a primary "something" from which these opposite qualities arose was an ongoing concern. The word used for this "something" is φύσις (*phusis*), which is often translated as "nature" (and from which, of course, our word "physics" derives), but according to Burnet, its original meaning is "stuff."[10] The search for a primeval *phusis*, and further exploration of the nature of the qualities, led to the development of humoral and temperamental theory.

Thales, living in the 6th century BCE, was the first of the Greek philosophers to identify water as the primal stuff: "He supposed that water was the first principle of all things."[11] Aristotle says that Thales came to this conclusion because:

---

8. Author of *Early Greek Philosophy*, first published in 1920; he is considered an early authority on this subject.
9. John Burnet, *Early Greek Philosophy* (Cleveland, O.:Meridian Books, The World Publishing Co., 1969), Introduction, Section VI, p. 8.
10. Ibid., Section VII, p. 10.
11. Diogenes Laertius, *Lives of the Philosophers*, quoted in Jonathan Barnes, *Early Greek Philosophy* (London:Penguin Books, 1987), p. 67. All quotes from this work are reproduced by permission of Penguin Books Ltd.

"the nourishment of everything is moist and that heat itself comes from this and lives by this (for that from which anything comes into being is its first principle) – he came to this belief both for this reason and because the seeds of everything have a moist nature, and water is the natural principle of moist things."[12]

Anaximander, who followed Thales chronologically (fl. ca. 550 BCE), also based his philosophy on finding a first principle, but it was not any of the four qualities or elements, but something else, which is "boundless."[13] However, it is clear that he used the four qualities as a taking-off point for his philosophical ruminations. The "boundless" separated off to form a world first differentiated into two opposites, hot and cold, from which our world eventually arises.[14]

Anaximenes (fl. ca. 540 BCE), a younger contemporary of Anaximander, considered the first principle to be "breath" (*pneuma*). He treats hot and cold thus, according to Plutarch:

"Or should we, as old Anaximenes thought, treat the hot and cold not as substance but rather as common properties of matter which supervene upon changes? For he says that matter which is concentrated and condensed is cold, while that which is rare and *slack* (that is the word he uses) is hot."[15]

Pythagoras (fl. 530 BCE) does not specifically consider the qualities in his philosophy, yet his ideas of combining opposites in a harmonious mixture (κρᾶσις, *krasis*) led to ideas later incorporated into the doctrine of temperaments ("temperament" is the Latin-derived cognate of the Greek κρᾶσις (*krasis*), which means "mixture," referring to harmonious balances among hot, cold, wet and dry).[16] Without such ideas, temperament theory would not have developed as it did, and phrases like "good-tempered person" would be meaningless.

Xenophanes of Colophon (fl. ca. 530 BCE) says "all things are earth and water that come into being and grow."[17] Heraclitus, remembered by Philosophy 101 students as the philosopher who said "Everything flows" (*Panta rhei*), also said "cold things become warm, and what is warm cools; what is wet dries, and the parched is moistened."[18] Thus, as Pythagoras, he also believed in the attunement (*harmonia*) of opposites. He also considered that opposites were not truly opposite, but two sides of the same process;[19] neither would be possible without the other.

"If there were no cold, there would be no heat; for a thing can only grow warm if, and in so far as, it is already cold. And the same thing applies to the opposition of wet and dry."[20]

---

12. Aristotle, *Metaphysics* 983b 17-27, quoted in Barnes, op. cit., p. 63.
13. Burnet, op.cit., Anaximander, Section 13, p. 53.
14. Ibid., Anaximander, Section 19, p. 62.15 Plutarch, The Primary Cold 947F, quoted in Barnes, op. cit., p. 79.
15. Plutarch, *The Primary Cold* 947F, quoted in Barnes, op. cit., p. 79.
16. Pythagorean ideas of harmony based on the intervals of the musical scale eventually resulted in the 'tempering' of the musical scale in the development of western music – consider Bach's pieces for an instrument so regulated, *The Well-Tempered Klavier*.
17. Xenophanes, Fragment 29, quoted in Burnet, op. cit., Xenophanes of Colophon, Section 57, p. 120.
18. Heraclitus, Fragment 39, quoted in Burnet, op. cit., Heraclitus of Ephesus, Section 65, p. 136.
19. Burnet, op. cit., Heraclitus of Ephesus, Section 80, p. 165.
20. Ibid.

This suggests the idea that qualities can change from one to the other in a circular process, an idea later expounded by Aristotle. This concept also became well-developed by astrology.

Burnet calls Alcmaeon of Croton the "founder of empirical psychology."[21] Alcmaeon followed Pythagoras in his view of things occurring in opposite pairs; and he believed that health was achieved by balance among the powers in the body – hot and cold, wet and dry, bitter and sweet, etc. It was the imbalance of one of these that created illness. We now begin to see the application of the qualities to functions of the body, which will become more pronounced in the writings of Empedocles first, and then Hippocrates, Aristotle, and later Galen.

Empedocles

It is with Empedocles that the full-fledged theory of the elements as the four building blocks of matter arises. Empedocles of Acragas, in Sicily, flourished in the middle of the 5th century BCE. He was a politician and also a religious teacher who followed some of the tenets of the Pythagoreans (although according to the Sicilian historian Timaeus, he was expelled from the Pythagorean Order for "stealing discourses").[22] He is best known, however, for founding a medical school which still existed in the time of Plato.[23] Plato and Aristotle, to say nothing of Hippocrates, were clearly influenced by his work.

Empedocles does not use the word "element" (Greek στοιχεῖον, *stoicheion*) in his writings: he refers to fire, air, earth and water as the "roots" (ῥιζώματα, *rhizōmata*) of all things.

"Hear first the four roots of all things: shining Zeus, life-bringing Hera, Aidoneus, and Nestis, who waters with her tears the mortal fountains."[24]

Theophrastus says Zeus is fire, Hera earth, Aidoneus air and Nestis water;[25] though even in antiquity there was disagreement about which element was assigned to which deity.[26] In any case, elsewhere Empedocles clearly talks about fire, earth, air and water: "…out of Water and Earth and Air and Fire mingled together, arose the forms and colors of all those mortal things…"[27] In Empedocles' view, it is Love and Strife which join and separate the "roots," later called elements by Plato and Aristotle. He considers the roots to be equal in strength and ultimate: that is, they cannot be further divided. They were identified with the hot, cold, wet and dry in Empedocles' school of medicine,[28] which paved the

---

21. Ibid., Alcmaeon of Croton, Section 96, p. 194.
22. Ibid., Empedocles of Acragas, Section 10, p. 200.
23. Ibid., Section 101, p. 201.
24. Empedocles, Fragment 6, quoted in Burnet, op. cit., Empedocles of Acragas, section 105, p. 205; and Barnes, op. cit., p. 174.
25. Peter Kingsley, *Ancient Philosophy, History and Magic: Empedocles and the Pythagorean Tradition* (Oxford:Oxford University Press, 1995), p. 14.
26. Peter Kingsley, op. cit., makes a rather convincing case for Zeus as air, Hera earth, Hades fire (given the amount of volcanic activity in Sicily) and Nestis water; see especially Chapter 4, "The Riddle."
27. Empedocles, Fragment 71, quoted in Burnet, op. cit., Empedocles of Acragas, Section 105, pp. 215-6.
28. Burnet, op. cit., Empedocles of Acragas, Section 101, p. 201, though he does not say exactly how they are correlated.

way for the more complex theories of Aristotle about the connections between the elements and the qualities.

Hippocrates

Hippocrates, following in the footsteps of Empedocles, devised the system of humors which evolved into temperament theory. He took the ideas of Empedocles and earlier philosophers about the formation of the world from the four elements and/or qualities and, perhaps inspired by Empedocles' medical school, formulated a theory that applied the elements/qualities to the human body. The components of the macrocosm (world) were correlated to the microcosm (body). As we will see, astrologers would do the same thing with their adoption of temperament theory.

Hippocrates of Cos was born about 460 BCE, which puts him in the generation after Empedocles. That he knew of Empedocles' work is certain, as he mentions him by name in his treatise *On Ancient Medicine*. Hippocrates has extended the theories of Empedocles and applied his roots of fire, earth, air and water to the four humors, or fluids, of the body: yellow bile, black bile, blood and phlegm. Further, he applies the qualities via the seasons to the humors, so that phlegm, which he associates with winter, is wet and the coldest humor; blood increases in the spring, which is wet and warm; yellow bile is associated with the hotness and dryness of summer (phlegm is at its weakest here); and black bile correlates with autumn, which is dry and beginning to cool (blood is at its lowest level here). He says:

> "All these substances, then, are always present in the body, but as the year goes round they become now greater and now less, each in turn and according to its nature. For just as every year has its share in all of them, the hot, the cold, the dry and the moist – none in fact would last for a moment without all the things that exist in this universe, but if one were to fail all would disappear, for they are all mutually interdependent. In the same way, if any of these primary bodily substances were absent from man, life would cease. In the year sometimes the winter is most powerful, sometimes the spring, sometimes the summer and sometimes the autumn. So too in man sometimes phlegm is powerful, sometimes blood, sometimes bile, first yellow, and then what is called black bile."[29]

Following the idea of balance espoused by Pythagoras and Alcmaeon, Hippocrates asserts that a healthy body is balanced in its proportion of the four humors:

> "The body of a man has in itself blood, phlegm, yellow bile and black bile; these make up the nature of his body, and through these he feels pain or enjoys health. Now he enjoys the most perfect health when these [things] are duly proportioned to one another in respect of compounding, power and bulk, and when they are perfectly mingled."[30]

---

29. Hippocrates, trans. Jones, *Hippocrates IV* (Loeb Classical Library, Cambridge, Mass.:Harvard University Press, 1931, 1998), *The Nature of Man*, VII, pp. 20; 22 (Greek text). Jones has supplied the word 'element' in his translation (it does not appear in the Greek) and been unclear in other parts, so I have translated this section myself.
30. Ibid., IV, p. 11.

Notice that we do not see the terms "choleric," "melancholic," "sanguine" and "phlegmatic" as types – he is only discussing the natures and names of the four humors, from which later the names of the temperaments derived – choleric from Greek χολή (*cholē*), the generic word for bile; melancholic from μέλαινα χολή (*melaina cholē*), black bile; phlegmatic from φλέγμα (*phlegma*), phlegm; and sanguine from the Latin *sanguis*, equivalent to Greek αἷμα (*haima*), blood.

In general, Hippocrates sticks to addressing physical, bodily symptoms in regard to the four humors, but even at this early date we can see some application of them to the soul: "Among psychical[31] symptoms are intemperance in drink and food, in sleep, and in wakefulness, the endurance of toil either for the sake of certain passions (for example, love of dice) or for the sake of one's craft or through necessity, and the regularity or irregularity of such endurance."[32]

Applying the qualities associated with the humors to the makeup of the soul becomes much more common later, but the germ of the idea is here in Hippocrates. His treatise *Humours* is a somewhat difficult text to read; it is written, really, as terse notes for a practicing physician and lacks any finesse in the writing. But examining it for the information it contains about humoral theory is very useful. Hippocrates makes very clear associations of humors to seasons, saying that the strength of each increases in the season it correlates with; and that men, too, adapt well or not to the season based on their own humoral constitution.[33] One can see in his *Aphorisms* similar correlations between season and constitution: "As for the seasons in spring and early summer children and young people enjoy the greatest well-being and good health; in summer and part of autumn, the aged; for the remainder of autumn and winter, the middle-aged."[34] There is a certain homeopathic effect here: spring is warm and moist and is associated with the blood (sanguine) as are children as a group; whereas the aged tend to dry out and become cold, as summer does when it moves into autumn; and the middle aged are drier but moving toward the phlegmatic, which is wet and cold, like winter.

The writings of Empedocles and Hippocrates had enormous influence on those who followed, philosophers such as Plato and Aristotle, physicians like Galen, and astrologers such as Ptolemy. Let us examine the further development of humoral and temperamental theory as seen through the lenses of these ancient writers.

Plato
Plato discusses the construction of the universe, and within that vast topic the nature of the four elements, in his dialogue *Timaeus*. (Coincidentally or not, this is also the Platonic dialogue that concerns itself with astrological philosophy in his descriptions of the creation of the heavens.) He is the first person to call fire, earth, air and water 'elements' (*stoicheia*), after the Greek word for a letter of the alphabet.[35] Fire, water, earth and air are "all visible bodies" (σώματα πάντα ὁρατὰ, *sōmata panta*

---

31. "Psychical" meaning "of the soul" – ψυχή (*psuchē*) meaning "soul" (but not in the religious sense) in Greek.
32. Hippocrates, op. cit., *Humours*, IX, p. 81.
33. Ibid., XIV – XVI, pp. 86-91.
34. Hippocrates, op. cit., *Aphorisms*, III, 18, pp. 128-9.
35. Plato, trans. Bury, *Plato IX* (Loeb Classical Library, Cambridge, Mass.:Harvard University Press, 1929, 1989), *Timaeus*, 48B, pp. 110-111.

horata), the soul being an invisible body.[36] He says that the body is composed of these four elements, and that diseases in it arise through an excess or deficiency of them.[37] He talks about the changes which arise through heating, cooling, moistening and drying, bringing in the humoral fluids involved in disease.[38] In this he sets the stage for Aristotle, his student, to delve into the four elements in depth, creating an entire system based on them and the qualities of hot, cold, wet and dry.

Aristotle

Aristotle of Stagira in Asia Minor was born in 384 BCE and died in 322 BCE. He studied with Plato at his school in Athens and was a tutor of Alexander the Great. It would not be an exaggeration to say that Aristotle has had more influence on Western philosophy and science than almost any other ancient thinker. With a prodigious output, he wrote on subjects ranging from physics to poetry. For our purposes, it is very useful to see what Aristotle has to say about the elements and qualities, for his thinking gets picked up by later astrological traditions and writers, including Ptolemy and Galen.

Aristotle was extremely interested in the theories of Empedocles, and he begins his treatise *On Coming-to-be and Passing-away* with a discussion of Empedocles' views about fire, earth, air and water, and the love and strife which bring them together and break them apart. Empedocles believed that the elements (which he calls "roots") exist now and forever,[39] and just as endlessly join and break apart. Aristotle goes a step (or more) further, and proposes a means by which this happens: elements (Aristotle's term for the "roots" of Empedocles) "come to be" and "pass away" because they are composed of qualities which allow them to do this. He explains his theory in great detail in Book II of *On Coming-to-be and Passing-away*.

First, he explains that each element is composed of a pair of qualities, the qualities being hot, cold, wet and dry. Hot and cold are active "contraries" and wet and dry are passive "contraries." By this he means that hot and cold can not be combined in an element, and neither can wet and dry, because their opposed natures do not permit them to be joined together. Therefore, there are four possible combinations of pairs: hot and wet, hot and dry, cold and wet, and cold and dry. Conveniently, each pair can be assigned to one of the four elements. "And, according to theory, they have attached themselves to the apparently simple[40] bodies, Fire, Air, Water and Earth; for Fire is hot and dry, Air is hot and moist (Air, for example, is vapour), Water is cold and moist, and Earth is cold and dry."[41]

---

36. Ibid., 46D, pp. 104-5.
37. Ibid., pp. 218-19.
38. Ibid., 82C-83C, pp. 220-5.
39. "If your trust was at all deficient on any of these matters – how when water and earth and ether and sun were blended, and the forms and colours of mortal things came into being *as many as there are now*, fitted together by Aphrodite" [italics mine]; Simplicius quoting Empedocles in *Commentary on the Heavens*, quoted in Barnes, op. cit., p. 175.
40. He calls them "apparently simple" because Empedocles does not say that they can be further divided, whereas Aristotle's arguments come from the position that the elements are in turn composed of the qualities.
41. Aristotle, trans. Forster and Furley, *Aristotle III* (Loeb Classical Library, Cambridge, Mass.:Harvard University Press, 1955, 1992) *On Coming-to-be and Passing-away*, Book II, 3, p. 275.

Next, he describes the process by which the four elements change into one another. He explains that water and fire are contrary, because they are made up of different qualities (fire being hot and dry, and water being cold and wet). By the same token, earth and air are also contrary (earth being cold and dry, and air being hot and wet). He asks, how can the elements change into one another? It is easier and quicker for the elements which have a quality in common to do this; those elements without a quality in common can change also, but it is longer and more difficult. Let's examine how these processes work.

The process by which elements with a quality in common change is a cyclical one. Air (hot and wet) comes to be out of fire (hot and dry) by moistness overcoming the dryness of fire. Water (cold and wet) comes from air by air's heat being overcome by cold. Earth (cold and dry) comes from water by dryness overcoming wetness and fire from earth by heat overcoming cold. The process is easy, because only one quality has to change. The reverse is also true; air becomes fire when wet decreases, fire becomes earth when hot decreases, earth becomes water when dry decreases, and water becomes air when cold decreases. These are Aristotle's words:

> "Now it is manifest that all of them are of such a nature as to change into one another; for coming-to-be is a process into contraries and out of contraries, and all the elements are characterized by contrarieties one to another, because their distinguishing qualities are contrary. In some of them both qualities are contrary, for example, in Fire and Water (for the former is dry and hot, the latter is moist and cold). Hence, it is clear, if we take a general view, that every one of them naturally comes-to-be out of every one of them and, if we take them separately, it is not difficult to see now to see how this happens; for all will be the

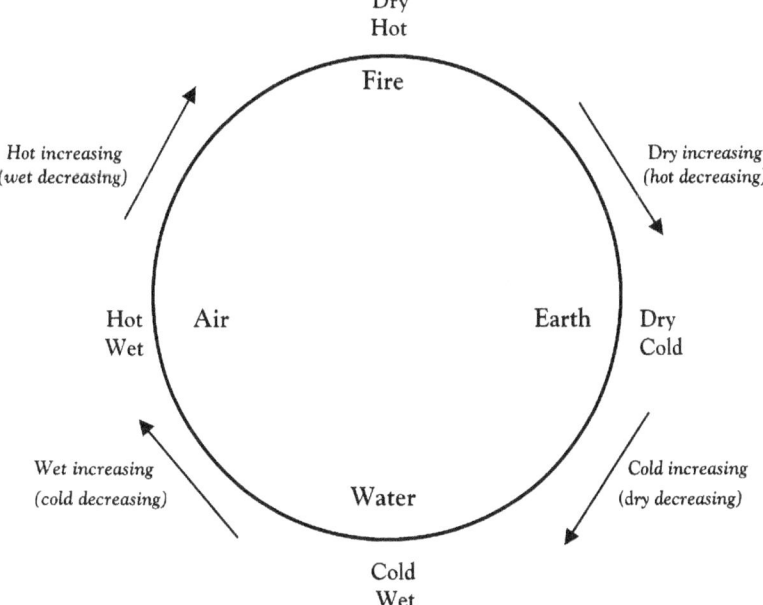

Figure 3. One example of how Aristotle's theory of the elements works

product of all, but there will be a difference owing to the greater and less speed and the greater and less difficulty of the process. For the change will be quick in those things which have qualities which correspond with one another, but slow when these do not exist, because it is easier for one thing to change than for many; for example, Air will result from Fire by the change of one quality; for Fire, as we said, is hot and dry, while Air is hot and moist, so that Air will result if the dry is overpowered by the moist. Again, Water will result from Air, if the hot is overpowered by the cold; for Air, as we said, is hot and moist, while Water is cold and moist, so that Water will result if the hot undergoes a change. In the same way, too, Earth will result from Water, and Fire from Earth; for both members of each pair have qualities which correspond to one another, since Water is moist and cold, and Earth is cold and dry, and so, when the moist is overpowered, Earth will result. Again, since Fire is dry and hot, and Earth is cold and dry, if the cold were to pass away, Fire will result from Earth.

It is clear, therefore, that the coming-to-be of simple bodies will be cyclical; and this manner of change will be very easy, because the corresponding qualities are already present in the elements which are next to one another."[42]

By contrast, the changing of those elements which do not have a quality in common is much more difficult, though it can be done. Fire can only become water by having two qualities change: it becomes water through the intermediate step of earth, or water through the intermediate step of air. The same is true for air becoming earth through fire or water. The change is still cyclical, but it involves two steps instead of just one, and therefore is slower and harder. These are Aristotle's words:

"The change, however, from Fire to Water and from Air to Earth, and again from Water and Earth to Air and Fire *can* take place, but is more difficult, because the change involves more stages. For if Fire is to be produced from Water, both the cold and the moist must be made to pass-away; and, again, if Air is to be produced from Earth, both the cold and the dry must be made to pass-away. In like manner, too, if Water and Earth are to be produced from Fire and Air, there must be a change of both qualities. This method of coming-to-be is, therefore, a lengthier process; but if one quality of each element were to be made to pass away, the change will be easier but not reciprocal; but from Fire and Water will come Earth and (alternatively) Air, and from Air and Earth Fire and (alternatively) Water; for when the cold of the Water and the dryness of the Fire have passed-away, there will be Air (for the heat of the fire and the moisture of the Water are left), but, when the heat of the Fire and the moisture of the Water have passed-away, there will be Earth, because the dryness of the Fire and the coldness of the Water are left. In the same manner also Fire and Water will result from Air and Earth; for when the heat of the Air and the dryness of the Earth pass-away, there will be Water (for the moisture of the Air and the cold of the Earth are left), but when the moisture of the Air and the cold of the Earth have passed-away, there will be Fire, because the heat of the Air and the dryness of the Earth, which are, as we saw, the constituents of Fire, are left. Now the manner in which Fire comes-to-be is confirmed by our sense-

---

42.   Ibid., Book II, 4, pp. 279-81.

perception; for flame is the most evident form of Fire, and flame is burning smoke, and smoke is composed of Air and Earth."[43]

We'll finish this section by considering an essay in the Aristotelian corpus on melancholy, which appears in *Problems XXX*, 1.[44] Klibansky, Panofsky and Saxl consider this writing to be the first time that physical or medical melancholy was connected with Platonic frenzy.[45] For *our* purposes it is interesting to see how Aristotle perceives melancholy. He talks about hot and cold, and says that nature is composed of these qualities: "…that in nature such a melancholic humor is already mixed; the temperament/mixture (κρᾶσις *krasis*) is both hot and cold, for from these two things nature is composed."[46] He adds that hot and cold cause the changes in the way a melancholy is expressed, cold black bile causing despondency and hot black bile causing cheerfulness.[47] (This essay is not exactly how Hippocrates would have put it!)

Aristotle claims that those outstanding in philosophy, politics, poetry and the arts are melancholic. Geniuses and heroes, he says, are melancholic.[48] (Did Aristotle fancy himself a melancholic?) Whether or not his arguments hold water, the interesting thing from our standpoint about *Problems XXX*, 1 is that he also clearly distinguishes between the humor melancholy and the temperament melancholy – "Now melancholy, both the humor (χυμὸς *chumos*) and the temperament (κρᾶσις *krasis*), produce air."[49] So he has gone a step further than Hippocrates, and talked about temperament as an adjunct to humor. It's also clear from reading this essay on melancholy that he is not only talking about physical melancholy, but psychological melancholy as well. He likely did not use "temperament" in the exact sense that later writers did, but rather meant to talk about the "mixtures" of qualities – but he was using the words that would later be used to describe what we know as temperament.

While it might seem as if we are spending too much time on these theories of Aristotle's, it will become clear that his work had a great influence on temperament, both physically and astrologically. Along with the ideas of the Stoics, the philosophical basis for astrology developed using these concepts, and temperament theory would not exist without them.

---

43. Ibid., pp. 281-3.
44. In fact, the essay may possibly be written by Theophrastus, but at any rate it is not later than the 1st century BCE. For the sake of simplicity, we will refer to the author as Aristotle.
45. Raymond Klibansky, Erwin Panofsky and Fritz Saxl, *Saturn and Melancholy* (New York: Basic Books, 1964), p. 17.
46. Aristotle, *Problems XXX*, 1; found in Klibansky, Panofsky and Saxl, op. cit., pp. 22-3. (Translation of this sentence by Dorian Greenbaum.)
47. Ibid., p. 23.
48. Ibid., pp. 18 and 19.
49. Ibid., p. 21.

The Stoics

So let us turn to the Stoics, whose school began with Zeno of Citium in around 300 BCE. Like Empedocles, Plato and Aristotle before him, Zeno believed in the theory of the four elements composing the physical world.[50] However, unlike Aristotle, only one quality was assigned to each of the four elements. Thus, fire is associated with hot and air with cold; fire and air are the "active" elements. Water and earth, the "passive" elements, are associated with wet and dry respectively.[51]

These associations have great ramifications for astrological theory. Both Stoic and Aristotelian philosophy were incorporated into Hellenistic[52] astrology, and the principles of both concerning elements (especially Aristotelian, for temperament) and cosmology (especially Stoic) were used by astrologers in the Greek-speaking world from Ptolemy to Olympiodorus and beyond. We shall explore the astrological 'take' on the elements as they relate to temperament theory, but first let us consider one final Greek philosopher/scientist, Galen, the great physician whose ideas dominated medicine for 1500 years.

Galen

Galen was born at Pergamum in Asia Minor (now Turkey) in 131 CE. Although his father wanted him to study philosophy or politics, he was inspired to study medicine by a dream he had where Asclepius appeared to him. He studied medicine for four years at the sanctuary of Asclepius in Pergamum. His first experience as a practicing doctor was as a physician to the gladiators of Pergamum. He later moved to Rome and became the attending physician for Marcus Aurelius and his son Commodus.

Through the huge *corpus* of Galen's extant work (over twenty volumes in Greek alone) we have a clear insight into his thought and philosophy. He was a follower of Aristotle and especially Hippocrates: a number of his works are commentaries on Hippocratic texts. Galen embraced both the humoral theory espoused by Hippocrates and the element/quality theories postulated by both Hippocrates and Aristotle. It is fair to say that what developed into medieval temperament theory was a direct result of the influence of Galen. Let us take a look at what he has to say on elements, qualities and humors.

It appears, from reading the relevant works, that Galen first discussed these topics in his work Περὶ κράσεων (*Peri kraseôn*), translated in Latin as *De temperamentis*, *On Temperaments*.[53] Incredibly, this work has never been translated into English. Perusal of the Greek original shows, however, that it is an attempt by Galen to order and elucidate the meanings of the qualities hot, cold, wet and dry and apply them to the humors. Galen is well aware that there are gradations of each of these qualities, so he attempts to differentiate between "pure" states, which are not possible in nature, and the actual

---

50. G.E.R. Lloyd, *Greek Science After Aristotle* (New York: W.W. Norton, 1973), p. 28.
51. Ibid. Also in S. Sambursky, *Physics of the Stoics* (Princeton, N.J.:Princeton Univ. Press, 1959, 1987), p.3.
52. I am using 'Hellenistic' here as an adjective, to describe the astrology practiced in the Greco-Roman world primarily from the 1st century BCE to about the 7th century CE.
53. Another perfectly plausible translation would be "On Mixtures."

mixtures as they occur in the physical world, and especially in humans. He talks about the "forms" (εἴδη, *eidē*) and the "kinds" (γένη, *genē*) of mixtures.[54]

> "For it is not possible for a living being (ζῷον, *zoion*) to actually be perfectly hot as fire nor perfectly wet as water. And in the same way neither utterly cold or dry, but to become the common names (προσηγορία, *prosēgoria*) from having a larger share in the mixture; so we call 'wet' that in which a greater degree is of wetness, 'dry' in which [it is] of dryness; 'hot' also in that way, in which the hot has a larger share than the dry; and 'cold' in which cold [has a larger share than] hot."[55]

He goes on to talk about the different kinds of mixtures, following the theories of Hippocrates, and explaining, for example, how heat dries and cold moistens (showing the Stoic idea that hot and cold are active principles, while wet and dry are passive). The humors themselves are somewhat tangential in this treatise; its primary focus is on the mixtures of hot, cold, wet and dry.

In *On the Natural Faculties*,[56] Galen also discusses the mixtures of the four qualities, though not in great detail, and does discuss the nature of the four humors:

> "…they also say that the blood is a *virtually* warm and moist humour, and similarly also that yellow bile is warm and dry, even though for the most part it appears moist. … And, similarly, phlegm has been called cold and moist; …is there none which is virtually cold and dry? …the black bile is such a humour."[57]

Galen discusses the difference between elements and qualities in his treatise *On the Elements According to Hippocrates*. He calls the qualities "first principles" and says:

> "For an element differs from a first principle in this way, namely, that first principles are not, of necessity, akin to the results to which they give rise; but elements certainly are akin."[58] "…an element…is not single and not unmixed and not by itself."[59]

He also connects the qualities to the four humors:

> "…Hippocrates expounded in his *On the Nature of Man*, saying that the elements common to all things are wet, dry, cold and hot. For he names the elements from their qualities, and through these qualities, the elements arise. For by means of matter, when there is an utmost

---

54. Clearly related to Aristotle's formal cause and material cause.
55. Galen, Περὶ κράσεων, *Peri kraseōn* (Stuttgart:B.G. Teubner, 1969), Book I, pp. 1-2. Translation by Dorian Greenbaum.
56. A better translation would be *On the Natural Powers*.
57. Galen, trans. Brock, *On the Natural Faculties* (Loeb Classical Library, Cambridge, Mass.:Harvard University Press, 1916, 1991), pp. 201-3.
58. Galen, trans. Lewis, Beach and Rubio-Fernandez, *On the Elements According to Hippocrates* (http://www.medicinaantiqua.org.uk/tr_GalElem.html, accessed 1 Mar 2004), Book I, Sections 469-471.
59. Ibid., Section 471.

innate heat, an element will come into being (i.e. fire), generally, and according to the same logic for coldness and dryness and wetness."[60]

This almost sounds Stoic in its assignment of one quality to each element, yet earlier he has reiterated the distinctions made by Aristotle:

"But if you seek what is simple, based on nature, it must necessarily be that which is unmixed and unblended, and utmost in quality. And so you come again to fire and air and water and earth. In these alone will you find the qualities unmixed and unblended; the utmost heat and dryness in fire, the utmost coldness and wetness in water, and in each of the others according to their particular natures."[61]

Finally, in *On Hippocrates' On the Nature of Man*, Galen coalesces his ideas about qualities, elements and humors. Again, he emphasizes the difference between "first principles," the qualities, and the elements.

"...there are four qualities, the extremes of coldness, dryness, heat and wetness. And indeed these are not the elements of the nature (φύσις, *phusis*)[62] of man or of others, but of the first principles. This was confused by the ancients who had not yet conceived of the idea of differences between 'first principle' and 'element,' since they were able to use the term 'elements' for 'first principles.'"[63]

And again, "...he [Hippocrates] discusses these things as being primary, from which all the others originate. These are hot and cold and dry and wet."[64]

Galen connects the four qualities to the elements/humors by stressing that the humors, which are each associated with an element, are *physical* manifestations of the workings of the four qualities.

"...that all things are generated from heat, cold, dryness and wetness, and for this reason these elements are common to all. Blood, phlegm, yellow bile and black bile are the particular elements of the nature of man. And yet, these things might not properly be called 'particular,' for they are common to all animals with blood. And it is quite clear that each of them comes from the four primary elements which we call wetness, dryness, cold and heat, naming them after their qualities; the specific terms fire, water, air and earth are from their substance.[65] ... So the hot, cold, dry and wet parts seen clearly in the human body, are not the elements of the nature of man, but compositions and generations of these elements; water, fire, air, and earth."[66]

---

60. Ibid., Sections 481-484.
61. Ibid., Sections 467-469.
62. Meaning the physical world.
63. Galen, trans. Lewis and Beach, *On Hippocrates' On the Nature of Man* (http://www.medicinaantiqua.org.uk/tr_GnatHom.html, accessed 1 Mar 2004), Sections 29-31.
64. Ibid., Section 38.
65. Ibid., Sections 51-53.
66. Ibid., Section 54.

Fire, earth, air and water are the physical representations of the four qualities—but even these do not exist in a pure state in the physical world.

> "…if the cold element were destroyed, everything would be fire; if the dry element were destroyed, everything would be water, and thus all the bodies in the universe would be destroyed. …For the extreme element is thought of, rather than actually existing; but a certain one of the existing elements is almost the same. Indeed, if you were to imagine that wetness and coldness in the extreme make water, then water would not yet be observed. For it would immediately solidify and stand still and cease flowing. And if you were to imagine earth as dryness and cold in the extreme, such a body would be harder than a diamond. … However, when the dry and cold elements are considered based on predomination, the earth in the universe is said to be a dry and cold body, and water is said to be a cold and wet body."[67]

Also in this work, Galen correlates the seasons to the humors and gives his opinion, supporting Hippocrates, that the various humors in man increase based on the season.

> "But just as among the seasons they say that this [spring] is wet and hot, so among the bodies of generated things, animals are wet and hot compared to plants….[68] … In summer blood is still strong, and bile rises in the body and extends into the autumn. And in the autumn blood becomes less, for autumn is opposite to it in nature.[69] … When winter takes over, the bile, being chilled, becomes less, and the phlegm increases again from the abundance of rain and from the length of the nights."[70]

Finally, we can be persuaded by the following that Galen's perception of the humors was at least partially psychological as well as physical. Again in his commentary *On Hippocrates' On the Nature of Man*, he says:

> "And there is a certain physical theory, possessing no small persuasiveness, according to which the four humors are shown to contribute to the formation of characteristics and aptitudes. And it is necessary for it to be explained again that in this account the characteristics of the soul depend on the mixtures in the body, concerning which we have written elsewhere. This being assumed, therefore, the sharp and intelligent character in the soul will be due to the bilious humor, the steadfast and firm character due to the melancholic humor, and the simple and stupid character due to blood. The nature of phlegm is most useless in the formation of character, and it appears to have its necessary origin in the first break-down of foods."[71]

---

67. Ibid., Sections 93-95.
68. Ibid., Section 83.
69. Ibid., Section 84.
70. Ibid., Section 86.
71. Ibid., Section 97.

It becomes clear from reading Galen that the four qualities, elements and humors inform all his conceptions and perceptions about physiology and medicine. Thus, with the ubiquity of his ideas throughout the European world through the end of the Renaissance, we can appreciate the importance of Galen's philosophy to astrology as well as medicine. As humoral and temperament theory continued to develop on what we would call a psychological plane as well as a physical one, medicine and astrology went hand in hand to emphasize its importance. As doctors were well-acquainted with the principles of astrology, they were in a position to share and discuss temperament/humoral theory with astrologers, as astrologers were with doctors.

So let us now turn to the interpretations of qualities, elements and humors by astrologers, and reveal the root of temperament from an astrological perspective.

The Roots of Temperament: Greco-Roman Astrology

Claudius Ptolemy

We'll begin with Ptolemy who, though not a practicing astrologer, could be fairly said to have done more for the codification of astrological principles than perhaps any other astrologer.[72] Ptolemy was about 40 years older than Galen, so we can probably safely infer that he was not influenced by the younger man's writing.[73] However, Ptolemy clearly was influenced by many of the same sources that so excited Galen: Hippocrates, Aristotle and the Stoics.

Though Ptolemy never uses the word "humor,"[74] nor does he refer to blood, yellow bile, black bile or phlegm, he echoes the teachings of Hippocrates in regard to mixtures and balances of the four qualities being necessary for good health; he refers to Zeus (Jupiter) and Aphrodite (Venus) as being "temperate" (εὔκρατον, *eukraton*, or well-mixed). Ptolemy follows Hippocrates when he says that the warm and the wet are the most fertile or generative qualities. (Galen also calls Spring "well-balanced," because of its hot and moist qualities.) Ptolemy also follows Hippocrates and Aristotle (as does Galen) in his characterizations of the seasons – spring is wet becoming hot, summer hot becoming dry, autumn dry becoming cold and winter cold becoming wet.[75]

Ptolemy assigns qualities to the signs (he never uses the word 'element') based partly on their place in the seasonal cycle and partly on their planetary rulers. Thus, Cancer and Leo are "most

---

72. Due to the ubiquity of his writings and his reputation throughout the ancient, medieval and renaissance world.
73. Though Galen could certainly have been influenced by Ptolemy; he was about 20 when Ptolemy died in 150 CE.
74. He does talk about the four "fluidities" – the qualities hot, cold, wet and dry. See Ptolemy, *Tetrabiblos*, trans. Schmidt (Berkeley Springs, W.Va.:Golden Hind Press, 1994, 1996), Book I, Ch. 5, p. 16. The other translator of the *Tetrabiblos*, Robbins (Loeb Classical Library, Cambridge, Mass.:Harvard Univ. Press, 1940, 1994), Book I, ch. 5, p. 39, mistranslates the word χύμα (*chuma*) as "humor;" its actual meaning is "that which is poured out or flows."
75. Ptolemy, op. cit., Book I, Ch. 10, pp. 24-5 (Schmidt translation); Book I, Ch. 10, p. 59 (Robbins translation).

productive of heat"[76] because they are closest to the summer solstice; Capricorn and Aquarius are the domicile of Saturn, which is cold, and they have cold and wintry weather; Sagittarius and Pisces are temperate because of Jupiter; Aries and Scorpio are dry like Mars; Taurus and Libra are temperate and fertile like Venus; the domiciles of Hermes, Gemini and Virgo, are not mentioned as having a particular quality or qualities.[77]

His application of the qualities is seen fully in his descriptions of the planets. The Sun heats and slightly dries; the Moon moistens, but also slightly warms because of the light it receives from the Sun. Saturn, because it is so far from the Sun cools and slightly dries; Mars dries and burns; Jupiter warms and moistens and is temperate; Venus is also temperate, though it moistens more than it warms. Hermes is dry at some times and moist at others, depending on where it is in relation to the Sun.[78] The Sun also gives different qualities to the parts of the diurnal cycle based on its position in the heavens.[79] The phases of the Moon and planets; seasons, solstices and equinoxes are also assigned qualities.

	ANGLES	SOLSTICE/EQUINOX	MOON PHASE	PLANET PHASE	PLANETS	SEASONS
Hot	M.C.	Summer Solstice	Full Moon	Opposition	☉♀♂♃ ☽(slightly)	Spring, Summer
Cold	I.C.	Winter Solstice	New Moon	Conjunction	♄	Autumn, Winter
Wet	DESC.	Vernal Equinox	First Quarter	1st Station/Square	☽ ♀ ♃	Winter, Spring
Dry	ASC.	Autumnal Equinox	Last Quarter	2nd Station/Square	☉ ♂ ♄	Summer, Autumn

Table 1. Ptolemy's Assignment of Qualities (Tetrabiblos, Book I)[80]

In Book I of the *Tetrabiblos*, Ptolemy sets forth his contribution to the idea that the astrological mixtures in a birth chart can be useful in understanding a person. Here is temperament applied by the astrologer, working with the criteria supplied by the philosopher (and used by the physician for the body). Ptolemy firmly believes that the "co-mixtures" in a person's birth chart describe that person's body and soul – in this we can see the application of "temperament" to soul as well as to body – the beginnings of its psychological application. He says, in his defense of the value of astrology:

---

76. Ptolemy, op. cit., Book I, Ch. 17, p. 79 (Robbins translation).
77. Ibid., Book I, Ch. 17, p. 83.
78. Ibid., Book I, Ch. 4, p. 39.
79. Ibid., Book I, Ch. 2, p. 7.
80. After Table by Robert Hand.

"Why can he not, too, with respect to an individual man, perceive the general quality of his temperament[81] from the ambient at the time of his birth, as for instance that he is such and such in body and such and such in soul....?"[82]

Ptolemy even compares the astrologer to the physician:

"In the case of events that may be modified we must give heed to the astrologer, when, for example, he says that to such and such a temperament, with such and such a character of the ambient, if the fundamental proportions increase or decrease, such and such an affection will result. Similarly we must believe the physician, when he says that this sore will spread or cause putrefaction...."[83]

Ptolemy also talks about the "composite" (σύγκριμα, sunkrima) as being the single beginning for an individual.[84] This is a Stoic term for the union of body and soul,[85] and also refers to the mixing of qualities in the body, which can be seen in the chart. He says the characteristics of this mixture for an individual, the constitution (σύγκρισις, sunkrisis) can be seen in the chart.[86]

In Book III of the *Tetrabiblos*, Ptolemy develops the way one identifies what the characteristics of an individual's mixture are, and what to look for in the chart to find this out. He uses the exact word κρᾶσις (krasis), mixture, that Galen uses - which will be translated into Latin as "*temperamentum*." First he talks about the shape of the body, looking at the Ascendant ("rising horizon"), planets there and the almutens (οἰκοδεσπότης, oikodespotēs). Planets either oriental or occidental will contribute varying amounts of the four qualities. Ptolemy also looks at the Moon to find the shape of the body; and to a lesser degree co-rising fixed stars and the places of the rulers of the Ascendant and the Moon.[87]

Ptolemy delineates his criteria for the "quality of soul" separately from those of the body. Hermes (Mercury) is in charge of the "rational and noetic part;" for the "sensitive and non-rational part" he looks to the Moon.[88] And here is where we see that the Moon has two astrological functions: it determines both the form of the body and the form of its "sensitive and non-rational" soul. Here is our first body/mind connection for temperament, though Ptolemy does not call it such and neither do later writers. Indeed, most writers up to the end of the Renaissance tend to use temperament strictly

---

81. σύγκρασις (sunkrasis), allied to κρᾶσις (krasis), mixture, from which eventually the word "temperament" arose. Robbins should not have translated the word *sunkrasis* as "temperament." A better translation of this word is "commixture" as in the Schmidt translation of the *Tetrabiblos*, p. 6.
82. Ptolemy, op. cit., Book I, Ch. 2, p. 13 (Robbins translation).
83. Ibid., Book I, Ch. 3, p. 27. Again Robbins translates σύγκρασις (sunkrasis) incorrectly, as "temperament" instead of "commixture."
84. Ptolemy, op. cit., Book III, Ch. 1, p. 2 (Schmidt translation).
85. Liddell & Scott, rev. Jones, *Greek-English Lexicon* (Oxford: Oxford Univ. Press, 1996) gives, as a specific reference for this word, Zeno in *Stoicorum Veterum Fragmenta*, I.40 (ed. von Arnim).
86. Ptolemy, op. cit., Book III, Ch. 1, p. 3 (Schmidt translation).
87. Ibid., Book III, Ch. 12, p. 47.
88. Ibid., Book III, Ch. 14, p. 56.

to describe bodily and physical characteristics. However, by the time of Marsilio Ficino in the 15th century, the words choleric, melancholic, sanguine and phlegmatic are used in relationship to psychological characteristics, not just physical ones. By the time of William Lilly, the psychological characteristics are a well-known part of popular culture (though they would not have been called 'psychological'), even though Lilly's formula for determining temperament is for the physical characteristics only. The Moon, however, is the connection in delineations of body and soul, and we will see this practiced by many astrologers in addition to Lilly.

Before we go on to these other times, however, let us take a brief look at the other astrologers of the ancient world who, like Ptolemy, interest themselves in the four qualities or elements as they relate to humans and the astrological chart.

Marcus Manilius

Manilius lived about 100 years before Ptolemy. Author of *Astronomica*, a poem written during the reigns of Augustus and Tiberius (ca. 10 C.E.), Manilius spends several lines of his poem speculating on the origin of the universe *à la* Heraclitus, Thales and, then, Empedocles:

> "...else it may be that neither earth nor fire nor air nor water acknowledges a begetter, but themselves consitute a godhead of four elements, which have formed the sphere of the universe and ban all search for a source beyond them, having created all things from themselves, so that cold combines with hot, wet with dry, and airy with solid, and the discord is one of harmony, allowing apt unions and generative activity and enabling the elements to produce all things."[89]

Manilius' combinations of cold with hot and wet with dry are not according to Aristotle! He finishes his description with the Stoic view of the creation of the cosmos from the four elements.[90] There is no mention of elements or qualities associated with signs or planets.

Vettius Valens

Vettius Valens, a younger contemporary of Ptolemy, was the earliest astrologer to assign elements to the triplicities: Aries, Leo and Sagittarius are "fiery," Taurus, Virgo and Capricorn "earthy;" Gemini, Libra and Aquarius "airy"; and Cancer, Scorpio and Pisces are "watery."[91] In a later book, Valens also refers to air as "ice-cold and opaque," a reference to the Stoic doctrine of characterizing air as cold.[92] Other than these descriptions, Valens does not concern himself with "bodily shape and mixture" as Ptolemy does.

---

89. Marcus Manilius, trans. Goold, *Astronomica* (Loeb Classical Library, Cambridge, Mass.:Harvard Univ. Press, 1977, 1997), p. 15.
90. Ibid., p. 17.
91. Vettius Valens, trans. Schmidt, *The Anthology* (Berkeley Springs, W. Va.:The Golden Hind Press, 1993, 1996), Book I, Ch. 2, pp. 7-16.
92. Ibid., Book IV, Ch. 4, p. 7. Almost the same phrase is used in Pseudo-Aristotle's Stoic treatise, *On the Cosmos*, 2 392b.

Antiochus of Athens

Antiochus of Athens, who is also 2nd century CE, wrote in his *Thesaurus* about the "mixtures" of the zoidia (signs); like Valens, he assigns elements to the triplicities.[93] He also clearly states that all things are composed of the four elements, and does not mention the four qualities in relation to the signs, though he does in connection to the planets, where he says Kronos (Saturn) is cold and dry.[94] There is no mention of humors.

Julius Firmicus Maternus

Surprisingly little about elements appears in the *Mathesis*, which was written about 334 C.E.[95] The section on the Nature of the Signs has a large lacuna, so only Aries and Pisces are presented in their entirety. Aries is called fiery and Pisces watery. The format of the descriptions that exist is similar to that in Paulus Alexandrinus; the two were rough contemporaries (Firmicus wrote about 40 years before Paulus). What Firmicus calls the "Lord of the Geniture" (he says it is the ruler of the sign following that of the Moon in its natal position)[96] will give indications as to the behavior of the person, though he gives no formula for temperament or quality of soul.

Paulus Alexandrinus and Olympiodorus

In his *Introduction to Astrology* (378 CE), Paulus does correlate the seasons to the elements: spring is "air," summer "fire," autumn "earth" and winter "water."[97] He does not have any sections on bodily form and mixture. Olympiodorus, in his commentary on Paulus (564 CE), occasionally refers to "watery" or "fiery" signs, though he does not specifically give an exposition of the signs in which he assigns elements to them.[98]

Hephaistio of Thebes

Hephaistio of Thebes (fl. 415 CE), like Ptolemy (in fact, he quotes Ptolemy heavily), also devotes a small portion of his *Apotelesmatics* to bodily form and mixture; and says, like Ptolemy, that the qualities of the soul are subsequent to the bodily mixture.[99]

---

93. Antiochus of Athens, trans. Schmidt, *The Thesaurus* (Berkeley Springs, W.Va.:The Golden Hind Press, 1993), Ch. 3, p. 6.
94. Ibid., Ch. 8, p. 10.
95. We know the date because Firmicus mentions an eclipse which occurred in that year.
96. Julius Firmicus Maternus, trans. Bram, *Matheseos Libri VIII* (Park Ridge, N.J.:Noyes Press, 1975; reprinted by Ascella Publications, 1995), Book 4, Section XIX.
97. Paulus Alexandrinus, trans. Greenbaum, in *Late Classical Astrology: Paulus Alexandrinus and Olympiodorus, with the Scholia from Later Commentators* (Reston, Va.:ARHAT, 2001), Introduction, Ch. 2, pp. 2-3.
98. Olympiodorus, trans. Greenbaum, in *Late Classical Astrology: Paulus Alexandrinus and Olympiodorus, with the Scholia from Later Commentators* (Reston, Va.:ARHAT, 2001), Commentary on Paulus.
99. Hephaistio of Thebes, trans. Schmidt, *Apotelesmatics* (Cumberland, Md.:The Golden Hind Press, 1998), Book II, Ch. 12, p. 47; also refer to p. 52.

Rhetorius

Rhetorius was an Egyptian who compiled extracts from a number of astrological writers. In his text (early 7th century CE), he takes a small step toward aligning planets with elements and humors; drawing from other ancient writers, he assigns a taste to each of the planets. Before this, no astrologer that we have been able to discover has used taste in describing planets or signs. Thus Saturn is cold and dry, and astringent; Jupiter is vital, fertile and of sweet taste; Mars is burning and drying through an overabundance of the power of fire; the Sun is hot and dry, its taste sharp and piquant; Venus is temperate and wet, with a fat taste; and Mercury is sometimes wet, sometimes dry, with a sour taste.[100]

With these astrologers, the era of Hellenistic astrology comes to an end. It is now time to turn to the flowering of temperament theory, which began with the Arabic astrologers of the medieval period and continued in the Renaissance era.

The Flowering of Temperament

We can thank the Arabic astrologers of the medieval period for keeping alive the astrology of the Greeks. Were it not for their translations of earlier authors, part of the Hellenistic tradition would have been lost. And clearly the Arabs owe much of what developed in their astrology to the ideas of the Hellenistic astrologers, especially Ptolemy. Although some of what they wrote distorted the actual Greek doctrines (and they also incorporated Persian teachings into their astrology), they kept astrology alive in the West.

Masha'allah

Masha'allah is the first "Arabized" astrologer in the west (he actually was a Jew from Basra, in Iraq). Flourishing from 762-815 CE, he wrote a *Book of Nativities* that incorporates much of the doctrine of Dorotheus[101] which he read in Persian translation. He does not specifically mention anything like temperament in the *Book of Nativities*, but he does discuss the "inclination" of the native. This appears to be a reworking of Ptolemy's criterion for the rational soul, as Mercury is heavily involved, though he also mentions the importance of the Ascendant and the Moon. He does not specifically mention qualities or elements in his descriptions.[102]

---

100. Rhetorius, "On the Nature and Virtue of the Planets," in *Catalogus Codicum Astrologorum Graecorum (CCAG) VII*, (Brussels, 1898-1953), pp. 213-224.
101. Dorotheus of Sidon was an important 1st century C.E. astrologer who wrote in verse on both nativities and katarchic astrology (horary and electional). His work has been translated from an Arabic version by David Pingree in *Carmen Astrologicum: Dorotheus of Sidon* (Mansfield, Notts:Ascella, 1993).
102. Masha'allah, trans. Hand, *Book of Nativities* (Berkeley Springs, W.Va.:The Golden Hind Press, 1994), "Of What Inclination is the Native," pp. 16-19.

Abu Mashar

In Arabic-era astrologers such as Abu Mashar, 787-866 CE (of the generation following Masha'allah), we can see the influence of both the Greek-speaking astrologers and the philosophers/physicians. While I have found nothing that precisely correlates the humors with the signs or planets in the extant Hellenistic literature, with Abu Mashar the connection is completely in place. For instance, he says of the sign Aries: "Its nature is hot, dry, fiery, yellow bile, its taste is bitter, and it is masculine."[103] He does the same for all the other signs, and for the planets.

SIGN	QUALITY				ELEMENT	HUMOR
♈	hot	dry			fire	choleric (yellow bile)
♉		dry	cold		earth	melancholic (black bile)
♊	hot			wet	air	sanguine (blood)
♋			cold	wet	water	phlegmatic (phlegm)
♌	hot	dry			fire	choleric (yellow bile)
♍		dry	cold		earth	melancholic (black bile)
♎	hot			wet	air	sanguine (blood)
♏			cold	wet	water	phlegmatic (phlegm)
♐	hot	dry			fire	choleric (yellow bile)
♑		dry	cold		earth	melancholic (black bile)
♒	hot			wet	air	sanguine (blood)
♓			cold	wet	water	phlegmatic (phlegm)

Table 2. The Nature of Signs According to Abu Mashar[104]

PLANET	QUALITY				ELEMENT	HUMOR
☉	hot	dry				
☽			cold	wet		
♀			cold	wet		phlegmatic (phlegm)
♂	hot	dry			fire	choleric (yellow bile)
♃	hot			wet	air	
♄		dry	cold			melancholic (black bile)

Table 3. The Nature of Planets According to Abu Mashar*[105]

*Mercury is "changeable," so does not appear in this table
(Note: Abu Mashar assigns humors only to Venus, Mars and Saturn; and elements only to Mars and Jupiter.)

---

103. Abu Mashar, trans. Burnett, *The Abbreviation of the Introduction to Astrology* (Reston, Va.:ARHAT, 1997), Ch. 1, pp. 2-3.
104. Ibid., Chapter 1, pp. 2-9. Thanks to Nadine Harris for the format of this table and the one on Abu Mashar's Nature of the Planets.
105. Ibid., Chapter 5, pp. 36-40.

Note that in Abu Mashar's system, Venus is cold and wet, whereas in Ptolemy, Venus is hot and wet. As a benefic, Ptolemy assigns the fertile qualities to Venus in moderate amounts (what makes the malefics malefic is that they possess *excessive* amounts of a quality). Abu Mashar still calls Venus a benefic, but considers her nature to be more phlegmatic (perhaps because the Moon, the other feminine planet, is cold and wet?). Abu Mashar does not delineate a means for finding a person's temperament, but the influence of planets and signs (and their "natures") clearly is there in the makeup of the individual.

Abu Mashar was one of the most famous of the Arabic astrologers, and his writings, eventually translated into Latin,[106] were considered authoritative by later astrologers such as Guido Bonatti.

Avicenna (Ibn Sina)

Known in the West as Avicenna, Ibn Sina (980-1037) was born in Bukhara, Iran, and was one of the great philosophers and physicians of the Arabic era. Avicenna's temperament scheme is laid out in his *Canon of Medicine*, using the Aristotelian view of the qualities and elements. The humors work in the body as material expressions of the elements. In contrast to many other practitioners of temperament, Avicenna assigns the fire signs (Aries, Leo, Sagittarius) to the sanguine humor, and the air signs (Gemini, Libra, Aquarius) to the choleric humor (earth/melancholic and water/phlegmatic remain the same in regard to the assignment of zodiac signs).[107] The modern-day Unani medicine system draws on the work of Avicenna.

Al Biruni

A contemporary of Avicenna who equalled him in skill is Al Biruni, who was born 15 September 973 in Kath, Khwarizm (now in Uzbekistan) and died 13 December 1048 in Ghazna (now in Afghanistan). His noted astrological work is translated in English as *The Book of Instruction in the Elements of the Art of Astrology*. The first two-thirds of the book are devoted to astronomy, leaving the last third as a dense compilation of astrological technique. As with Abu Mashar, the humoral system seems entirely in place (was it copied from Abu Mashar?). Al Biruni says:

	DRY	*MOIST*	*DRY*	*MOIST*	*DRY*	*MOIST*
HOT	Aries	Gemini	Leo	Libra	Sagittarius	Aquarius
COLD	Taurus	Cancer	Virgo	Scorpio	Capricorn	Pisces

Table 4. The Qualities of the Signs According to Al Biruni[108]

---

106. Adelard of Bath translated the *Abbreviation* into Latin ca. 1100.
107. For more information on the concepts dealt with in Avicenna's *Canon of Medicine*, see *The Traditional Medicine Network* online, in particular "Avicenna's Canon of Medicine," http://www.traditionalmedicine.net.au/canonavi.htm (accessed 4 July 2004).
108. Al Biruni, trans. Wright, *The Book of Instruction in the Elements of the Art of Astrology* (London: Luzac and Co., 1934; reprinted Ballantrae), p. 211.

"When therefore you know the active virtues of a sign whether heat or cold, and the passive virtues, whether dryness or moisture,[109] it will not be concealed from you what particular element of the world and what particular humour of the body each sign resembles. Each sign that is hot and dry is related to fire and yellow bile, each that is cold and dry, to earth and black bile, each that is hot and moist to air and blood and each that is cold and moist to water and phlegm."[110]

PLANET	QUALITY				ELEMENT	HUMOR
☉	(more) hot	(less) dry			lower part of fire	
☽				wet		phlegm
☿		moderately dry	moderately cold			black bile
♀			moderately cold	moderately wet		
♂	extremely hot	extremely dry			upper part of fire	yellow bile
♃	moderately hot			moderately wet	air	blood
♄		extremely dry	extremely cold		earth	black bile

Table 5. The Nature of the Planets according to Al Biruni

Though he provides no formula for ascertaining the temperament, Al Biruni does maintain that "the signs are also indicative of various diseases of man, of his complexion, figure, face and the like...."[111] In addition, he provides a table of signs and description of planets which show their "manners."[112] These descriptions clearly show psychological qualities in addition to the physical ones enumerated elsewhere.

Guido Bonatti

The fame of Guido Bonatti in the medieval world was such that Dante placed him in the eighth circle of hell in the *Inferno*. Born in 1210, Bonatti wrote his *magnum opus*, the *Liber Astronomiae*, sometime after 1282. It runs to over 800 pages, which shows its encyclopedic scope. We could hardly do better for a textbook of medieval astrology. Bonatti has studied the works of the Greeks and Arabs who went before him, and often quotes them by name. His descriptions of both signs and planets incorporate qualities, elements and humors. To give examples:

---

109. Calling hot and cold active, and wet and dry passive, are, of course, both Stoic and Aristotelian designations: see p. 10 and p. 14.
110. Al Biruni, op. cit., p. 211.
111. Ibid., p. 216.
112. Ibid., pp. 217 and 250.

> "Aries, Leo and Sagittarius make up the first triplicity. ... This triplicity is called hot and dry because each of the three signs is fiery, hot, dry, masculine, oriental, diurnal, choleric, and bitter with respect to taste. ... Taurus, Virgo and Capricorn make up the second triplicity because each one of these signs is earthy, cold and dry, feminine, nocturnal, melancholic, southern, and sharp or acid with respect to taste. ... Gemini, Libra and Aquarius make up the third triplicity because each of these signs is airy, hot and moist, masculine, diurnal, sanguine, occidental and sweet with respect to taste. ... Cancer, Scorpio and Pisces make up the fourth triplicity because each of these signs is watery, cold and moist, feminine, nocturnal, phlegmatic and salty with respect to taste, though some say insipid."[113]

In Tractate 3, Bonatti spends a lot of time going through the natures of the seven planets and their interactions with each other. Here again, he associates humors with the planets. A few examples:

> "And Saturn speaks of all that signifies the oppression of cold and distemperate dryness. Of the humors he signifies melancholy; and of the complexions of bodies he signifies the melancholic type; and probably that melancholia will be with an admixture of phlegm.[114] And according to his [Jupiter's] own nature he produces heat and humidity; [he is] airy and sanguine.[115] Alchabitius[116] said Mars is a masculine, nocturnal planet. By his fiery and choleric nature he produces heat and distemperate dryness; [he is] bitter in flavor.[117] Alchabitius said that the Sun is a masculine, diurnal planet, a fortune by aspect, but by bodily conjunction evil; he produces heat and dryness through his own nature.[118] Venus produces cold and moisture according to her own nature in a proper mixture.[119] Albumasar[120] and Alchabitius said that the Moon is a feminine, nocturnal fortune; she produces by her nature cold and moisture.... ...And Alchabitius said there is moderate phlegm in the Moon."[121]

Mercury, of course, is mixed, though Alchabitius, Bonatti says, asserts that Mercury "signifies things of the earth and the increase of things by growing."[122] By pointing out Mercury's earthy quality, we can infer a certain dryness at least.

In Book 9, Bonatti gives his philosophy behind using the ascendant and ascendant almuten as significators of the constitution, also taking into account the geographical and cultural background of the person. He enumerates what must be taken into consideration:

---

113. Guido Bonatti, trans. Zoller, *Liber Astronomiae, Second Tractate* (Berkeley Springs, W.Va.:The Golden Hind Press, 1994), Ch. 11, pp. 1-2.
114. Guido Bonatti, trans. Hand, *Liber Astronomiae, Third Tractate* (Berkeley Springs, W.Va.:The Golden Hind Press, 1995), Ch. 1, p. 2.
115. Ibid., Ch. 2, p. 8.
116. Alchabitius was an Arabic-era astrologer (d. 967) who wrote *Introduction to the Art of Judgments of the Stars*, popular in the West in the translation of John of Seville. He also gave his name to a system of house division.
117. Ibid., Ch. 3, p. 12.
118. Ibid., Ch. 4, p. 17.
119. Ibid. Ch. 5, p. 23.
120. A variant spelling of Abu Mashar.
121. Ibid., Ch. 7, pp. 34-5.
122. Ibid., Ch. 6, p. 29.

"…because the forms and figures of the bodies of the natives are comprehended from the nature of the figures of the ascendant and from the planets and from the conjunction [aspect] of them with others; and from the signs and fixed stars which are in these places."[123]

He also gives descriptions of the effect significating planets and combinations of planets have on the person's constitution.

Ramon Lull
Lull was a Spanish philosopher and Christian advocate from Majorca, born about 20 years after Bonatti. After a religious conversion in 1263, he spent the rest of his life creating an intricate system, the *Ars Combinatoria*, for analyzing ideas, concepts and their interrelationships, in order to defend and advance the cause of Christianity. Astrology and its philosophy was one of the ideas Lull incorporated into his system, especially using the four elements and qualities applied to the planets and signs. Through Lull's analysis of what he calls "proper" and "appropriated" qualities, we find that his logic creates the same wheel of elements and qualities that we saw in the beginning of this paper using Aristotle's cyclic ideas about the combinations of qualities to make elements (see over.)[124]

In Lull's scheme, the wheel rotates clockwise, and the quality preceding (to the left of) each element is the quality that is fully established but beginning to pass away; this is the "proper" quality. The quality following (to the right of) each element is coming into being and becoming stronger; this is the "appropriated" quality. Thus, in Air, wet, the proper quality, is beginning to pass away and hot, the appropriated quality, is becoming stronger. In Fire, hot is beginning to pass away and dry is becoming stronger. In Earth, dry is beginning to pass away and cold is becoming stronger; and in Water, cold is beginning to pass away and wet is becoming stronger. Lull also assigns a hierarchy of dominance to the element which goes counter-clockwise, so that Air dominates Water, which dominates Earth, which dominates Fire, which dominates Air, and so on.

With this system, Lull has devised an intricate methodology for ascertaining the predominance of elements/qualities in combination with each other, as planets in various signs and combinations mix together. It is not relevant to go into detail here about this system, but merely to point out that Lull has used the elements and qualities as part of a complex system that ends, in astrological terms at least, with one element or another becoming dominant through its association with both planets and signs. In this way, temperament also comes into the picture, since Lull gives interesting psychological descriptions of the temperaments in his delineation of the planets and their dominant element. These are in many ways psychological rather than physical. For example:

"The man born under Mars is subtle and learns and understands quickly, but by nature he does not have a good memory and forgets as quickly as he understands and wishes. This

---

123. Bonatti, *Liber Astronomiae* (Erhard Ratdolt, 1491), Book 9, Ch. 2 (translation by Dorian Greenbaum).
124. This analysis of Lull's theories is taken from Robert Hand's introduction to Lull's *Treatise on Astronomy, Books II – V* (Berkeley Springs, W.Va.:The Golden Hind Press, 1994), pp. v - vii.

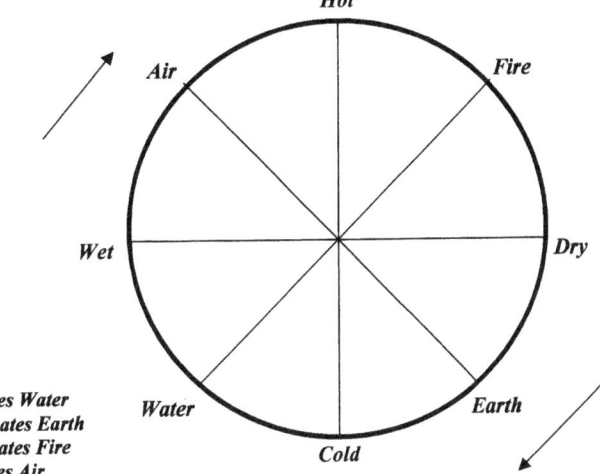

Figure 4. Lull's System of Elements and Qualities

happens through the imagination, which is too dry in the choleric man, for the great heat of the fire dries it out...."[125]

Lull's influence on the philosophy and thought of the medieval and Renaissance world is not perhaps as great as it ought to be, because a papal bull in 1376 condemned his teachings. His reputation was restored somewhat by another papal bull rehabilitating his work in 1416, but it is unclear how much influence he had, at any rate, on astrological thinking.[126] Even so, it is important to recognize his place in the history of temperament theory.

Antonius de Montulmo

Antonius de Montulmo flourished about a hundred years after Bonatti, so we are getting to the end of the medieval period and encroaching on the Renaissance. Montulmo's book, *On the Judgment of Nativities*, was written ca. 1396. In it, he discusses methods of determining life expectancy and, in the second half of his treatise, writes a fairly long section on determining both temperament and the quality of soul. Montulmo adheres to the philosophical traditions of Aristotle and Ptolemy, and his work was later referenced by Regiomontanus, Schoener and Lilly.[127]

---

125. Ramon Lull, trans. Shapar, *Treatise on Astronomy* (Berkeley Springs, W.Va.: The Golden Hind Press, 1994), p. 14. Appendix C extracts more of Lull's descriptions of temperaments.
126. Robert Hand, ibid., introduction to *Treatise on Astronomy*, p. v.
127. Robert Hand, introduction to Antonius de Montulmo, *On the Judgment of Nativities, Part 1* (Berkeley Springs, W.Va.:1995).

Chapter VIII is devoted to the "Form of the Body and the Complexion." In the first part of the chapter, Montulmo outlines ethnic and genetic characteristics of children as creations of their parents and products of a specific culture, echoing Ptolemy in his distinctions between the genetic and the celestial. Next, he enumerates what to look for in the chart to ascertain the "form and complexion:"[128]

> "The Ascendant of the nativity is the factor which always signifies the body of the native; wherefore consider first what it may signify concerning forms and complexion. Second, consider the Almuten of the Ascendant and the sign in which it is, and what each may signify concerning forms. Third, you will consider the place of the Moon because the Moon [also] signifies the body of the native. Also see whether there is any planet in the degree of the Ascendant especially if it should have any dignity in these places…. …you shall judge the form of that Ascendant according to that which predominates, mixing together the form of the Moon and of the other planets which aspect said places. Consider also which forms of the images of the fixed stars may be in the Ascendant…. Indeed consider the time of the nativity, whether it may be day or night, and in which quarter of the year he may have been born…."[129]

We can see Montulmo's debt to Ptolemy in the above criteria. Everything except the time of day of the nativity and the season of birth is enumerated in the *Tetrabiblos* Book III. For quality of soul, Montulmo expands on Ptolemy; and his description of the three kinds of soul, vegetative, sensitive and rational, are straight from Aristotle (*De Anima*, Book II). His criteria are clearly linked, and even similar, to those for determining bodily form, especially for the vegetative and sensitive soul, so again, as with Ptolemy, we find a 'psychological' connection to temperament. Montulmo says:

> "The principal significators of the vegetative soul first are the Ascendant, Moon, and the Almuten of the Ascendant, [any] planet which is in the Ascendant, especially if it should have any dignity here, the triplicity lord of the Ascendant, and the place which has been chosen as the Hyleg. However, the principal significators of the sensitive power are the Moon, the Almuten of the Ascendant, and [that] planet which is in the Ascendant, and the luminary whose is the authority. The principal significators of the intellective power are Mercury, the Almuten of the Ascendant, and the Moon. And although Ptolemy and others chiefly consider the place of Mercury for the native's reason and intellect, and they consider the Moon as it concerns the complexion and harmony which the body has toward the soul, because the soul having the proper dispositions and instruments in the body properly operates also on the reason. Wherefore it was according to the intention of Ptolemy that the Moon should signify the passions of the body, and should signify joyousness and quickness, and that which is obedient to the soul; wherefore it will be necessary to consider the Moon in performing the operations of the sensitive power because without the power of sense, either mediate or immediate, understanding cannot occur in created beings. Likewise Ptolemy considered the place of the Moon and Mercury when one had to understand the

---

128. Antonius de Montulmo, trans. Hand, *On the Judgment of Nativities*, Part 2 (Berkeley Springs, W.Va.:1995), p. 26.
129. Ibid., pp. 26-7.

operative power of the native's intellect. According to his intention it seems that you ought to consider the Ascendant because it signifies the body and disposition of the native's soul, and following the disposition of the aforesaid and their places, from this the astrologer can judge concerning the aforesaid powers."[130]

Here Montulmo considers the very same criteria for the vegetative soul as he does for bodily form: Ascendant, Almuten of the Ascendant, planets in the Ascendant and the Moon (in addition to which he adds the triplicity lord of the Ascendant and the Hyleg). Further, the same criteria for complexion are used as significators for the sensitive soul: Moon, Almuten of the Ascendant and planets in the Ascendant, plus the luminary ruling the chart (Sun for diurnal charts and Moon for nocturnal). We can conclude, since such similar criteria are given, that it is the *order* of those criteria which is important. Thus, for bodily temperament the Ascendant and its sign are most important; for vegetative soul the same; and Moon is most important for the sensitive soul. It seems clear that the temperaments of body and psyche are inextricably entwined.

A Literary Digression

That such was the case can also be seen in the popular culture of the time. Chaucer is roughly equivalent chronologically with Montulmo: *The Canterbury Tales* were written around 1387, only about 10 years before *On the Judgment of Nativities*. Images of the happy sanguine and the sorrowful melancholic can easily be found:[131]

> **(The Sanguine)**
> There was a franklin in his company;
> White was his beard as is the white daisy.
> Of sanguine temperament by every sign,
> He loved right well his morning sop in wine.
> Delightful living was the goal he'd won,
> For he was Epicurus' very son,
> That held opinion that a full delight
> Was true felicity, perfect and right.
>
> **(The Melancholic)**
> But telling of his sorrow brief I'll be.
> Had never any man so much torture,
> No, nor shall have while this world may endure.
> Bereft he was of sleep and meat and drink,
> That lean he grew and dry as shaft, I think.
> His eyes were hollow and ghastly to behold,

---

130. Ibid., pp. 42-3.
131. Geoffrey Chaucer, *The Canterbury Tales*, Prologue. The Knight's Tale. http://www.litrix.com/canterby/cante001.htm#1, http://www.litrix.com/canterby/cante002.htm (accessed 1 Mar 2004).

His face was sallow, all pale and ashen-cold,
And solitary kept he and alone,
Wailing the whole night long, making his moan.
And if he heard a song or instrument,
Then he would weep ungoverned and lament;
So feeble were his spirits, and so low,
And so changed was he, that no man could know
Him by his words or voice, whoever heard.
And in this change, for all the world he fared
As if not troubled by malady of love,
But by that humor dark and grim, whereof
Springs melancholy madness in the brain,
And fantasy unbridled holds its reign.

In addition, Chaucer reveals his knowledge of humors and temperament in his description of the doctor (and, incidentally, shows the deep connection between astrology and medicine):

With us there was a doctor of physic;
In all this world was none like him to pick
For talk of medicine and surgery;
For he was grounded in astronomy.
He often kept a patient from the pall
By horoscopes and magic natural.
Well could he tell the fortune ascendent
Within the houses for his sick patient.
He knew the cause of every malady,
Were it of hot or cold, of moist or dry,
And where engendered, and of what humour;
He was a very good practitioner.
The cause being known, down to the deepest root,
Anon he gave to the sick man his boot.
Ready he was, with his apothecaries,
To send him drugs and all electuaries;
By mutual aid much gold they'd always won-
Their friendship was a thing not new begun.
Well read was he in Esculapius,
And Deiscorides, and in Rufus,
Hippocrates, and Hali, and Galen,
Serapion, Rhazes, and Avicen,
Averrhoes, Gilbert, and Constantine,
Bernard and Gatisden, and John Damascene.

In diet he was measured as could be,
Including naught of superfluity,
But nourishing and easy. It's no libel
To say he read but little in the Bible.
In blue and scarlet he went clad, withal,
Lined with a taffeta and with sendal;
And yet he was right chary of expense;
He kept the gold he gained from pestilence.
For gold in physic is a fine cordial,
And therefore loved he gold exceeding all.

Marsilio Ficino

About one hundred years after Chaucer, Marsilio Ficino, the great Renaissance thinker, wrote a tremendous exposition as a tribute to his biological father, a doctor, and his spiritual father and patron, Cosimo de Medici. This has come down to us as *De Vita Libri Tres*, or *Three Books on Life*. In them Ficino sets forth his views on medicine, astrology and philosophy.

A great part of Book I is devoted to describing and explaining the melancholic temperament. Ficino's interest in this particular complexion comes from his own experience: Saturn, the planet of melancholy *par excellence* rises in his birthchart, in Aquarius, one of the signs it rules. In a letter to his friend Giovanni Cavalcanti, he describes his birthchart:[132]

> "Saturn seems to have impressed the seal of melancholy on me from the beginning; set, as it is, almost in the middle of my ascendant Aquarius, it is influenced by Mars, also in Aquarius, and the Moon in Capricorn. It is in square aspect to the Sun and Mercury in Scorpio, which occupy the ninth house. But Venus in Libra and Jupiter in Cancer have, perhaps, offered some resistance to this melancholy nature."[133]

We present Ficino's chart for interested readers (see over). Ficino was blessed or cursed by his own melancholic temperament, so he knows whereof he speaks. Here, perhaps striving to make lemonade from his Saturnine lemons, he makes a great case for the benefits of being melancholic: intelligence, even genius, and scholarly pursuits; ability to investigate things fully; good perception and judgment; an instrument of the divine.[134] Accordingly, he shows Saturn in the same light, the wise councillor rather than the malefic heavyweight.

---

132. He says erroneously here (he corrects himself in another letter, however) that Venus is in Libra and Jupiter in Cancer; Venus is actually in Virgo and Jupiter in Leo, but the mitigation he mentions still applies: Jupiter opposes Saturn; and Venus, though in fall, is in its own triplicity and in mutual reception with Saturn by term and Mercury by face.
133. Marsilio Ficino, *Meditations on the Soul, Selected Letters of Marsilio Ficino* (Rochester, Vermont:Inner Traditions International, 1997), p. 160.
134. Marsilio Ficino, trans. Kaske and Clark, *Three Books on Life* (Tempe, Ariz.:Medieval and Renaissance Texts & Studies *In conjunction with* the Renaissance Society of America, 1998), Book I, pp. 121-3. Perhaps Ficino had also read the Aristotelian treatise on melancholy mentioned on pp. 13-14 of the present book.

34 *Temperament: Astrology's Forgotten Key*

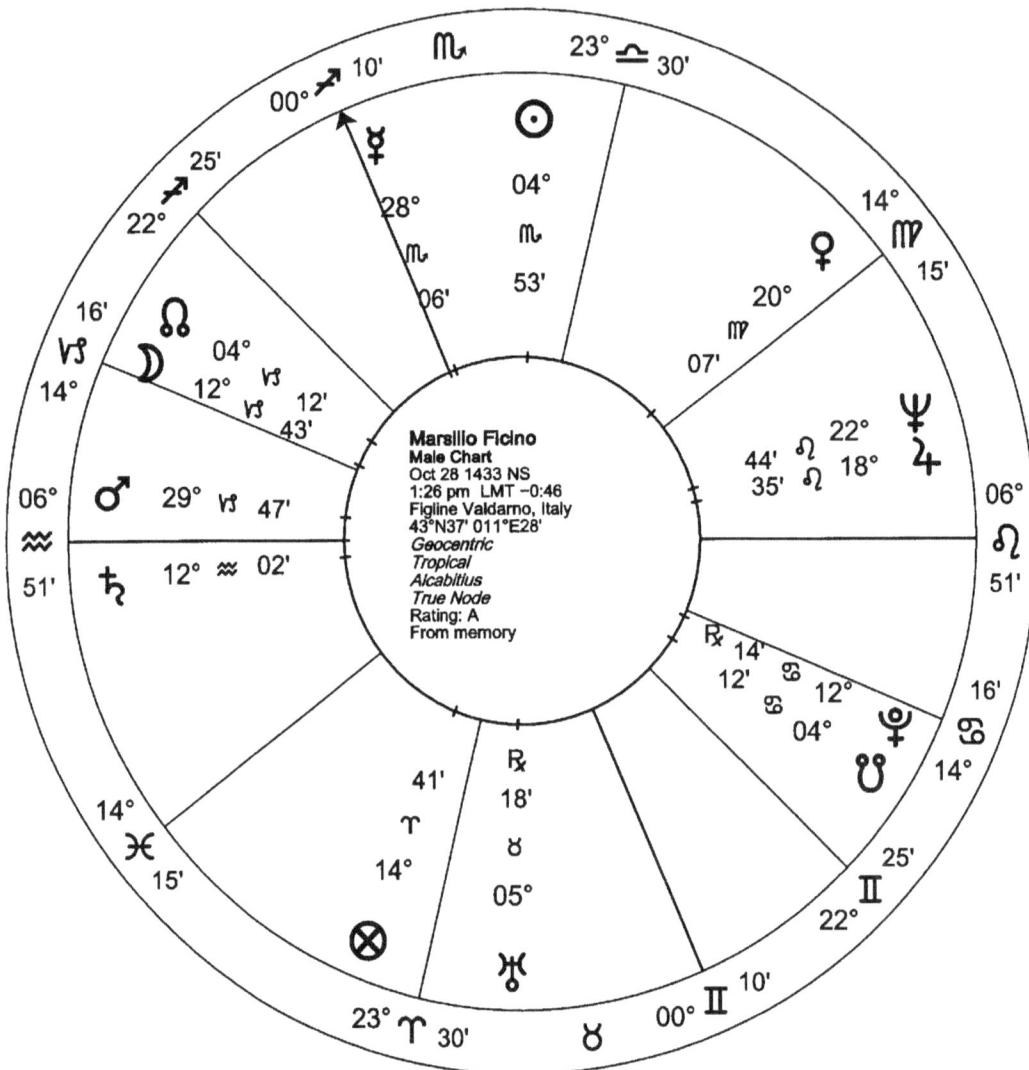

The third book, "On Obtaining Life from the Heavens," embraces Ficino's view of astrology, complete with sections on each of the seven planets and a large amount of ritual magic, invocations and talismans. He also gives astrological instructions for finding a person's ruling "*daemon*," that is, the planetary spirit that guides the person into finding his/her proper place in life. He advocates Firmicus' position, using both the Lord of the Geniture (in this case, the planet into whose sign the Moon moves after birth), either the Sun or Moon based on the sect of the chart, and the term ruler of the Part of Fortune. Look also at the houses the planets fall in; angular is best, then the 11th or 5th, then the 9th or 3rd. In Ficino's case Saturn would be Lord of the Geniture, the Sun is ruler by sect of the chart (a diurnal chart) and Mercury is the term ruler of the Part of Fortune. Adding the placement of the planets in question, Saturn is clearly the winner, placed as it is in the first house and in its own sign, Aquarius.

That Ficino spent so large a portion of his treatise discussing temperament is surely testimony to its importance in the worldview of the time. And Ficino was not even a practicing astrologer!

With Ficino we have left the medieval period and entered the Renaissance. It was during this time that people began to look not only outwards, toward the heavens, but within, and to question and investigate the relationships between God, humans and nature. For Ficino, the planets are gods who have lent their names to the heavenly bodies, and through correspondences we can invoke their powers within ourselves. The heavenly bodies, as living things, mediate between the material (man) and the divine (God).[135] From this point of view it is but a short step to the idea of microcosm (humans) reflecting the macrocosm (the heavens and the divine). This idea is enunciated by the great physician and philosopher Paracelsus.

Paracelsus
Paracelsus (1493-1541) rejects the humoral structure of the Greeks, but certainly embraces the idea of symbolic correspondence between the macrocosm and the microcosm:

> "*Ens naturale* is this: in astronomy you know the influence, the firmament, and all the heavenly bodies, and how to explain the stars, planets, and the nature of the heavens down to the smallest detail; there is an identical constellation and firmament in man. We should not mind calling man the microcosm, but you should understand this correctly. Just as the heavens with their firmaments and constellations are free and independent, so man is constituted completely independently without any linkage."[136]

However, in treating disease, it is important to find the remedy that correlates the heavenly to the earthly:

> "The physician should know how to bring about a conjunction between the astral Mars and the grown Mars (i.e. the herbal remedy). In this sense the remedy should be prepared in the star and should become a star.... The physician must...understand medicine in the light of the heavens, namely that there are stars both above and below. As a remedy cannot act without the heavens, it must be directed by them."[137]

Though Paracelsus rejects humoral theory (believing instead that Sulphur, Mercury and Salt are the substances of the body), he still accepts the idea that a man's constitutional makeup has an effect on his ability to withstand certain diseases, and that the planets have a part in this constitution.

---

135. Kaske and Clark, ibid.,"Introduction" to *Three Books on Life*, p. 44.
136. Paracelsus, trans. Goodrick-Clarke, *Paracelsus: Essential Readings* (Berkeley, Ca.:North Atlantic Books, 1999) "Volumen Medicinae Paramirum", p. 51.
137. Ibid., "Das Buch Paragranum," p. 75.

"But beyond all these anatomies, there is also a uniform science in the anatomy of medicine, and beyond them all stand heaven, earth, water and air, and the heavens and stars have their part in the new anatomy. For Saturn must give his *saturnum*, Mars his *martem*, and until these are discovered, the art of medicine has not been found."[138] "Therefore man is his own physician; for as he helps Nature she gives him what he needs, and gives him his herbal garden according to the requirements of his anatomy."[139]

Johannes Schoener

Johannes Schoener provides a means for finding that "anatomy" in his *Three Books on the Judgment of Nativities*.[140] In Book I, Chapter 5, he gives two methods of determining the form, figure and constitution of the body.[141] He lists the usual suspects: the Ascendant, the Almuten of the Ascendant, the Moon and planets which fall in or aspect the Ascendant, fixed stars in the Ascendant and the quarter of the year. The first of his methods, in addition to the above, also calls for the determination of the Part of Stability (aka the Part of Basis) and the Part of Future Things (the Part of Spirit). The second method subtracts the Parts and fixed stars, and adds Moon Phase, planets aspecting the Moon and the Almuten of the Geniture.[142]

For quality of soul, Schoener, like Ptolemy, looks at Mercury and its almuten; and like Montulmo, adds the Moon, the Almuten of the place of the Moon, the Ascendant and its almuten. He also considers the second and third triplicity lords of the 12th house, and the third triplicity lord of the 7th house.

Schoener published *Three Books on the Judgment of Nativities* in 1545, two years before his death. The tradition was carried on, however, by Johann Gartze, known as Garcaeus.

Garcaeus (Johann Gartze)

Garcaeus was of the generation after Schoener (1530-1574). In his work, *Astrologiae Methodus...*, published in 1574, he lists the qualities of planets by phase, Moon by phase and Sun by season.[143] Garcaeus considers temperament to be an important component of chart analysis. He says:

"Just as there are four principal humors in the bodies of animals, so four temperaments (*crases*) correspond to these: the sanguine which is hot and temperately moist; the phlegmatic which is moist and cold; the choleric which is hot and dry; and the melancholic which is cold and dry. Furthermore, once the temperament is recognized, one can judge more correctly and certainly with regard to manners, erudition, illnesses and similar matters. ... One must

---

139. Ibid., p. 84.
140. This is not to imply that he was necessarily a follower of Paracelsus.
141. Johannes Schoener, trans. Hand, *On the Judgments of Nativities*, Book I (Reston, Virginia:ARHAT, 2001).
142. For Schoener, this would be the planet with the most essential dignity in the places of the Sun, Moon, Ascendant, Part of Fortune and prenatal syzygy.
143. This information is taken from an unpublished translation of Garcaeus by Robert Hand.

combine [the indications] of all of these places together most carefully, and one should pay careful attention as to which of these intensify the temperament, and which diminish it and remit it."[144]

	ORIENTAL	*OCCIDENTAL*
♄	cold & wet	dry
♃	hot & wet	wet
♂	hot & dry	dry
♀	hot & wet	wet
☿	hot	dry

Table 6. Qualities of the Planets, by phase (Garcaeus)

New Moon to 1st Square	Hot & Wet
1st Square to Full Moon	Hot & Dry
Full Moon to Last Square	Cold & Dry
Last Square to Next New Moon	Cold & Wet

Table 7. Qualities of the Moon, by phase (Garcaeus)

SEASON	**SUN IN SIGNS**	**QUALITIES**
Spring	♈ ♉ ♊	hot & wet
Summer	♋ ♌ ♍	hot & dry
Autumn	♎ ♏ ♐	cold & dry
Winter	♑ ♒ ♓	cold & wet

Table 8. Qualities of the Sun, by phase (Garcaeus)

These are Garcaeus' criteria for determining temperament: the Ascendant and its almuten, planets in the Ascendant, planets partilely aspecting a planet in the 1st house, planets and nodes aspecting the degree of the Ascendant, the Moon, planets aspecting the Moon, the quarter (season) of the year, the Lord of the Geniture, any planet sharing rulership with the preceding, and fixed stars in the 1st house.

A Literary Digression
Let us take another look, now, at how temperament was portrayed in popular culture at this time. As Chaucer did in the *Canterbury Tales*, Shakespeare shows a thorough acquaintance with the qualities

---

144. Robert Hand's Garcaeus handout, p. 2.

of the various temperaments, from the melancholy of Hamlet to the sanguinity of Falstaff. Shakespeare's contemporary Ben Jonson even wrote a play entitled "Every Man in his Humour."[145]

Ben Jonson on the well-balanced person:[146]

> A creature of a most perfect and divine temper;
> One, in whom the Humors and Elements are peaceably met,
> without an emulation of Precedencie: he is neither too fantastickly
> Melancholy; too slowly Phlegmatick, too lightly Sanguine,
> or too rashly Cholerick, but in all, so compos'd and order'd; as it is
> cleare, Nature was about some full worke, she did more then
> make a man when she made him; His discourse is like his behaviour,
> uncommon, but not unpleasing; he is prodigall of neither:
> He strives rather to be (that which men call) Judicious,
> then to be thought so; and is so truely learned that he affects
> not to shew it: He will think, and speak his thought, both freely;
> but as distant from depraving any other mans Merrit, as proclaiming
> his owne: For his valor, it is such, that he dares as little to
> offer an Injury, as receive one. In sum, he hath a most Ingenious
> and sweet spirit, a sharp and season'd wit, a streight judgement,
> and a stronge minde; constant and unshaken: Fortune
> could never breake him, or make him lesse, he counts it his
> pleasure to despise pleasures, and is more delighted with good
> deedes then Goods, It is a competencie to him that he can be
> vertuous. He doth neither covet, nor feare; he hath too much
> reason to do either: and that commends all things to him.

Shakespeare on Melancholy:

Hamlet, Act II, Scene 2

> HAMLET. I have of late,—but wherefore I know not,—lost all my
> mirth, forgone all custom of exercises; and indeed, it goes so
> heavily with my disposition that this goodly frame, the earth,
> seems to me a sterile promontory; this most excellent canopy, the
> air, look you, this brave o'erhanging firmament, this majestical
> roof fretted with golden fire,—why, it appears no other thing
> to me than a foul and pestilent congregation of vapours.

---

145. This can be found at http://digital.library.upenn.edu/webbin/gutbook/lookup?num=3694 (accessed 30 Dec 2004).
146. From *Cynthia's Revels*, which can be found at http://www.gutenberg.org/catalog/world/readfile?fk_files=5176&pageno=49 (accessed 30 Dec 2004).

Shakespeare on Choler:

Comedy of Errors, Act II, Scene 2

ANTIPHOLUS OF SYRACUSE. I'll make you amends next, to give you nothing for something. But say, sir, is it dinnertime?
DROMIO OF SYRACUSE. No, sir; I think the meat wants that I have.
ANTIPHOLUS OF SYRACUSE. In good time, sir, what's that?
DROMIO OF SYRACUSE. Basting.
ANTIPHOLUS OF SYRACUSE. Well, sir, then 'twill be dry.
DROMIO OF SYRACUSE. If it be, sir, I pray you eat none of it.
ANTIPHOLUS OF SYRACUSE. Your reason?
DROMIO OF SYRACUSE. Lest it make you choleric, and purchase me another dry basting.
ANTIPHOLUS OF SYRACUSE. Well, sir, learn to jest in good time; there's a time for all things.
DROMIO OF SYRACUSE. I durst have denied that, before you were so choleric.

Robert Burton and *The Anatomy of Melancholy*

In 1621, the new century's equivalent of Ficino's book on melancholy was written by mathematician, vicar and astrologer Robert Burton, whose *The Anatomy of Melancholy* was to be an influence on writers for generations to come.[147] In this almost 1000 page book, Burton explores the definition of melancholy, its causes, its cures, and variations of melancholy, including love-melancholy, jealousy, and religious melancholy, all freely embellished with the opinions of other writers Burton has encountered in his liberal education.

For the purposes of this discussion, we shall only consider the medical and astrological links to melancholy mentioned by Burton. He follows the standard humoral theory of the time, and accepts the three faculties of soul: vegetal, sensitive and rational. He says that melancholy is an overabundance of black bile, probably affecting the brain, without fever, because the humor is mostly cold and dry. He says "Fear and Sorrow are the true characters, and inseparable companions, of most melancholy…"[148] He suspects that most melancholics have the Moon, Saturn and Mercury "misaffected in their geniture,"[149] among other causes.

Burton considers the "heavens, planets, stars &c. by their influence" to be primary causes of melancholy.[150] He bases his opinion on the writings of Paracelsus and Melanchthon, among others. (In fact, it is quite astonishing to see the amount of astrological sources he mentions in this section of the book: Jovianus Pontanus,[151] Leovitius,[152] Cardanus, Garcaeus, Schoener, Albubater,[153] Junctinus,

---

147. The frontispiece of this book, and a copy of Burton's birthchart, may be found in Appendix B.
148. Robert Burton, *The Anatomy of Melancholy* (New York: Tudor Publishing Co., 1927), p. 149.
149. Ibid., p. 150.
150. Ibid., p. 179.
151. Italian humanist and poet, 15th century.
152. Cyprien Leowitz, Bohemian astronomer, astrologer and almanac-maker, 16th century.
153. Another name for Rhasis; a *Hermetic Centiloquy* by Albubater was published in Venice in 1501.

Ranzovius, Lindhout, Origan, Gauricus. And these are just the astrologers!) He also mentions numerous scientists, physicians and philosophers such as Ficino. The chief signs, says Burton, are these: consider the Lord of the Geniture, or when there is an aspect between the Moon and Mercury, but neither aspects the Ascendant; or Saturn or Mars rule the present (lunar) conjunction or opposition in Sagittarius or Pisces, whether ruling the position of the Sun or Moon in the syzygy. The melancholy will occur when the significators of a chart (the Ascendant, Moon, Hyleg, etc.) are directed to Saturn or Mars by aspect, or the terms of Saturn or Mars, or to any fixed star of the nature of Saturn or Mars; or if transiting Saturn aspects the significators.[154]

That such a book as Burton's could be as popular as it was (it went through six editions in Burton's lifetime alone) is testimony to how ingrained temperament theory was to the Elizabethan world. By understanding the popularity of such a book, we can also see the influence of astrologers such as William Lilly, Nicholas Culpeper and John Gadbury.

So let us now look at the astrologers of the Elizabethan era and beyond. We will begin with William Lilly, who can be fairly said to have had the most influence on our modern interpretation of traditional techniques since Ptolemy.

William Lilly

Lilly's *Christian Astrology* is almost encyclopedic: in this 832 page work he delves into both natal and horary astrology, with numerous case studies, plus an "introduction" to the art of Astrology in about 100 pages.

Delineations of temperament, both of body and of soul, were clearly important to Lilly, as he devotes quite a few chapters (105-113) of *Christian Astrology* to this subject. First, he finds the Lord of the Geniture by considering the planets with the most essential and accidental dignity in the entire chart, and makes sure that such a planet is also placed well in the chart and "elevated."[155] The planet that comes in second place in this scheme may also participate as a ruler. Next, he ascertains the temperament of the body, as well as discussing the qualities of the planets and signs. For temperament of the body, Lilly uses the sign of the Ascendant and its lord (almuten), planets in the Ascendant, or partilely aspecting the Ascendant (including the Moon's nodes), the Moon and planets aspecting her, the season of the year, and the Lord of the Geniture. (His assignment of quality based on phase and season are the same as those used by Garcaeus.) By considering the qualities of the planets involved, one can find the temperament: more hot and moist = sanguine, more cold and moist = phlegmatic, more hot and dry = choleric and more cold and dry = melancholic. In this system he also triples the qualities of the Lord of the Geniture if it is the same as the lord of the Ascendant, and doubles those of the Moon if it is in the 1st house.

Lilly next considers the "Manners" of the person. He immediately points out the connection between temperament and manners:

---

154. Burton, op. cit., p. 181.
155. Presumably essentially dignified on its own.

"Wee may not doubt, but that the manners and motions of the mind, and the greatest part of our principall humane actions and events of life, doe accompany, or are concomitant with, and acted according to the quality of the *Temperature* and *inclinations*; for the *accidents* of Mind are twofold, some *rationall*, others *irrationall*, or more proper to the Sensitive power."[156] (italics Lilly's)

To determine manners, Lilly looks at planets in the Ascendant's sign or 1st house (and also the planet's dispositor), and considers the nature of that planet and its aspects (benefic or malefic). If there is more than one planet in the Ascendant, all contribute, but the one with the most dignity predominates. If there is no planet in the Ascendant, look at planets aspecting the Moon or Mercury. If no planets aspect the Moon or Mercury, use the Lord of the Ascendant (that is, the almuten). Also look at the fixed stars aspecting the significator of Manners. He ends the chapter with descriptions of each temperament:

"Again, a Sanguine temperament shewes men or person cheerfull, liberall, faithfull, affable, peace-makers, open hearted, modest, religious.
Cholerick people are full of anger, quarrelsome, revengefull, ambitious, importunate, imperious, hardy, rash, involving themselves into unnecessary troubles, seditious, many times ingenious, and easily changing their opinions.
Melanchollick persons are slow in resolutions, fraudulent, keeping close their counsels, prudent, severe, covetous, suspicious, sorrowfull, fearfull, froward, seldome forgetting injuries, inexorable, ambitious, loving no mans esteem but their owne.
Phlegmatick, are very cowards, uxorious people, mutable, not capable of keeping secrets, dull fellowes and sluggards in performing any businesse."[157]

Other chapters deal with descriptions of the planets as significators of Manners, the "Wit or Understanding of the Native" (using Mercury and its relationship to the Moon)[158] and finally, the person's physical appearance using planetary positions, signs and almutens. He concludes this section on a cheerful note with the general "Fortune or Misery of the Native."[159]

Nicholas Culpeper

A contemporary of Lilly's who also placed great importance on temperament was Nicholas Culpeper (1616-1654).[160] Trained as a physician, Culpeper was the first to write a medical book in English, thus enraging those who thought such ideas should never be read by the vulgar unlearned in Greek and Latin. Undeterred, Culpeper went on to write other books in English, culminating in *The English Physician*, now better known as *Culpeper's Complete Herbal*, which has never been out of print since it was first published in 1652.

---

156. William Lilly, *Christian Astrology* (Exeter:Regulus Publishing Co., Ltd., 1985), p. 534.
157. Ibid., p. 539. I suppose we can safely say that Lilly was not a phlegmatic!
158. Ibid., p. 543.
159. Ibid., pp. 551 ff.
160. For those interested in more about Culpeper, Graeme Tobyn has written *Culpeper's Medicine*, highly recommended.

Culpeper followed the humoral and temperamental system of his day. He considered the temperament to be completely manifest by age 30.[161] We can assume that the common astrological rules for delineating temperament were used by him also. Culpeper described the four temperaments in his book *Galen's Art of Physick* (1652).[162] He also considered the fact that not all people would be a "pure" temperament, and so described eight compound temperaments as well (the first one more predominant): melancholic-sanguine, sanguine-melancholic, sanguine-phlegmatic, phlegmatic-sanguine, choleric-melancholic, melancholic-choleric, choleric-phlegmatic and phlegmatic-choleric.[163]

We can see with the work of Culpeper that delineating temperament was being honed to a high degree. Was this to be the last gasp before the extinguishing of humoral and temperamental theory in the 18th and 19th centuries?[164] With the exceptions of the work of such astrologers as Gadbury, Coley and Partridge, unfortunately the answer is yes.

John Gadbury

John Gadbury was an admirer of both Lilly and Culpeper (though he later had a falling out with Lilly over politics; he was a royalist, while Lilly supported Parliament). He was born in 1628 and died in 1704, so his is the generation following Lilly's and Culpeper's. He adheres to the principles of both Lilly and Culpeper in determining temperament, and even did a temperamental chart delineation of Culpeper,[165] where he described Culpeper's temperament as melancholic-choleric. (Culpeper himself said he was "exceedingly melancholy of complexion. …I had the Sun opposite to Saturn in my nativity, which probably may be the natural cause of it.")[166] The following is Gadbury's descriptions of the temperament types:

> "Those persons that are of a sanguine Complexion, are generally the emblems of honesty; liberal, cheerful, affable and faithful; peace-makers, true, open-hearted and modest; very vertuous and religious. …gentle, courteous, affable disposition and temper.
> Melancholy persons are full of mental reserves, ponderous and slow in conception and resolution; fraudulent, suspicious, inexorable, fearful, sorrowful, froward, ambitious, seldom

---

161. Graeme Tobyn, *Culpeper's Medicine: A Practice of Western Holistic Medicine* (Rockport, Me.: Element Books, 1997), p. 50.
162. See Appendix D for his descriptions, and Appendix E for poems on the temperaments from the *Regimen of Health* (John Harrington, 1607).
163. Appendix F gives the characteristics of each of these temperaments. Culpeper omitted compound temperaments whose zodiacal correlation showed them not to be consecutive (i.e. Aries/Gemini, fire/air/, choleric/sanguine; or Taurus/Cancer, earth/water, melancholic/phlegmatic. Culpeper only considered the compound temperaments of those whose signs/elements were consecutive: thus e.g. choleric/melancholic = Aries/Taurus, fire/earth; or melancholic/sanguine = Taurus/Gemini, earth/air. A treatment of Culpeper's compound temperaments can also be found in Tobyn, *Culpeper's Medicine*, pp. 58-9.
164. Hastened by the theories of Vesalius and Harvey which doomed the humoral model.
165. John Gadbury, *Culpeper's School of Physick*, 1659. The chart of Culpeper is described in detail in Appendix 1 of Tobyn, op. cit., pp. 229-237.
166. Quoted in Tobyn, op. cit., p. 232.

forgetting injuries, loving no mans esteem but his own; very close and subtle in all their actions....of a mental reserved and close disposition.

The cholerique person is imperious, tyrannical, full of revenge, quarrelsome, apt to anger, importunate, hardy, rash, involving himself in many unnecessary troubles and vexations; a seditious Fellow, yet in many things ingenious and wittily apprehensive: but a very *Proteus* in his Opinion...of a rugged, surly and tyrannical disposition.

The Phlegmatic person is uxorious and a busie-body, a mutable person, not capable of keeping secrets; a vaporing, bragging, boasting, cracking person, yet a very coward; wonderful slow, dull and sluggish in the performance of any business...yet he is sometimes given to Mirth."[167]

Henry Coley and John Partridge

Coley (1633-1707) was a friend of Lilly's, and was given the rights to Lilly's almanac after his death. His system of delineating temperament is very similar to Lilly's.[168] Partridge (1644-1715) also gives a list of astrological indicators for temperament in his *Mikropanastron, or an Astrological Vade Mecum*, published in 1679. He looks for the Ascendant and its lord; planets in the Ascendant and planets partilely aspecting it, including the Nodes; the Moon; planets aspecting the Moon within orb; the season, or the sign of the Sun; and the lord of the nativity.

With Coley and Partridge, we come to the end of the use of astrological temperament for all intents and purposes until the end of the 19th century. The Enlightenment was about to erase the previous world view, to be replaced by the mechanist-materialist universe. Astrology entered a decline which would not reverse until the 20th century. Temperament theory would also reappear, but in disguise. We shall examine that disguise in the next section. For this one, it remains only to touch on the work of Immanuel Kant, who wrote a section on temperament in his book *Anthropology from a Pragmatic Point of View*, written about 1796.

Immanuel Kant

Kant considered the temperaments to be primarily psychological, but "influenced mysteriously by the physical condition of a person."[169] Kant classified the temperaments by *feeling* and *activity*: sanguine and melancholic fall into the feeling continuum, and choleric and phlegmatic on the activity continuum. The sanguine has quick and fleeting sense impressions, while the melancholic's are deeper and long-lasting. Cholerics are characterized by much activity and impetuous behavior; the phlegmatic is apathetic and hard to arouse to activity. Kant relates the temperaments to the physical body by connecting different kinds of blood to each: sanguines are light-blooded, melancholics heavy-blooded,

---

167. Gadbury, *Doctrine of Nativities* (1658; Ballantrae Reprint, no date), Chapter XII, secs. 5 & 7, pp. 94, 97. We can only surmise, when realizing the similarity of the descriptions between Gadbury and Lilly, that imitation was the sincerest form of flattery, not plagiarism!
168. See Appendix A, p.146.
169. Immanuel Kant, trans. Dowdell, *Anthropology from a Pragmatic Point to View* (Carbondale & Edwardsville, Ill.:Southern Illinois University Press, 1978), p. 197.

cholerics hot-blooded and phlegmatics cold-blooded. There is a certain elegance in Kant's system and it is clearly based on Greek theory. Kant does not allow for the compound temperaments choleric/sanguine or melancholic/phlegmatic – whose qualities, he says, neutralize each other.[170] He is not an advocate of compound temperaments in general, saying "We do not know what to make of the person who claims to have a mixture of temperaments.[171]

The Offshoots of Temperament

Kant's work on temperament is one of only a few to gain prominence during the Enlightenment. We might say that both astrology and temperament theory went into hibernation for about the next 200 years. The Enlightenment, followed by the materialism and urbanization of the Industrial Age, served almost to sever humanity's connection between cosmos and psyche. With the creation of psychology as a 'science' at the end of the 19th century, a chink appeared in the armor of materialism (only a small chink, given psychology's 'hard science' boosters), and not one, but two 'modern' concepts correlating to temperament came into existence. These are the theories of Carl Jung and Rudolf Steiner. Others in this time frame also developed similar ideas, but this discussion will focus primarily on Jung and Steiner and their followers, as representatives of temperament in the modern world. We will also take a brief look at one 20th century astrologer who used temperament in his work, Marc Edmund Jones.

Carl Jung

Carl Jung was born July 26, 1875 in Kesswil, Switzerland.[172] Trained as a doctor, he was the descendant of a long line of preachers, including his father, and early on had an interest in spiritual matters. For the earlier part of his medical career he was a disciple and then colleague of Freud, though their paths began to diverge in 1909. Jung went on to develop, among many other things, the concept of the collective unconscious and, more pertinent for our investigation, a new theory of temperament divided into *attitudes* (extravert and introvert) and *functions* (thinking, feeling, sensation and intuition). Jung believed that we experience the world from two fundamental viewpoints: extravert and introvert.[173] Extraverts, says Jung, focus their interests outward into an object-oriented existence, while introverts tend to put their awareness inward and see the world subjectively[174] Everyone is classified as having one or the other of these types predominant.

In addition to these types, there are also four ways of functioning in the world. Jung calls these thinking, feeling, sensation and intuition. Combined with either extraversion or introversion, there come to be eight different possible psychological types: extraverted-thinking, extraverted-feeling,

---

170. Ibid., pp. 201-202.
171. Ibid., p. 202.
172. Chart data for Jung are from *Astrodatabank*. Rating, A: from memory.
173. Carl Jung, op. cit., p. 3.
174. Ibid., p. 5.

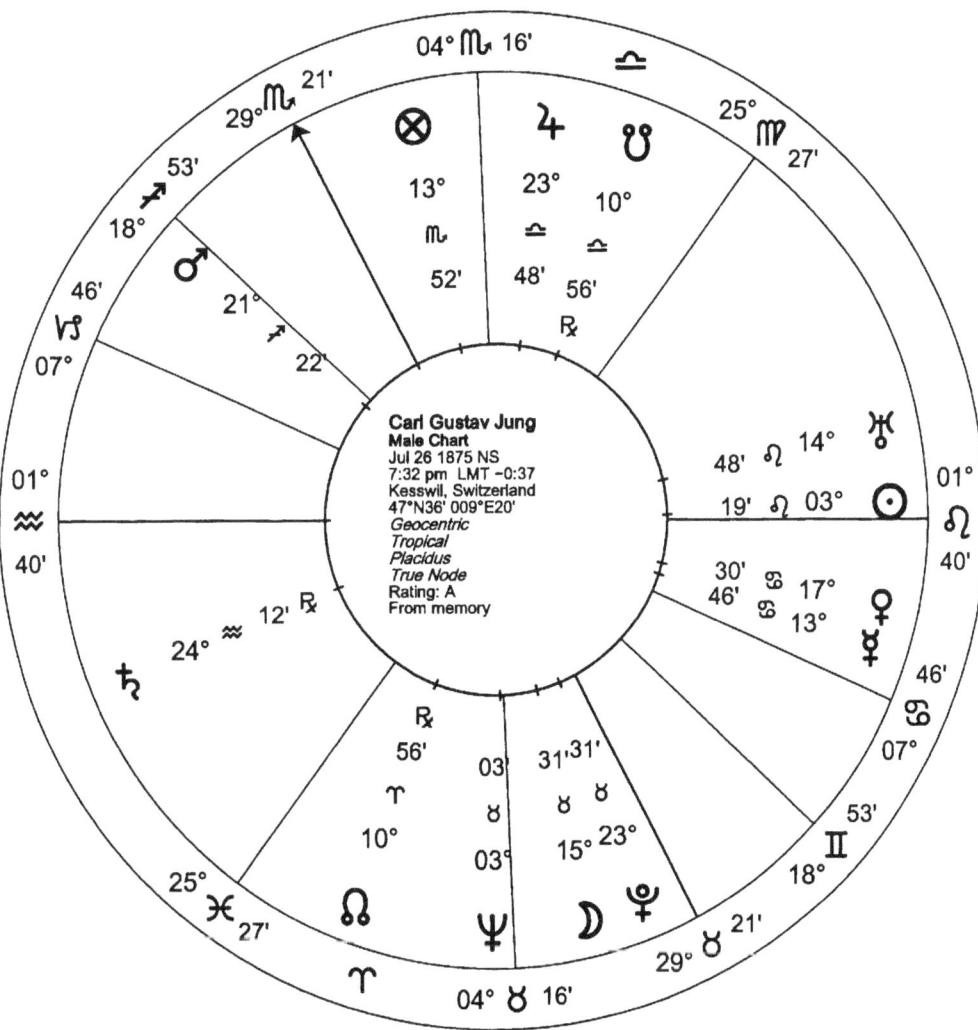

extraverted-sensation, extraverted-intuition, introverted-thinking, introverted-feeling, introverted-sensation and introverted-intuition.

Thinking says Jung, is "the function of intellectual cognition and the forming of logical conclusions."[175] Thinkers find it hard to adapt to a situation they cannot understand intellectually, whether in an extraverted or introverted way. The extraverted thinker functions by reducing all actions to an intellectual, objective, reality-based level, whereas the introverted thinker, though still influenced by ideas, bases those ideas on his own subjective, personal experience. Jung gives Darwin as an example of an extravert thinker and Kant as an introvert thinker.

---

175. Ibid., p. 518. For other material in this paragraph, see also pp. 519, 346-7, 383.

Feeling is a "function of subjective valuation,"¹⁷⁶ meaning that feelers make value judgments not necessarily logically, as thinkers think they do, but based on whether their impression of a situation is positive or negative. Again, there are two forms: extravert and introvert feeling. Extraverted feelers divorce themselves from the subjective – for example, they might go to the latest play or movie not because they have a personal interest in it, but because everyone else is going. The world of fashion is a perfect example of this, with its emphasis on being 'in style' by wearing the latest clothing. In a more positive way, philanthropic and cultural institutions survive on this kind of approach. Introverted feeling, by contrast, divorces itself from the object and even devalues it. Though they may appear as cold and reserved on the outside, introverted feelers are in fact guided by their subjective feelings which can be deep and intense; as Jung points out, the phrase 'still waters run deep' perfectly expresses the underlying sentiment of the introverted feeling person.

Both thinking and feeling are called *rational* by Jung, because they involve the process of reasoning. Sensation and intuition, on the other hand, are called *irrational* because they involve perception, not reason.

Sensation, in fact, refers to "perceptions by means of the sense organs."¹⁷⁷ In extraverted sensation, an object that arouses the strongest sensation is what affects the person's psychology the most. Jung says that extraverted sensers are the most realistic of the types, and feel themselves to be extremely rational, though this may not in fact be the case; their sensations may simply overwhelm them when experiencing an irrational or chance event. Introverted sensers do not judge rationally, but form their judgements based on what happens and how strong their response to it is. Their reactions, unlike those of the extraverted sensers, come from a subjective stance. The introverted component may cause them to seem unable to express themselves, or they may come across as calm and passive. Whether extraverted or introverted, it is the external object or event and their perception of it that influences the senser's psychology.

Intuition is "perception by way of the unconscious, or perception of unconscious contents."¹⁷⁸ Intuitives may find themselves always thinking about the possibilities in a situation, enthralled with 'what might be.' The extraverted intuitive directs unconscious perception outwards, and it is consciously expressed by feelings of expectation, or by envisioning something new just on the horizon. We might characterize Bill Gates as an extraverted intuitive. These types are cramped and bored by stability, and lack judgment. Jung lists business tycoons and politicians as likely extraverted intuitives. The introverted intuitive, however, has trouble differentiating visions or articulating them from among the many images teeming in his/her unconscious mind. Jung gives as types of introverted intuitives "the mystical dreamer and seer on the one hand, the artist and the crank on the other."¹⁷⁹ Unlike the visionary extraverted intuitive, whose ideas may be welcomed, the introverted intuitive is a voice crying in the wilderness, the dreamer who is years ahead of his time.

---

176. Ibid., p. 518. For other material in this paragraph, see also pp. 519, 355, 388.
177. Ibid., p. 518. For other material in this paragraph, see also pp. 363-3, 395.
178. Ibid., p. 518. For other material in this paragraph, see also pp. 519, 366, 368-9, 400-402.
179. Ibid., p. 401.

The four functions, in Jung's scheme, come in pairs that naturally oppose each other: thinking and feeling are opposite functions, and sensation and intuition are opposite functions. In an ideal state, all the functions would be balanced, but in reality one type tends to predominate, with its opposite as the most repressed *inferior* or *shadow* function, and one of the other two functions perhaps playing a secondary role to the principal function :

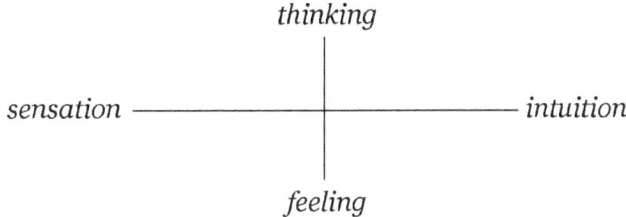

Figure 5. Jungian Functions

As character types, one could be a combination, say, of thinking-sensation, or feeling-intuition, but not thinking-feeling or sensation-intuition.

Psychological Types is clearly a *tour de force* of Jung's intellectual and intuitive powers. He acknowledges a debt to ancient temperament theory, as providing at least a foundation and continuum from which his new typology can emerge (though he says temperament theory "hardly rates as a psychological typology since the temperaments are scarcely more than psychophysical colourings").[180] Having studied the actual development of temperament theory up to 1700, I must respectfully disagree. He also states that temperament arose from astrology,[181] when actually astrology picked up temperament from philosophy and medicine. However, he wants to show that his psychological types are less 'metaphysical' in order to give them legitimacy in the scientific community. So in the end he must discard any vestige of the ancient system.

Is this indeed the case, or can we perhaps show some correlations between Jung's types and the ancient temperaments/elements? Liz Greene has attempted this in her book *Relating*, where she equates thinking with air, feeling with water, sensation with earth and intuition with fire.[182] She makes some very valid points, but goes against astrological/temperamental/philosophical principles when she says that air and water are thus opposite types, as are earth and fire. Since air is hot and wet and water is cold and wet, they are not true opposites; the same is true for earth, cold and dry, and fire, hot and dry.

My colleague Joseph Crane has made other correlations between Jung's psychological types and the temperaments, which seem to keep their philosophical integrity intact. In his unpublished lectures, Crane has characterized the two attitudes, extravert and introvert, as hot and cold respectively. (You will remember that these are Aristotle's and the Stoics' "active" qualities.) He characterizes the four functions as either wet or dry. Thinking and sensation are dry; feeling and intuition are wet. So, the oppositions still make sense:

---

181. Ibid., "A Psychological Theory of Types," p. 531.
182. Liz Greene, *Relating* (York Beach, Me.:Samuel Weiser, 1978), Chapter 3.

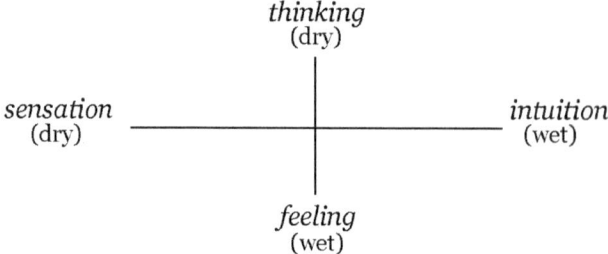

Figure 6. Functions correlated with qualities

When hot and cold (extravert and introvert) are added, we get:

    extraverted (hot) thinking or sensation (dry) = choleric
    extraverted (hot) feeling or intuition (wet) = sanguine
    introverted (cold) thinking or sensation (dry) = melancholic
    introverted (cold) feeling or intuition (wet) = phlegmatic

An intriguing way to blend the old and the new! (And could easily be a study on its own.) Other psychologists have taken up Jung's ideas on psychological type, and created the Myers-Briggs Temperament Index (Katharine Briggs and her daughter Isabel Briggs Myers) and the Keirsey Temperament Sorter (David Keirsey and Marilyn Bates). With the click of a mouse, it is possible to take the Keirsey questionnaire on the internet and instantly come up with a temperament indicator. The seeds planted by Jung have been sown far and wide.

Marc Edmund Jones

Jones' work with temperament[183] seems to be an amalgam of astrology with theosophy, producing a system that divides the mind into three: mind as mood, mind as personality and mind as sensation. Temperament is associated with mind as mood.

    Jones calls temperament the "actuation of the physical expression of selfhood." He believes that temperament can be both underlying and transient (a mood); this would correspond to the idea the we have temperament overlays at various times in our lives (e.g., childhood is sanguine). So all individuals possess all temperaments at certain phases and moments. He describes five temperaments, the usual four plus what he calls the "volatile." Each temperament is associated with a particular sign of the zodiac, and since all signs are contained within a birthchart, all individuals have the potential for any temperament, even if they manifest another one. Temperament, according to Jones, is a functioning of what he calls the astral body, and not a physical characteristic. It is inner rather than external.

---

183. Found in his typed notebooks entitled *Lecture Lessons, Hermetic Astrology I-VI* (Privately typed, 1933), but not widely available. This system is quite different from the "temperament types" described by Jones' definitions of chart patterns (bowl, bucket, locomotive, etc.). The descriptions of Jones' temperament system in the following paragraphs come from these *Hermetic Astrology* Lessons: II, p.3; III, pp. 3-6; IV, p. 7; V, pp. 9-10; VI, p. 11.

To discover the temperament in the chart, Jones suggests looking at the rising sign, at an emphasis in the chart on one of the signs associated with the five temperaments, at planets in those signs, including the parts and nodes if there are no planets in those signs. If there is no direct emphasis on a temperament, the default temperament is phlegmatic.

He describes the five temperaments in great detail; I will give here a few highlights, supplemented by a table showing the temperaments' relationships to signs, glands, humors, etc.

Volatile Temperament. This temperament is closely allied with the astral body, and finds it easy to be independent from physical actuality. There is a loyalty to selfhood; that is, the sense of self as different from other is important, and people with this temperament use life situations to demonstrate their sense of self. There is also a desire for practical wisdom.

Choleric Temperament. This temperament projects the astral body and is an example of the fundamental nature of the astral body. It is easily able to accomplish things, and may feign anger to accomplish its purpose. It has a desire to assert itself and to be recognized and honored as an individual.

Phlegmatic Temperament. This temperament uses the astral body in a role of self-discovery. It has an inward focus, and tries to rely solely on itself so that it can separate itself from the interactions of daily life. It desires a luxury or security for itself.

Sanguine Temperament. This temperament looks to present consciousness of the astral body. It is the embodiment of normality, has conventional ideals, and desires the excitement of self-expansion. It is able to successfully adapt the social pattern to its own purposes.

Melancholic Temperament. This temperament strives for intense development of the astral body. The melancholic has a "cosmic loneliness;"[184] it is similar to the phlegmatic, but where the phlegmatic is self-sufficient, the melancholic is dependent on what it separates itself from. Jones remarks on the melancholic's capacity for spiritual enlightenment.

SIGN	GLAND	HUMOR	PRINCIPLE	TEMPERAMENT	DESIRE	INCLINATION
Cancer	Pituitary	Spirit	Air	Volatile	Wisdom	Self-awareness
Gemini	Thyroid	Yellow bile	Lymph	Choleric	Honor	Self-sharing
Taurus	Adrenals	Phlegm	Mucus	Phlegmatic	Luxury	Self-isolation
Aries	Spleen	Blood	Blood	Sanguine	Excitement	Self-exercise
Pisces	Liver	Black bile	Gall	Melancholic	Affection	Self-judgment

Table 9. Marc Edmund Jones' Temperament System [185]

---

184. Marc Edmund Jones, *Lecture Lessons, Hermetic Astrology VI*, p. 11.
185. Modified from table in Marc Edmund Jones, *Lecture Lessons, Hermetic Astrology IV*, p. 8.

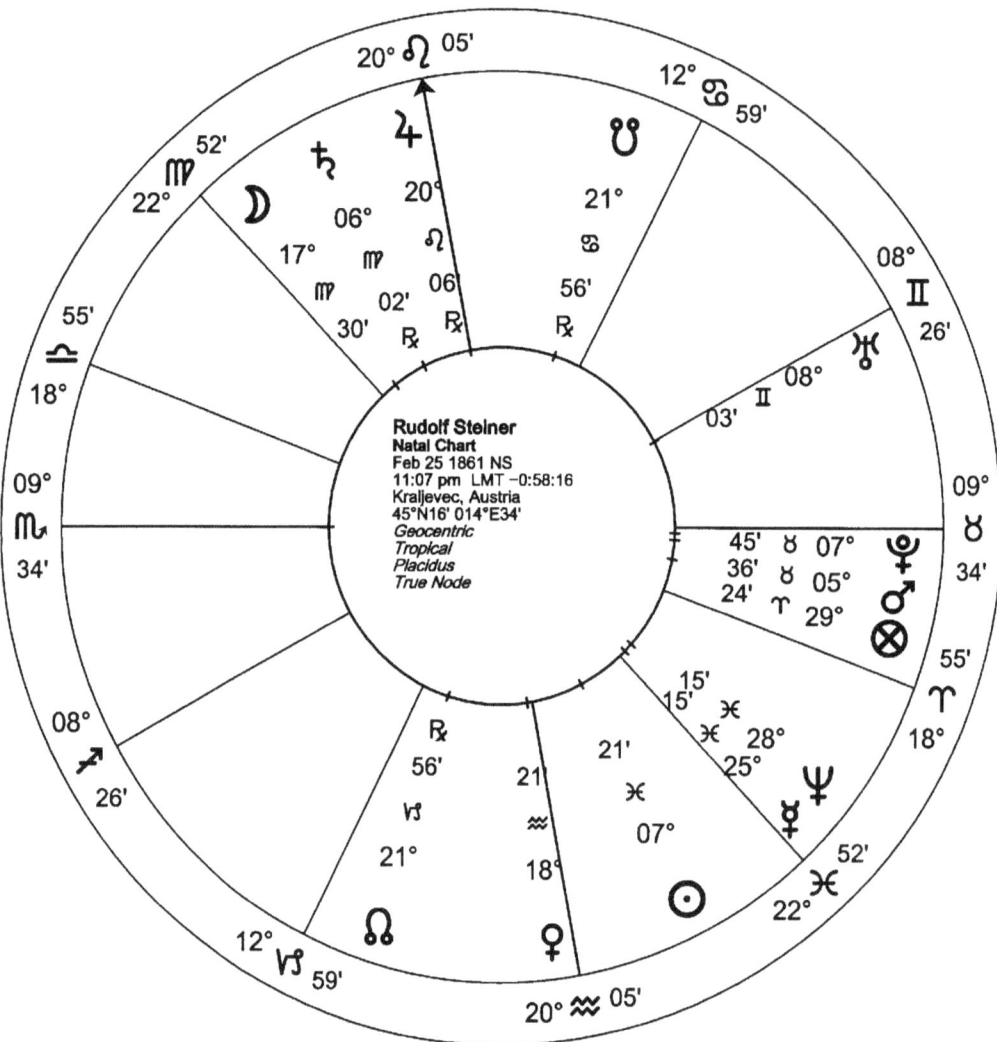

Rudolf Steiner

Born 14 years before Jung, on February 25, 1861,[186] Rudolf Steiner formulated ideas about temperament beginning in 1909. Steiner was trained as a mathematician and philosopher, and was especially influenced by Goethe, whose works he edited. His first philosophical work, *Intuitive Thinking as a Spiritual Path: A Philosophy of Freedom*, was published in 1894. Steiner was deeply interested in the spiritual component of human beings, nature and the universe. For a while, he was a Theosophist, but

---

186. Birth data for Steiner from Lois Rodden, citing Birth Record and personal letter from Steiner (AA).

when they declared Jiddu Krishnamurti the reincarnation of Christ in 1912, he, and the German section of Theosophy that he had formed, broke off from the Theosophists and created a movement called Anthroposophy – the wisdom of man.

Today, Steiner is best known as the originator of biodynamic agriculture and Waldorf education. Both of these were based on the philosophical principles of Anthroposophy, which holds that the spiritual world is every bit as real as the physical one. It was in the formulation of Waldorf education that Steiner articulated his concept of the four temperaments, which he clearly modelled after the Greek and medieval/renaissance definitions. His primary exposition of temperament theory can be found in his essay, "The Four Temperaments," a lecture given in Berlin on March 4, 1909. In the following three pages, I will explain Steiner's ideas on temperament both from this essay (printed in *Anthroposophy in Everyday Life*[187]) as well as his further elucidations of temperament in *Discussions with Teachers*.[188]

Steiner calls temperament "that fundamental coloring of the human personality, [which] plays a role in all manifestations of individuality that are of concern to practical life."[189] He believes that temperament combines what he calls the "spiritual-psychic stream,"[190] (that is, the spiritual consciousness that a soul carries with it through each incarnation) together with the physical heredity passed through our parents. In this way both the eternal inner essence of a person and ancestral inheritance manifest through the temperament; it is poised between what endures and what does not.

Steiner uses both the words "disposition" and "characteristic constitution"[191] to describe temperament. For him, both the physical and psycho-spiritual components are important. His view is that external physical characteristics can point the way or, in fact, correlate, to internal psychic manifestations. He has his own system of psychic-spiritual-physical connections in the *four bodies* which make up the human being. These are the physical body; the etheric body which contains the

BODY PRINCIPLE	EXPRESSION IN PHYSICAL BODY	TEMPERAMENT
Ego	*blood*	*Choleric*
Astral	*brain, nervous system*	*Sanguine*
Etheric	*glandular system, fluids*	*Phlegmatic*
Physical	*bones, mineral nature*	*Melancholic*

Table 10. Steiner's correlation of Body and Temperament

---

187. Rudolf Steiner, trans. Kelly, *Anthroposophy in Everyday Life* (Hudson, N.Y.:Anthroposophic Press, 1995), pp. 67-81; especially refer to pp. 67, 70-71, 74-79.
188. Rudolf Steiner, trans. Fox, *Discussions with Teachers* (N.Y.:Anthroposophic Press, 1997), refer to pp. 13-14, 18-20, 29-33, 36-38, 63-64.
189. Rudolf Steiner, trans. Kelly, *Anthroposophy in Everyday Life* (Hudson, N.Y.:Anthroposophic Press, 1995), p. 67.
190. Ibid., pp. 70-71.
191. Steiner, *Discussions with Teachers*, p. 13.

life-force, regulates growth and separates from the physical body at death; the astral body which bears instincts, drives, passions, desires, sensation and thought; and the Ego body which gives us our self-awareness.[192] Each of these bodies is associated with a temperament: the Ego body with cholerics, the astral body with sanguines, the etheric body with phlegmatics and the physical body with melancholics. (In children, a different body is aligned with each temperament: Ego body/melancholic, astral body/choleric, etheric body/sanguine and physical body/phlegmatic. The actual characteristics of the temperament, however, do not change.)[193]

That Steiner built on the system created by the Greeks is clear in the way that he diagrams the temperaments:

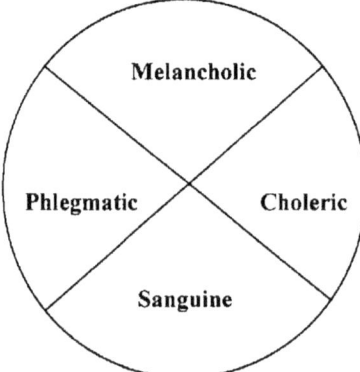

Figure 7. Steiner's circle of Temperaments [194]

This is both the seasonal cycle, with spring at the bottom and the seasons going counter-clockwise; and Aristotle's concept of the elements changing into one another easily when one of their qualities is the same. Steiner says:

> "Sanguine and phlegmatic temperaments are frequently found together, and you will see that they are next to each other in the diagram. You will never find a phlegmatic temperament passing easily into the choleric. They are as different as the North and South Poles. The melancholic and sanguine temperaments are also polar opposites."[195]

How does Steiner describe each temperament? He notes both physical and psychological characteristics, again, clearly influenced by traditional temperament theory:

Cholerics tend to be short, because their Ego body is so strong that it stunts the growth of the other bodies. Their features are cleanly defined, and when they walk they plant their feet firmly on

---

192. Steiner, *Anthroposophy in Everyday Life*, p. 71.
193. Gilbert Childs, *Balancing Your Temperament* (London:Sophia Books, 1999), p. 16.
194. Chart after Steiner's diagram in *Discussions with Teachers*, p. 19.
195. Ibid.

the ground. They are strong-willed, sometimes inclined to bluster, and have trouble controlling their tempers. Steiner suggests that musically, choleric children will do best with percussion, rhythm and solo instruments. They need someone as a teacher whom they can respect, and they like challenging situations.

Sanguines' sensations and feelings constantly fluctuate, and their features are "mobile, expressive and changeable."[196] Their step is springy and they tend toward the svelte and sleek. They have an interest in many things, but a short attention span. Sanguines will do best with wind instruments, melody and being part of a whole orchestra. They need a teacher they can admire, even love, or they will become bored or resentful. When sanguine children love their teachers, they are willing to do anything for them and can make great strides in their educations.

Melancholics, who are ruled by the physical body, sometimes feel overwhelmed by that very physicality. Since the physical body is supposed to be the "instrument"[197] of the other bodies, the inversion of the hierarchy can make the melancholic frustrated and despondent. They may stoop or hang their heads, and walk with a leaden gait. They tend to be tall and thin. Melancholics musically do best with strings, counterpoint and solo singing. They tend toward inner reflection and brooding, and are convinced that no one has ever had experiences like theirs, and that no one can understand their pain. Thus, they need a teacher who can show them that he or she has been through the same pain and trials as they have.

Phlegmatics, being ruled by the etheric body, which regulates growth and metabolism, tend to be preoccupied by their own internal processes. They feel a sense of well-being from contemplating their inner workings. They seem somehow out of touch with their surroundings and have a "static, indifferent physiognomy,"[198] tending to the plump. They have a loose and somewhat shambling gait, and may be shy. Musically, they do best with the piano, harmony and choral singing. It is important for them to have playmates who can show them a range of interests, and get them to come out of their shells.

Steiner is careful to point out that there is great diversity in human beings, and that no temperament exists in a totally pure state. Thus one temperament will tend to predominate, with one or two more as sub-temperaments, and the other as somewhat unconscious or repressed.

In addition, stages of life are overlaid by specific temperaments (this is true in the traditional system also). Childhood is sanguine, adolescence and young adulthood choleric, mature adulthood melancholic and old age phlegmatic. Steiner says, "…you must remember above all that the human being is constantly *becoming*, always changing and developing."[199] Usually, people retain vestiges of these temperaments as they age. Thus, a poet, for example, might retain some of the sanguinity he had as a child, but also, experience and the wisdom gained from it shows a certain phlegmatic quality. "A

---

196. Steiner, *Anthroposophy in Everyday Life*, p. 75.
197. Ibid., p. 74.
198. Ibid., p. 75.
199. Steiner, *Discussions with Teachers*, p. 36.

harmonious temperament, along with some of the phlegmatic's unexcitability is the best combination for business life."[200]

Countries and languages can also show a predominance of a temperament: for example, Steiner describes Russia as melancholic. Interestingly, he considers both Greek and German to have strong sanguine components, mentioning the German proclivity toward philosophy – which could equally apply to Greece. (Though German, he says, has a melancholic component as well.) He describes English as "thoroughly phlegmatic."[201]

The concept of temperament suffuses Waldorf pedagogy. Teachers seat their students according to temperament, which Steiner says has a homeopathic effect in calming down cholerics and enlivening phlegmatics.[202] Lessons and stories told by teachers can be geared toward the different temperaments; even drawing lessons have a different focus based on temperament.[203]

As one might expect, Waldorf educators have embraced and expanded on Steiner's concepts. Gilbert Childs has written two books on temperament, describing the characteristics of each, discussing compatibility of different types, and comparing the temperament system to others such as Sheldon's theories of body type (endomorphic, mesomorphic and ectomorphic). His mottoes and theme tunes for each temperament are evocative and apt:[204]

TEMPERAMENT	MOTTO AND THEME TUNE
Choleric	Motto: When the going gets tough, the tough get going. Theme Tune: *My Way*
Sanguine	Motto: Promises, promises! Theme Tune: *Blue Skies*
Phlegmatic	Motto: Procrastinate tomorrow! Theme Tune: *Home Sweet Home*
Melancholic	Motto: Life is real, life is earnest. Theme Tune: *Yesterday*

Table 11. Childs' mottoes, theme tunes and temperaments

Childs also brings in the ideas of Jung when he calls phlegmatics and melancholics introverted and cholerics and sanguines extraverts. He expands on the connection to traditional temperament theory in the following chart:[205]

---

200. Ibid., p. 38.
201. Ibid., p. 64.
202. Ibid., p. 20.
203. Ibid., p. 36.
204. Gilbert Childs, *Understand Your Temperament!* (London:Sophia Books, 1995), pp. 31, 39, 47, 57.
205. Ibid., p. 18.

Theory and History of Temperament   55

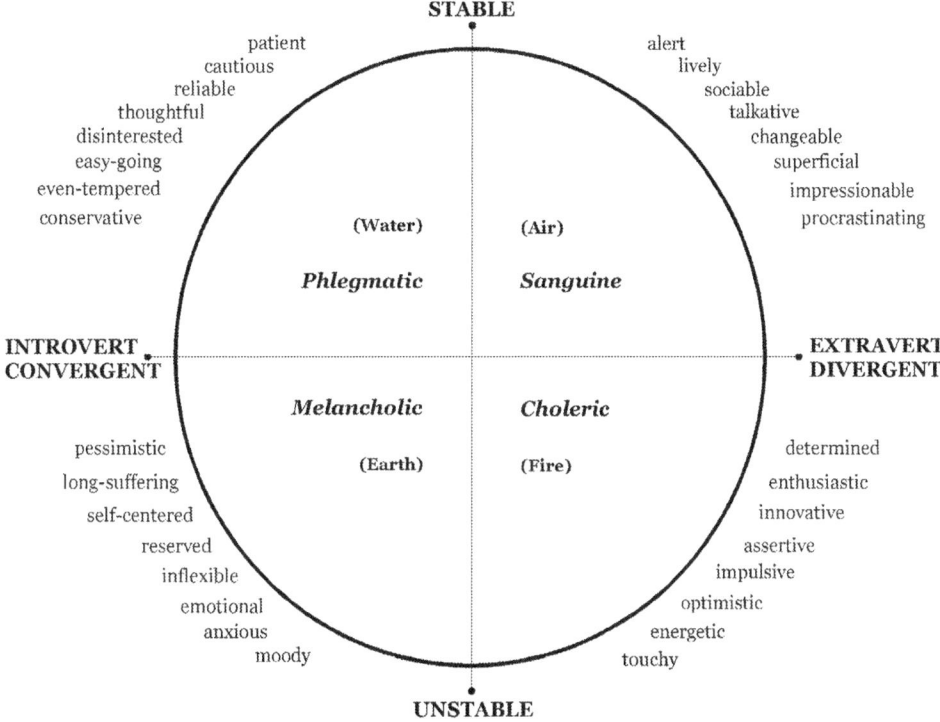

Figure 8. Childs' Temperament Diagram

Marieke Anschütz, in her book *Children and their Temperaments*, even gives a history of the Greek temperament system and creates a chart which clearly has astrological and medical connections:[206]

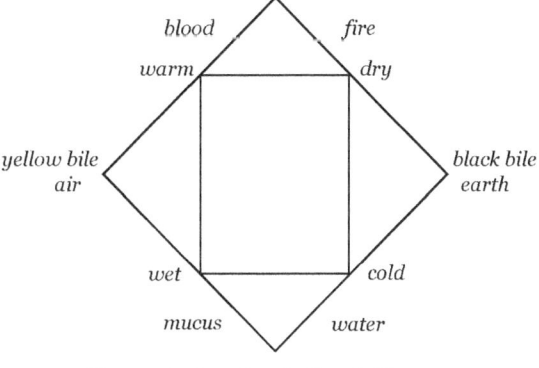

Figure 9. Anschütz's Greek Humors

---

206. Marieke Anschütz, trans. Langham and Peters, *Children and their Temperaments* (Edinburgh: Floris Books, 1995), p. 24.

Roy Wilkinson, another Waldorf educator, has developed the use of temperament typing in the classroom with *The Temperaments in Education*. He has created a handy chart for identifying each temperament, along with reactions of children according to their temperament and teaching tips for each temperament (see Appendix G).

With Steiner and Jung, we can see the two main evolutions of traditional temperament theory in the 20th century. Thanks to Myers-Briggs and Keirsey, Jung's system is better known than Steiner's, especially in psychological typing in the work environment. The Waldorf education movement has been the primary carrier of Steiner's system.

It is Steiner's system, I believe, that is truer to the traditional model and has more connection to us as practicing astrologers. In the next section we will consider how temperament theory can be best used with the astrological chart, and we will illustrate, in a real-life study of schoolchildren, how Steiner's temperament system worked when correlated with traditional astrological models of temperament.

Part 2

Temperament Theory Applied: The Waldorf Study

Introduction

It was a fortuitous and fortunate set of circumstances that allowed me to create the following study. I taught Classical Languages at a Waldorf School for six years, and both of my children spent three years at the school. It was during that time that I was first exposed to Steiner's temperament theory, both on a personal level (with my own children) and in the classroom (with my students). As a practicing astrologer I was excited by the idea that temperament, as identified by the Class Teacher,[1] could perhaps be correlated to the student's birthchart. As fairly pure types, my own children (melancholic and sanguine) provided further impetus, since their birthcharts bore out their temperamental identities.

Of course, this is not the first study that has attempted to correlate the birthchart or sun sign to a psychological system. The following are some of those who have contributed to the literature in this field:

- Beverly Fodor, in "A Model of Carl Jung's Psychological Functions in Relation to the Annual Cycle," has done a statistical study correlating season of birth to Jungian psychological type.[2] Fodor has also done a study of the relationship between Myers-Briggs type preferences and astrological factors in birthcharts.[3]
- The Gauquelins have also done studies of character or personality in relationship to planetary factors in the birthchart.[4]
- Jane Lee has done a study on introversion/extraversion and astrological motifs.[5]

No doubt there are other studies of which I am not presently aware. However, I believe this *is* the first published study which attempts to connect astrological temperament considerations with those of Rudolf Steiner.

---

1. The Class Teacher is the student's main teacher during the day. Subject Teachers, such as I, came in to the classroom for classes in specific subjects like French or Handwork.
2. Beverly Fodor, "A Model of Carl Jung's Psychological Functions in Relation to the Annual Cycle," self-published, 1993.
3. Unpublished, 1991, quoted in Jane Lee, "Character Traits," in *Astrological Research Methods*, vol. 1, p. 326.
4. Mentioned in Françoise Gauquelin, "The Character Traits Controversies," in *Astrological Research Methods*, vol. 1, p. 330.
5. Jane Lee, "Character Traits," in *Astrological Research Methods*, vol. 1, p. 329.

This is not a statistical study but an anecdotal one. I worked with the charts of only 35 children, yet valuable information has been gained even from this small number of charts; certainly a statistical follow-up study could be prepared if a large enough number of Waldorf Schools and parents were willing to participate.

The Waldorf Study: Gathering Data

The goal of this study was to see if the usual astrological factors employed in determining temperament had any correlation with the temperaments of the students as identified by their Class Teachers. I looked at a number of astrological methods in my assessment; I also talked with the teachers about many of the children, so as to understand how they chose a temperament for the child in the first place. None of the teachers had more than a superficial knowledge of astrology, and none had any birth times for the children prior to identifying their temperament types. I myself did not look at the children's charts (except for my own biological children) until after I had been given their temperament types.

As a middle school teacher, I decided to use students in the 5th – 8th grade, and asked teachers in those grades to give me the primary temperament types, and secondary if appropriate, of their students. (Some children were hard to type, or were thought to be of varying temperaments by different teachers. Further interviews with teachers uncovered the rationale by which they made their choices.) This information was added to the administrative class lists provided by the school office.

I wrote to the parents of all the children in these grades, explaining the study, asking for permission to use their child in the study and requesting details of birthdates, times and places. Of 37 parents contacted, 28 provided birth information for their children and gave permission for them to be included in the study. There were four parents who provided birth information for two siblings, including one set of fraternal twins (a boy and a girl). I also included my own children (who had earlier been typed by their teacher), and one of my son's friends (he is a very pure type, and since this is an anecdotal study I felt it was appropriate to include him for purposes of education). Thirty-five children were included in the study. All children were provided with aliases created and known only by me. All the children used in the study were at least ten years old at the time of the study, ten being the age at which the teachers felt comfortable in determining the temperament accurately.[6]

The next step was to produce birthcharts for all of the children in the study using Astrolabe's *Chartwheels 2* and *Solar Fire* (see Appendix H for each child's chart). Once I had these, I created a list of methods used to determine temperaments. The methods selected were those of Ptolemy, Montulmo, Schoener, Garcaeus, Lilly and Partridge. (See Appendix B.) As a first test, I used these methods on the chart of a child agreed by all the teachers to be strongly melancholic.

Once this first step had been accomplished, I selected chart factors for testing the other childrens' charts by collecting those which were prevalent in most or all of the methods for determining temperament. I used the following factors:

---

6. Before age ten, I was told, many children have a strong sanguine overlay which makes true typing difficult.

- Sun sign
- Ascendant sign
- Moon sign
- Ascendant ruler
- Ascendant almuten[7]
- Moon phase (both Ptolemy and Lilly)
- Moon ruler
- Lord of the Geniture[8]
- Season of birth

These factors would each be equated to a temperament, in order to test which ones showed promise of being useful in determining temperament from the birthchart. Two methods were used to equate a factor with a temperament: either the sign and its element = temperament, or the intrinsic quality of a planet = temperament. In the first method, for example, the sun sign's element would be equated with temperament: fire sun signs = choleric, earth sun signs = melancholic, air sun signs = sanguine and water sun signs = phlegmatic. In the second method, for example, the Ascendant Ruler's intrinsic quality would be equated with a temperament by its qualities: hot and dry = choleric, hot and wet = sanguine, cold and dry = melancholic, cold and wet = phlegmatic.

Next, I created a table listing every child with his/her temperament (primary/sub), plus the above factors (see Appendix I), and I analyzed the data in the following ways:

- Analyzed each factor individually as a reflection of the temperament: that is, e.g. Sun sign = temperament, Moon sign = temperament, Ascendant sign = temperament, etc. Factors which matched in more than 50% of the charts (with a match to either primary or secondary temperament) were analyzed further, in combination. Also analyzed rulers of temperament factors based on intrinsic quality, sign and phase.
- Considered matches of primary temperament versus secondary temperament: should they be weighted differently? What can we learn from them?
- Analyzed combinations of factors in relation only to primary temperament.
- Using standard elemental weighting system, analyzed that system in relation to temperament.

As a result of the analysis I ended up with these fundamental questions:

- If we use only the ASC/Moon/Season factors, does this pick up the dominant temperament?

---

7. I used Ptolemaic triplicity rulers (Mars rules water day and night) and Ptolemaic terms to find the almuten. This is the prevalent system for Lilly and the English astrologers of his period.
8. The calculation of the Lord of the Geniture was chosen, using Ibn Ezra's formula, as the planet with the most essential and accidental dignity (using the 5-point system) in the positions of the Sun, Moon, Ascendant, Part of Fortune and prenatal syzygy.

- Although many children fit the model using combined chart factors for determining temperament, there were some who did not fit the pattern as well as we would like. Who are they, and what can we learn from them?
- Do pure types show up more obviously in the chart? What percentage are pure types?
- When teachers have a hard time typing a child, or disagree about which temperaments a child is, does this show up as a quality balance in the chart?
- Do children with a compound temperament that involves the same quality show more of that quality in the chart: are sanguine/phlegmatics more wet, sanguine/cholerics more hot, melancholic/phlegmatics more cold and melancholic/cholerics more dry?
- Are children with compound temperaments that do not duplicate a quality more balanced in overall qualities (the melancholic/sanguine and the choleric/phlegmatic)?
- What about the modern elemental analyses found in many astrological computer programs? Are they valid predictors of temperament?

We will discuss the analysis of the data collected and answer the questions raised by the data in the following section.

The Waldorf Study: Analyzing Data and Results of the Study

Testing the Methods on One Example Chart

The chart of a child all teachers considered to be strongly melancholic was chosen arbitrarily (in that any child with a strongly manifested temperament could have been selected), as an example chart to 'test the waters.' I felt that a strongly manifested temperament would be more likely to show results with one of the methods than a child with a compound temperament. We will call the melancholic child selected 'Fern.'

Fern

Fern is an almost classic melancholic according to her teachers. Thin, gangly and slightly stoop-shouldered, she believes that life is a series of disappointments. She feels that no one understands her (which among her peers may in fact have elements of truth; a fellow student described her as "strange. She talks about weird things. She calls her friend 'dog' and once ate a dog biscuit. She laughs at her own jokes because no one else thinks they're funny.") During her 4th grade year, she cried almost every day at recess because of one slight or another. She had no concept of empathy or how to be social. In Latin, which I taught her, she had a real knack, which might be expected for a melancholic: with its structure and order, Latin lends itself to the cold and dry. Here follows the application of each method to Fern's chart:

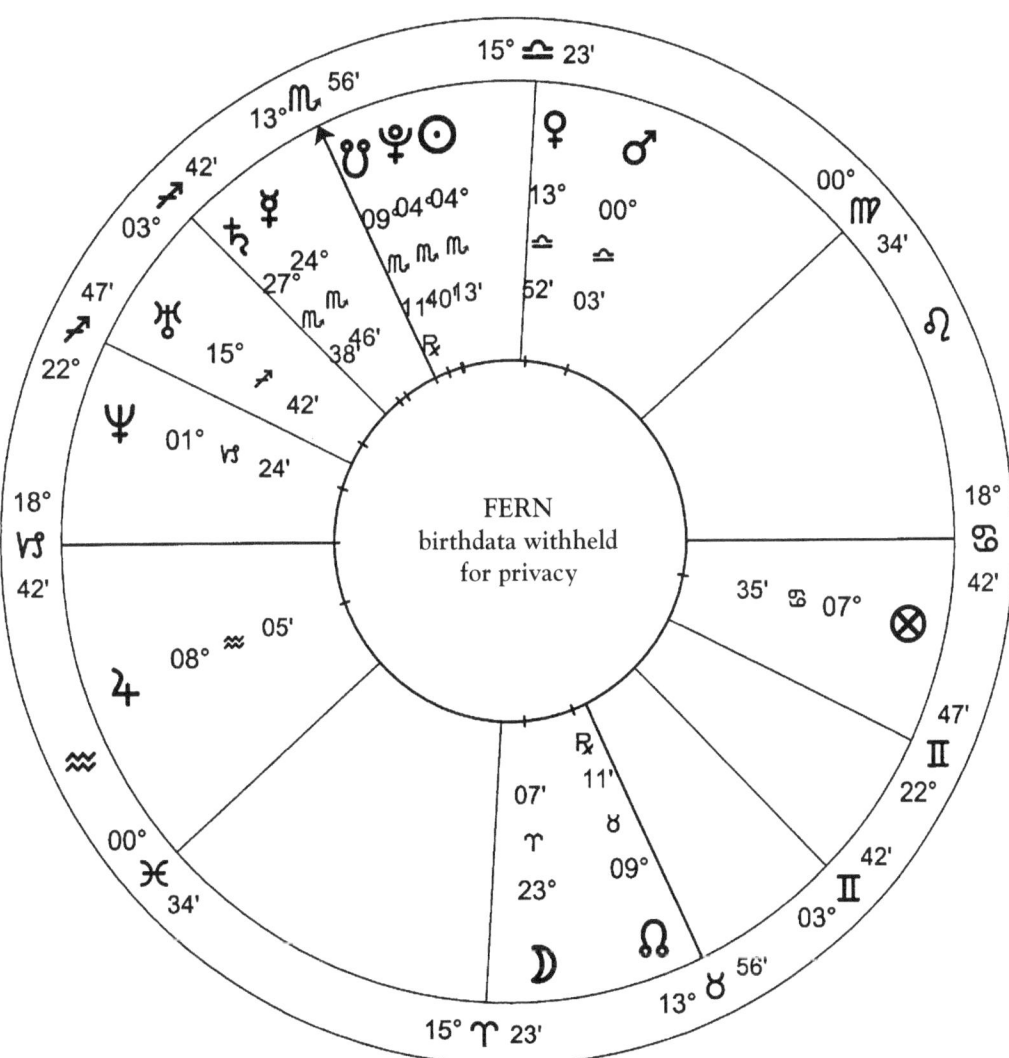

Application of Each Method to Fern's Chart

Ptolemy (c. 120 CE)

ASC sign:	Capricorn cold and dry
Planets in ASC:	none using whole sign houses
Ruler of ASC:	Saturn in Scorpio; by phase dry and cold
Moon sign:	Aries hot and dry
Moon phase:	1st quarter (not yet full) hot and wet in Ptolemaic system
Moon ruler:	Mars in Libra (by phase occidental – dry)
Moon aspects:	opposes Venus in Libra (oriental – hot and wet)
	opposes Mars in Libra (oriental – hot and dry)
Fixed stars co-rising with significators:	(Saturn and Moon): no Ptolemaic fixed star rises with Saturn; Fomalhaut with Moon (Ptolemy says head of southern fish nature of Hermes and somewhat of Kronos; thus basically dry, because Mercury is also conjunct Saturn in the chart)
Scores:	Hot=4 Cold=2 Wet=2 Dry=6
	Dry is most represented, then hot.

Montulmo (c. 1396)

ASC sign:	Capricorn cold and dry
Almuten of ASC:	Saturn cold and dry by phase, cold and wet by sign (Montulmo does not use a point system and does not use face as a dignity; both Saturn and Mars have essential dignity in the place of the Ascendant; Montulmo says that Ptolemy places dignity of domicile in the forefront [Book I, p. 3]. Montulmo also says that if planets are "equal in fortitude" then choose the one which aspects the place; if they "aspect equally," choose the one which is stronger in an angle. [Book I, p. 4] Since Saturn is in the 10th house and Mars in the 9th, we have chosen Saturn.)
Place of Moon:	in Aries, hot and dry; waxing, temperate and moist
Planet in ASC:	none
Fixed stars in ASC:	Rukbat, alpha star in Sagittarius, nature of Jupiter and Saturn
Fixed stars in place of almuten of ASC:	none visible at birth latitude
Time of nativity:	day
Quarter of the year:	Autumn cold and dry
Scores:	Hot=1 Cold=4 Wet=2 Dry=4 (not using qualities for the fixed star because the nature of Jupiter and Saturn would actually be distemperate (Saturn cold and dry, Jupiter hot and wet) – if these were added in we would have Hot=2 Cold=5; Wet=3 Dry=5.

Diurnal chart would make complexion lighter rather than darker.
Autumnal quarter gives yellow color, lean, long hair, great shoulders, melancholic complexion
In either scoring option, cold and dry predominate.

Schoener (c. 1539)

ASC sign:	Capricorn cold and dry
Almuten of ASC:	Mars and Saturn equal using point system
	Mars oriental hot and dry
	Saturn occidental dry
Place of the Moon:	in Aries, hot and dry; almuten of 24 Aries is Mars; phase hot and dry
Planet on the ASC:	Jupiter in Aquarius, hot and wet; phase occidental, wet
Planets asp. ASC:	Moon by phase hot and dry
	Mercury, occidental with Saturn dry
	Venus oriental and in Libra hot and wet
Season of the year:	Autumn, cold and dry
Fixed stars on ASC:	Rukbat, nature of Jupiter and Saturn; " posterior part of Sagittarius – temperate and fortunate"
Fixed stars with Saturn:	none visible at birth latitude
Part of Stability (Basis):	10 Aq 55; almuten Saturn dry by phase
Part of Future Things (Spirit):	29 Can 49; almuten Moon, by phase hot and dry
Scores:	Hot=6 Cold=2 Wet=3 Dry=9

Dry predominates, followed by hot.

Garcaeus (1574)

ASC sign:	Capricorn cold and dry
Almuten of ASC:	Mars (oriental – hot and dry; in Libra – hot and wet; therefore only hot); and Saturn (occidental – dry; in Scorpio – cold and wet; therefore only wet)
Planets in 1st house:	Jupiter (occidental – wet; in Aquarius – hot and wet)
Planets or nodes aspecting degree of ASC:	none
Moon:	Aries - hot and dry; by phase hot and dry (acc. Garcaeus)
Lord of the Moon:	Mars (oriental – hot and dry; in Libra – hot and moist; therefore only hot)
Planets aspecting Moon within orb:	none
Quarter of the year:	Autumn cold and dry

Lord of Geniture
(Almuten Thematis):   Mars (oriental: hot and dry; in Libra – hot and wet; therefore only hot)
Participating Rulers: none
Fixed stars in 1st house: none
Scores: Hot=5 Cold=2 Wet=2 Dry=3

Hot is most represented, then dry.

Lilly (1647)

ASC sign: Capricorn cold and dry
Lord of ASC: Saturn occidental dry
Planets in the ASC: Jupiter occidental wet
Planets in partile aspect to ASC: none
Moon: in Aries; by phase hot and dry
Planets aspecting Moon within orb: none
Quarter of the Year: Autumn – cold and dry
Lord of the Geniture: (planet with most essential and accidental dignities in entire chart; and well placed): Saturn occidental dry x 3 (Triple the qualities of the Lord of the Geniture because it also rules the Ascendant)
Scores: Hot=1 Cold=2 Wet=1 Dry=7

Dry far outweighs the other qualities.

Partridge (1675)

ASC sign: Capricorn cold and dry
Lord of ASC: Saturn occidental dry
Planets in ASC: Jupiter in 1st house, occidental wet
Planets partile aspecting ASC: none
Moon: in Aries, phase hot and dry
Planet aspecting Moon: none
Quarter of the heavens: Autumn cold and dry
Lord of the Nativity: Saturn occidental dry
Scores: Hot=1 Cold=2 Wet=1 Dry=5

Again, dry predominates.

Fern fares best (or rather, her melancholic nature is exposed best) by the system of Montulmo, ca. 1396. Cold and dry predominate, and Montulmo says that the "autumnal quarter" gives a yellow color, lean, long hair, great shoulders and melancholic complexion."[9] Fern's hair is light brown and somewhat lank; she is thin but surprisingly strong (Does she have great shoulders? Perhaps....), and she walks as if dragged down by a weight. One can't help but think of Eeyore in *Winnie-the-Pooh*.

In Ptolemy she comes out as mostly dry; in Garcaeus hot; in Lilly dry; in Schoener dry and hot; and in Partridge dry.

This was an interesting exercise with which to begin the study of the data. It took nearly two days to gather up and interpret the data according to the various temperament-determining methods. In practice, it is doubtful that a working astrologer would have the time to painstakingly ferret out the phases, fixed stars, arcane 'parts' and other necessary criteria for these methods, even assuming that one is always more accurate than another. However, as an exercise, working with the various criteria of each method began to put certain of them in a stronger light, as criteria that could be investigated more with the other charts in the study. This was done in the next stage of investigation.

Which Factors? Selecting and Testing Chart Factors in Temperament Analysis

I looked at all the factors used to determine temperament in traditional analysis, and selected ones to test for based primarily, but not exclusively, on their prevalence in all the methods. (These factors are listed on p. 59.) Once I had decided on which factors to use, I created a table with the following categories: name of child, assigned temperament, Sun sign, Ascendant sign, Ascendant ruler, Ascendant almuten, Moon sign, Moon phase, Moon ruler, Lord of the Geniture and season of birth. (See Appendix I.) This became a useful tool for plucking factors from a chart and experimenting with them. It was decided, in the case of compound temperaments, to count each one equally for the time being. Each factor was first tested separately to see if it matched with the dominant or sub-dominant temperament. The following table shows each factor tested, the number of charts out of 35 which matched the factor with a temperament, and converts this fraction to a percentage of the total charts tested.[10]

Table 12
Temperament Matches by Individual Factors (counting compound temperaments equally)

By Sun Sign: 15/35 or 43%
By ASC Sign: 19/35 or 54%
By ASC ruler (sign): 11/35 or 31%
By ASC ruler (intrinsic quality*): 22/35 or 63%
By ASC almuten (sign): 14/35 or 40%

---

9. Montulmo, *Judgment of Nativities Part 2*, p. 27.
10. To use the first line of the table as an example: of the 35 charts being tested, in 15, or 43%, the Sun sign of the chart matched the dominant or sub-dominant temperament assigned to the child. I.e. if, say, the Sun was Leo, the child had a dominant or sub-dominant choleric temperament.

> By ASC almuten (intrinsic quality*): 23/35 or 66%
> By Moon Sign: 18/35 or 51%
> By Moon ruler (sign): 20/35 or 57%
> By Moon ruler (intrinsic quality*): 14/35 or 40%
> By Lord of Geniture:† 17/35 or 49%
> By Season: 20/35 or 57%
> By Moon Phase (Ptolemy): 15/35 or 43%
> By Moon Phase (Lilly)‡: 16/35 or 46%
>
> *using dry for Mercury and cold & wet for Venus
> †using Ibn Ezra's formula: planet with most essential and accidental dignity in the places of the Sun, Moon, ASC, Part of Fortune and prenatal syzygy
> ‡ Some children matched one of their temperaments in both the Ptolemaic and Lilly systems

To get a manageable amount of factors to work with, I looked for factors which matched the dominant or sub-dominant temperament in at least 50% of the charts. I found that six factors individually had a hit rate of over 50%: Ascendant sign (54%), Ascendant ruler - intrinsic quality[11] (63%), Ascendant almuten – intrinsic quality (66%), Moon sign (51%), Moon ruler – sign (57%) and Season (57%). Admittedly, this was a somewhat scattershot approach, not taking into account a predominant temperament and not looking at charts individually to see how many factors matched. Still, it was good for eliminating factors that did not show much promise of being ultimately useful for determining temperament from the chart.

I decided to combine these six factors to see how many charts would show at least one, and preferably more than one, of the six. Putting the six factors together yielded 19 of 35 charts (54%) showing 4-6 of the six factors tested, 27 of 35 (77%) showing 3 or more, and 34 of 35 (97%) showing at least one. So we can determine that looking just at these six factors has a high likelihood of yielding useful information about a person's temperament, though not necessarily their dominant temperament.

If looking at six factors seems like too much for a not certain result, testing for just three factors, the 'traditional' ones of Ascendant sign, Moon sign and season, yielded a result almost as good: 33 of 35 charts (94%) had at least one hit, and 21 of 35 (60%) 2 or more. That is, 94% of the charts matched the temperament by at least one factor, and 60% matched the temperament by 2 or more factors. The following table shows the breakdown:

---

11. By intrinsic quality, I mean the planet's traditional nature: Sun hot and dry, Moon cold and wet, Mercury dry, Venus cold and wet (though Ptolemy says hot and wet), Mars hot and dry, Jupiter hot and wet and Saturn cold and dry.

Table 13
Temperament Matches by ASC sign, Moon sign, ASC ruler, ASC almuten, Moon ruler, Season

By 0 factors: 1 (2.8%)
By 1 factor: 3 (8.6%)
By 2 factors: 4 (11%)
By 3 factors: 8 (23%)
By 4 factors: 8 (23%)
By 5 factors: 11 (31%)
By 6 factors: 0

Table 14
Temperament Matches by ASC sign, Moon sign and Season

By 0 factors: 2 (5.7%)
By 1 factor: 12 (34%)
By 2 factors: 18 (51%)
By 3 factors: 3 (8.6%)

Of course, this is still a blunderbuss approach: we are not distinguishing a dominant temperament, if there is one. For that we need to examine the data in more detail. And we also need to consider those who don't, or only barely, fit these models. Again, since we are not totally relying on statistics to give the definitive answer, it becomes useful to look at those who model the paradigm perfectly and those who don't fit it at all. And we should also consider that those children who have a more balanced temperament will skew the results to a certain extent, as more factors fit one of their temperaments. Keeping these things in mind, let us return now to the original questions posed earlier in this section (pp. 59-60), and consider them one by one.

- **If we use only the ASC/Moon/Season factors, does this pick up the dominant temperament?**

Generally, yes. In 30 of 35 charts the dominant or co-dominant temperament was found in one of those 3 factors. The dominant temperament was not picked up in 5 charts, and in 2 the correct temperament was not picked up at all.

- **Although many children fit the model using combined chart factors for determining temperament, there are some who do not fit the pattern as well as we would like. Who are they, and what can we learn from them?**

'Abby' is one of the class leaders, ambitious and talented. All her teachers agreed she was a primary choleric with the social skills and friendliness of a secondary sanguine temperament. She is born in the springtime, and her Ascendant ruler is Jupiter, intrinsically warm and moist. But where is her choleric drive and ambition? It can be seen only in her Moon phase, 1st Quarter, which in the Lilly system is hot and dry, and in the Lord of the Geniture, Mercury, which is oriental in phase, thus hot. Her Ascendant almuten, Venus, is also combust.

'Charlie' has the boisterous, opinionated, loud manner of the choleric who may be trying too hard, possibly as compensation for his sub-melancholic temperament. His melancholic side can be found in his Virgo Moon (and Taurus Sun), but again we have to look for the choleric in his Ascendant ruler and almuten, Mars. This may be the example which points out to us the importance of the ruler and almuten of the Ascendant (in Charlie's case they are the same, but this is not always true), as well as the importance of a planet's intrinsic quality in reflecting temperament

We can find 'Nathaniel's' choleric side in his Moon and Season, but his likely melancholic component[12] can only be seen in his Ascendant ruler and almuten, Saturn.

Now, we come to two children whose temperaments are not picked up at all by the Ascendant, Moon or Season. 'Derek' was typed as a melancholic (though not a totally pure one in my opinion). However, his Gemini Ascendant, Leo Moon and birth season of winter (cold and wet) do not show this. We can find some dryness in his occidental Mercury, the Ascendant ruler and almuten (though it is in Pisces!), but in fact his chart remains somewhat of a mystery in regard to his temperament.

And 'Stacy,' who is a true sanguine, is even more of a puzzle. Fine, pretty features, sociable, graceful, flitting from interest to interest and never remaining long on anything. So where is the hot and wet in her chart? Her chart is actually very interesting, because it has 29° 30' of Aries rising. In two minutes by the clock the Ascendant will move into Taurus, with lovely temperate Venus as its ruler. Tempting as it is to rectify her chart, we will refrain and work with what is there. Her birth season is cold and wet, and Moon and ASC in Aries, hot and dry. Her chart is actually balanced, which could be an indication of the 'temperate' sanguine. Still, it would be nice to see more significators in air!

What can we learn from those who don't fit the easy pattern? That there is more to a chart and a person than a few isolated factors. Though some might argue that we are only trying to justify ourselves astrologically, in fact it is useful to emphasize that astrology is not an art of dissection but of integration.

- **Do pure types show up more obviously in the chart? What percentage are "pure" types?**

There are eight children, or 23%, typed as predominantly one temperament in this study. Looking at their charts in more detail provides much insight as to how temperament actually manifests in a chart.

We have mentioned Fern, the 'quintessential' melancholic child, earlier in this study, so without repeating ourselves, it is useful to point out that in addition to her earth Ascendant and birth season, the Ascendant ruler and one Ascendant almuten is Saturn; and Saturn is in the 10th house, conjunct Mercury and sextile its co-almuten, Mars.

We have also discussed Stacy, the sanguine, above. Let's consider another sanguine, my own daughter, 'Darcy,' whose social skills and ability to make friends I have admired since she was three. In

---

12. I use the word "likely" because this is a case where not all teachers agreed.

her life she has been involved in ballet, swimming, softball, acting, horseback riding, learning French and music – this is a child with too much on her plate who enjoys every minute of it! In her chart, it is easy to spot the sanguine – both her Ascendant and Moon are in air. There's no need to look for more subtle factors in her chart – sanguine sticks out a mile.

Her brother, 'Daniel,' is as melancholic as Darcy is sanguine. Especially in the social whirl of school, his Eeyore disposition was painfully obvious, and caused him much distress until he learned that he could find and make a few good friends who didn't care if he dressed in the latest style or not, and who valued his steadiness, loyalty and good-heartedness. The Taurus Ascendant is a big tipoff here, but we also should look at Moon ruler Mars conjunct Saturn in Virgo in his chart.

Daniel's friend 'Kevin' defines the phlegmatic. Of ponderous gait and weight, he speaks slowly, often hesitating between words, and would drive a sanguine or choleric mad. He sails through life little caring what others think as long as he has his own pursuits uninterrupted. Again, his Ascendant in Scorpio is the clue to his temperament, plus three other planets including Sun and Mercury in Scorpio, plus the intrinsically cold and wet Moon in Aquarius (the coldest of the air signs), squaring the Ascendant.

Finally, let us consider three more quintessential 'phlegs,' 'Gretchen,' 'Deirdre' and 'James.' They oblige us by having charts which ooze water from every pore.

Gretchen has both the round body type of the phlegmatic and the phleg's tendency to laziness. Getting her to put effort into a task was like pulling teeth, though when roused (not often) she could do excellent work. Her entire chart is overwhelmed by the Moon in Cancer – it rules and is almuten of the Ascendant (in Cancer of course), and is also just two degrees from the Ascendant, where it also aspects four other planets.

Deirdre's chart at first glance would not make anyone run for an umbrella, as they would with Gretchen's chart, though both Moon sign and season of birth are cold and wet. But when one considers that out of all signs and planets involved in determining temperament, not one is intrinsically dry, it becomes clear how much the embodiment of the phlegmatic Deirdre is. Again, she has the round body and slow gait of the phlegmatic, and she always had to be given more time to finish an assignment – a lot more time.

James also lacks a quality in the signs and planets which determine temperament – not one is intrinsically hot! So instead of the total wet phlegmatic like Deirdre, James is the cold phlegmatic, and like Gretchen, also has the Moon in Cancer, his sextiling the Ascendant and aspecting five planets. The same phlegmatic body and endless deliberation over assignments.

Before we move on, let's consider an antidote to this surfeit of wetness, three children of compound temperament (but primarily melancholic) who have a surfeit of dry in their charts.

'Sasha' is primarily dry due to the dry qualities of her Moon (by sign), Ascendant and season of birth; The ruler and almuten of her Ascendant is Mercury, naturally a somewhat dry planet. This dryness supports the melancholic part of her temperament, but she also has some hot qualities which make her more outgoing than the usual melancholic.

'Jared' and 'Michael' are truly dry – dry wit, great at detail, true academics and thinkers. They are the kind of students teachers love – they can always be counted on to supply the right answer when everyone else is stuck. With meticulous focus and attention to detail, they will wring every last drop of information from whatever it is they're interested in. How fascinating it is that both have Virgo rising with Mercury the ruler and almuten of the Ascendant. Jared's Mercury conjuncts the Ascendant and Michael's Mercury conjuncts Saturn in the 4th.

- **When teachers have a hard time typing a child, or disagree about which temperaments a child is, does this show up as a quality balance in the chart?**

Again, generally yes. Let's look at a few of the children in this category, which I have nicknamed 'The Blends.'

'Adam' – good-natured, excellent student, conscientious, neat, athletic, popular with other students and with teachers, well-rounded. Teachers had some disagreements on how to type him – all agreed he was not a pure type. Some saw him as melancholic/sanguine; others as choleric/phlegmatic. One who said he was choleric/phlegmatic also said strong social skills showed a sanguine component. A fellow student said about him: "Excited about things, notices everything, makes jokes and can be goofy; has a temper, especially if you accuse him unjustly." Another described his excessive drive and obsessive doing as choleric, but also has the even-temper and liveliness of a sanguine. Methodical habits and order are phlegmatic; ability to absorb details and separate wheat from chaff melancholic.

He is an excellent Latin student. No surprise to find that no one quality predominates in his chart; slightly more cold and dry, but not excessive.

'Courtney' – another one who could not be easily typed. Her teacher said "she shifts a lot. Her movement of body is phlegmatic," but she also has good sociability and the pert features of a sanguine. Also a good student, popular, a hard worker. Somewhat bony physique suggests melancholic also, but has the shortness of a choleric. She is also very even in qualities; slightly more hot and dry, also not excessive.

Courtney's brother 'Christopher' is also a blend, with no one quality or temperament predominating. A fellow student comments, "Likes to be best and first. He's pretty funny, but can also be really serious." Chris has more hot than cold, but Sun and Moon both in Aquarius (the coldest of the air signs). Wet slightly more than dry – the hot and wet showing his sanguine part.

'Cameron' and 'Nathaniel' – two hard to type boys. Are they phlegmatic, or melancholic/choleric? Teachers had some difficulty distinguishing one from the other in certain students. The phlegmatic is self-contained, almost in their own little world, and doesn't really care about the opinions of others. True of both. Both have a short, thin body type; Cameron more confident and outgoing, Nathaniel more reserved. Nathaniel's mother thinks he's a melancholic/choleric – he loves sweets and for a long time only ate 5 foods; she described him as having a sense of "aggrieved entitlement." A teacher noted "he doesn't look you in the eye, which is phlegmatic behavior." And the strong will of the choleric can also be felt. Cameron has the same strong will, perhaps more easily seen than in Nathaniel. He also has more social skills, more leadership ability – so more choleric quality. Cameron has an abundance of dry, good amount of hot, but Venus is his Ascendant ruler nicely dignified in Libra (there is the social skill!). Quality-wise, Nathaniel is more balanced, though with a small excess of hot and dry, but his Ascendant ruler is Saturn, the king of melancholy.

The twins – are they a blend too? Both teachers who worked closely with them saw their phlegmatic qualities – in Eve's face and Evan's physicality. Both slow and unruffled, though both good athletes; Evan showing more choler. One of Evan's teachers wondered, "is melancholic his temperament or just a personality overlay?" One thought Eve was melancholic/phlegmatic and Evan melancholic/choleric; the other thought Eve phlegmatic/choleric and Evan choleric/phlegmatic. Interesting that, with essentially the same chart, they are each doing different aspects of it, as twins often do. In fact, there is no clear consensus among teachers! The one who said they were phlegmatic/choleric and choleric/phlegmatic thought Eve was *not* melancholic because she didn't hold on to things; and that Evan had the intensity of the choleric. The one temperament both teachers agreed upon, phlegmatic, is shown by the preponderance of wet over dry in their chart; and they also have more cold than hot.

- **Do children with a compound temperament that involves the same quality show more of that quality in the chart: are sanguine/phlegmatics more wet, sanguine/cholerics more hot, melancholic/phlegmatics more cold and melancholic/cholerics more dry?**

There are mixed results on this one, perhaps to be expected as we divide a small sample into even smaller portions. Are sanguine/phlegmatics more wet? The two clear sanguine/phlegmatics, 'Bobby' and 'Jeremy,' do have more wet than dry, but not by a large margin. Most of the obvious sanguine/cholerics do have more hot than cold, but only one ('Morgan') to a pronounced degree. None of the melancholic/phlegmatics have a preponderance of cold. The melancholic/cholerics on the other hand do seem to be rather dry, with one (Sasha) having no wet at all.

- **Are children with a compound temperament that doesn't duplicate a quality more balanced in qualities (the melancholic/sanguine and the choleric/phlegmatic)?**

Again, results are mixed, and actually these types are in the minority. Two of the clear melancholic/sanguines, 'Ethan' and 'Sarah' do seem to be more balanced, while the third, 'Ginny,' does not. There are no clear choleric/phlegmatics in the study. This category overlaps somewhat with 'The Blends,' whom we have already discussed above.

- **What about the modern elemental analyses found in many astrological computer programs? Are they valid predictors of temperament?**

On first inspection, the answer appears to be "yes." Using the elemental analysis provided in Printwheels,[13] which showed hits for one of the temperaments, using the two top elemental scores, in 21 of 35 or 60%. However, when assigning a compound temperament of the basis of the top two elemental scores, and a single temperament if the top elemental score was very high (more than 4 points higher than the next highest score), many wrong temperaments were given (24 of 35 or 69%).

---

13. This schema gives Sun, Moon, Ascendant and Midheaven 3 points; Mercury, Venus and Mars 2 points; and Jupiter, Saturn, Uranus, Neptune and Pluto 1 point each. Only sign is used, not intrinsic quality.

A few wrong could be expected, but not in that quantity. In fact, only in 26% (9 charts) was the correct temperament given based on elemental distribution. Clearly, the traditional approach has more to offer us.

Conclusions

I must admit that when I began this study, I was looking for a magic bullet that would predict the correct temperament all the time. I was also searching for a short, elegant solution that would not involve hours of the astrologer's time. Alas, there is no easy, foolproof method. Like anything else, especially in astrology, analyzing separate components of a chart must be combined with looking at the whole picture. The apple is just one piece of fruit in the bowl. Any method that involves adding up points and tallying the results is only a part of the picture; using our intuition and skill as trained astrologers to examine and draw conclusions from a *whole* chart is the other part.

Having said, that, there are some 'quick and dirty' checks we can make to get us started on determining temperament from the birthchart, remembering that most people are not pure types and may be at a stage of life where different expressions of temperament color their outlook. The first check we can make is to look at the Ascendant, Moon and season of birth. If two of those are the same element, an imaginary bell should go off. A second check would involve looking at the other factors that had a hit rate over 50%, namely the intrinsic qualities of the Ascendant ruler and almuten, and the sign of the Moon ruler. All these will provide more information which may or may not match with one of the first three factors. These are, however, only intermediate steps. In the final analysis, temperament is only one component. We must integrate it into a picture of the whole chart.

The same is true of this study. After all the mathematical and statistical analyses had been done, what was equally useful was the evaluation of the charts that 'worked' and the charts that didn't. Astrology is not digital. Components of a person's psyche are not either 'on' or 'off.' There are shades of meaning and waves that ebb and flow. Temperament is no exception to this. While it is intrinsic, it too is part of a continuum that moves toward and away from balance at different times, and is different for every person. We can make educated guesses about standards and norms, but in the end we have to take into account the uniqueness of every person and chart we work with. Our practice is, in the end, not a science but an art.

Part 3
Using Temperament in Modern Astrological Practice

Why Temperament?

The Waldorf Study provided a number of indications for developing a temperament formula that modern astrologers can use in their own work. In doing the study, it became more and more clear to me that delineation of temperament ought to be an important part of chart interpretation. Yet it has been virtually ignored by modern astrology, especially since the advent of 'psychological' astrology – when element scores took the place of temperament.

There are likely a number of reasons for this: first of all, most traditional formulae for determining temperament involve many steps and factors. Second, there is no one universally agreed-upon technique for determining temperament; between Ptolemy and Partridge, for instance, 7 techniques were variously in or out of fashion, with no particular one predominating over all times. Third, the Enlightenment put an end to humoral theory as a valid medical concept. And finally, the modern technique of adding up planet and chart points by element, and weighting some factors more heavily than others, is certainly easier for the modern astrologer than delving into the arcane methods used by the medievals. Astrology's love affair with Jung, and the subsequent equation of elements to Jungian functions, further submerged any vestige of temperament and meant that modern psychological techniques took hold in astrology and have dominated it ever since.

Even with the astrological renaissance now occurring, as we rediscover our past, modern psychological astrology is what is practiced by a majority of Western astrologers. This is not to denigrate all that modern psychology has done for the practice of astrology; but it is, in the end, a separate discipline from astrology, and one that has, in some cases, either tried to make astrology over in its own image, or been grafted (not always successfully) onto astrological technique.

By contrast, when we use temperament delineation in astrological practice, we are using astrology's *own* technique, not a warmed-over, modified version of a technique from another discipline that's somehow been made to fit. Temperament assessment is whole in itself, and furthermore, it is completely consistent with the fundamental principles of astrology. After using temperament in my own astrological work for several years, I am confident that it has something valuable to provide to our clients and students. Those astrologers who practice primarily traditional astrology have always known the merits of including temperament in an astrological consultation.[1] The following sections will, I hope, convince you of its merits as well.

---

1. John Frawley, Graeme Tobyn and Lee Lehman come to mind.

Separating the Wheat from the Chaff:
Developing a Useful Temperament Assessment Formula

As we have seen in our journey through the history of temperament, many astrologers developed complex methods for discovering it from the birthchart. Some of these methods were seen in the Waldorf Study to be more successful than others, but they still involved many steps and coordination of dozens of factors. Even then, the formula did not always 'work.' Probably the most well-known example of this is illustrated in *Christian Astrology*. On pages 532-534 (Chapter 106), Lilly gives specific instructions for finding the temperament; yet immediately after doing so, he hedges his bets:

> "You must deale warily in the collection of the testimonies of the four Humours, of Heat, Humedity, Cold and Drinesse...."[2]

The reason for the hedge becomes clear when we see Lilly's "practicall" example on page 742 – by his formula,[3] the man is sanguine/choleric – yet Lilly adds:

> "I cannot perceive any superabundance in any of the four Humours;[4] so much as may be discerned in the Native is, that he is Sanguine, Melancholly Sanguine, by reason ☉ ☿ ♀ and ☽ are in ayëry Signes. Melancholy, because ♄ Lord of the ascendant is naturally so, and is also posited in a Signe concurring with his own naturall disposition."[5]

Then, on page 746, he continues his description with "Our Native absolutely is a melancholy person (*per se*) grave, austere, of a firm resolution, solitary, laborious, taciturne, nothing loquacious &c." So Lilly, in fact, *knows* that the man is a primary melancholic, secondary sanguine, but his method for determining temperament does not pick it up; so he is forced to rationalize his direct observations of the man by emphasizing the inner planets in air signs, and the sign of the Ascendant and its ruler, Saturn, being in a cold and dry sign, Taurus.

If even the great William Lilly crashes on the rocks of temperament assessment, is there any hope for us? I must answer (like a true phlegmatic) with a cautious "yes." We have seen in the Waldorf Study that certain factors showed promise in calculating a temperament in accord with the teacher's assessment. In particular, the ASC sign, Moon sign and season of birth often indicated a correct primary or secondary temperament. I have now worked with this material for three years, looking at example charts and trying to come up with a formula that gives fairly consistent good results. (My colleague Garry Phillipson has been of invaluable help in working on this problem with me. I could not have arrived at this stage in my research without his helpful comments and suggestions.)

The following sections cover the usual criteria for temperament analysis. I will discuss each of them in turn, highlighting which ones I think might be more useful in developing a streamlined

---

2. William Lilly, op. cit., p. 534.
3. Note that the table which adds up the testimonies is missing the qualities for the Moon in Gemini (probably a printer's error); adding them in will give a score of 8 hot, 7 moist, 6 cold, 7 dry.
4. Which is true if one goes by the table.
5. William Lilly, op. cit., pp. 743-4.

formula for temperament assessment, and why I believe they are philosophically or theoretically valid as components of such a formula. Choosing only a specific set of factors does not mean that I think the others should be discarded permanently – but the specific ones I have chosen do appear to work reasonably well for giving a general fundamental temperament assessment, which can then be the foundation of more intensive analyses in terms of manners or personality, aspirations, and all the other things that make astrology such a rich discipline for mining human potential and actuality.

Which criteria?

The first step is to determine which factors we should use in finding temperament expressed in the birthchart. It is clear that all traditional methods of determining temperament involve the Ascendant and the Moon. Many also look at planets *ruling or aspecting* the Ascendant or the Moon, or *in the 1st house*. Some methods involve *almutens* of the Ascendant or the Moon. Some methods use the *sign* (by element) of a significating planet to lend its qualities to the temperament; some use its *intrinsic quality*, or its quality based on whether it is *oriental or occidental*. Some methods incorporate *the Sun*, using the qualities of its season. Some use the *Lord of the Geniture*. Some use *fixed stars* in combination with significators. Some use *Moon Phases*. All methods add up all the factors by *quality*, then assign a *temperament* based on which qualities are strongest.[6] Let's examine each of these criteria in turn.

Essence and Accident (a brief digression)

In the following discussion of criteria I will be using the concepts of essence and accident as I describe astrological techniques used in temperament analysis. I will designate some criteria as essential, and some as more accidental. Essence and accident are related, though they are at opposite ends of a continuum which deals with the characteristics of planets as they appear in the birthchart. If we were to look at criteria like the sign of a planet, or its intrinsic quality, those things would fall on the more essential side of the continuum, while planet phase or planet aspects would fall on the more acccidental side. But what exactly do 'essence' and 'accident' mean, and where did these terms come from?

Hellenistic astrology codified a dignity system for planets, based on their sign and degree within that sign. These kinds of dignity, which were by domicile (what we call 'rulership'), exaltation, triplicity, bound (or term) and face, were later called 'essential' dignities by the Medievals, to differentiate them from the 'accidental' dignities of placement by house or solar phase, proximity to the Sun, speed, aspect and other factors. 'Essential' comes from the Latin word *essentia*, which derives from *esse*, the verb to be. So essence is about being, about cosmic state. Essential dignity based on sign connects a planet to its place in the zodiac, and the zodiac was seen as a realm beyond the changeable world of humans, a place of the eternal, unchangeable, infinite and divine. A planet in a particular sign and degree partakes of that eternal and divine essence or state of being.

---

6. Though Montulmo does not specifically instruct the astrologer to add up factors by quality (there is no worked out example or table of factors), it seems likely that his method, too, would do this. Ptolemy, Schoener, Garcaeus, Lilly, Coley and Partridge all add up qualities.

'Accident,' on the other hand, comes from the Latin word *accidere*, to happen, to come to pass, to befall.[7] We think today of an accident as something unpleasant, unwished for and mostly unforeseen, but its original meaning has no negative connotation. Where essence is being, accident is becoming. Accident is more relative than essence, being based on where something happens to fall.[8] The things of the world are random, including the moment of birth. So the moment for when a chart is cast incorporates both the essential (planets in signs, and also their intrinsic qualities), and the accidental (where they fall in the wheel of the chart, and how they relate to other planets).

Sign/Element

The sign of the Ascendant, delineated by its element, is an essential factor in temperament analysis. Thus, for example, fire sign Ascendants impart heat and dryness/choler to the temperament, water sign Ascendants impart cold and moisture/phlegm, etc. The Ascendant, as a point in the chart, has no intrinsic quality other than that imparted by its sign.

The Moon as well, as an indicator of temperament, affects that assessment more by the sign it is in than by its intrinsic quality of wetness and cold. The Moon's nature is changeable and inconstant, as evidenced by its rapid movement through the zodiac and by its changing appearance during its monthly cycle. So it makes sense that on its own, the Moon should also be assessed by the element of its sign. (We will examine the Moon by phase later.)

What about the other planets? How important is the sign in which they fall? In traditional temperament analysis, significating planets are usually judged by their orientality or occidentality to the Sun. But in other cases (in Lilly's example on page 742, but not his method on page 533), planets aspecting or ruling the Ascendant or the Moon, and the Lord of the Geniture, are given qualities based on the Sign they are in, not their intrinsic quality or their phase position. The planet's sign is important because it is on sign position that the planet's essential dignity is based. Its authenticity comes from essential dignity. So in a way, the sign of the planet in a particular birthchart is a truer indication of what that planet is like *in that chart* than its phase or its intrinsic quality, even though both sign and intrinsic quality are components of its essence.

Intrinsic Quality vs. Oriental/Occidental

However, all planets have an intrinsic quality independent of anything else that may be going on in the chart. Almost every astrological writer from Ptolemy to Partridge talks about the innate, or intrinsic, qualities of the planets. Those qualities were important because they were a baseline from which things could be measured or compared. Intrinsic quality was also taken into account when considering sect (at least when considering the sect of the malefics, Saturn and Mars, whose essential nature is contradicted by their sect), and when deciding how benefic or malefic a planet was. A cold and wet

---

7. This last word might be the best translation of *accidere*, which is a compound verb *ad* + *cadere*, lit. "fall towards."
8. We could make the case that a planet also 'happens to fall' in a zodiac sign, but the zodiac, outside the realm of the human world, is already a more perfect and eternal place to be, and a place which supports a planet's essence.

planet like the Moon, when in a hot and dry sign, will be tempered to some degree by that sign (and that may be reflected in its essential dignity score), but its basic nature is still cold and wet. In a way, intrinsic quality for a planet is analogous to temperament for a person: it never really goes away. The Sun's basic nature is hot and dry. Saturn's is very cold and dry, and Mars' is hot and very dry. (The malefics have an excessive quality.) Jupiter's is hot and wet, the fertile qualities befitting the greater benefic.

What do we do about Venus and Mercury? All agree that Venus is wet; it's how hot or cold it is that is an issue between the Greeks and the medievals. Above all, Venus, as a benefic, is temperate. Robert Hand suggests that Venus can either warm you up if you're too cold, or cool you down if you're too hot. Venus always strives for balance. Mercury is variously described by different authors as being hot, cold, wet or dry! It is also described as 'changeable;' its nature is different based on where it is in relation to the Sun. In addition, we get the sense, perhaps based on Mercury both ruling and exalted in Virgo, that Mercury tends to those same cold and dry qualities. This is Mercury as exemplar of the logical mind: just the facts (in order), ma'am. But Mercury is also about making connections (this is where logic comes from, after all), so perhaps we need also to look at applying the qualities of Mercury's other sign, Gemini, which is hot and wet – the fertile, connecting qualities.

It seems to me that a way to solve the dilemma about the intrinsic qualities of Mercury and Venus is to take their orientality/occidentality into account. They are the two planets closest to the Sun, after all. If we say that Venus, when oriental, is hot and wet, and when occidental, cold and wet, we include the positions of both the Greeks and the medievals. If we call Mercury oriental hot and wet, and Mercury occidental cold and dry, we acknowledge both its signs of rulership and the fact that Mercury indeed does encompass all the qualities in some fashion or another.[9] We also acknowledge its changeability.

If orientality/occidentality becomes an important factor when ascertaining the nature of Mercury and Venus, what about the other planets? Most of the methods for temperament assessment use the phase relationship of the planet to the Sun; the qualities of the significating planet by phase, not necessarily their intrinsic quality or their sign, are added to the list. But what exactly are we talking about when we refer to the relationship of a planet to the Sun? Is this an essential quality, or an accidental quality? How is phase different from sign in that regard?

Phase is accidental in nature, while sign is essential. The planets in signs are not dependent upon their relationship to the Sun, but to the (tropical) zodiac. The sign (and degree within that sign) of the planet is the factor on which essential dignity depends. Phase, by contrast, is accidental, because the planet just *happens* to be in a particular relationship with the Sun. Certainly for any superior planet this is true, where the planet can also be in any aspect to the Sun. Thus, I think it is not correct to judge a significating planet by its phase qualities alone, when these are accidental conditions and

---

9. Dane Rudhyar, in *An Astrological Study of Psychological Complexes* (Berkeley, Calif.:Shambala Pub., 1976), Chapters 8 and 11, discusses the phases of Mercury and Venus, calling Mercury at the inferior conjunction Promethean, and Mercury at the superior conjunction Epimethean. These correlate with orientality and occidentality, though Rudhyar does not use those words. Rudhyar's oriental Venus is Lucifer, while Venus occidental is Hesperus.

78   *Temperament: Astrology's Forgotten Key*

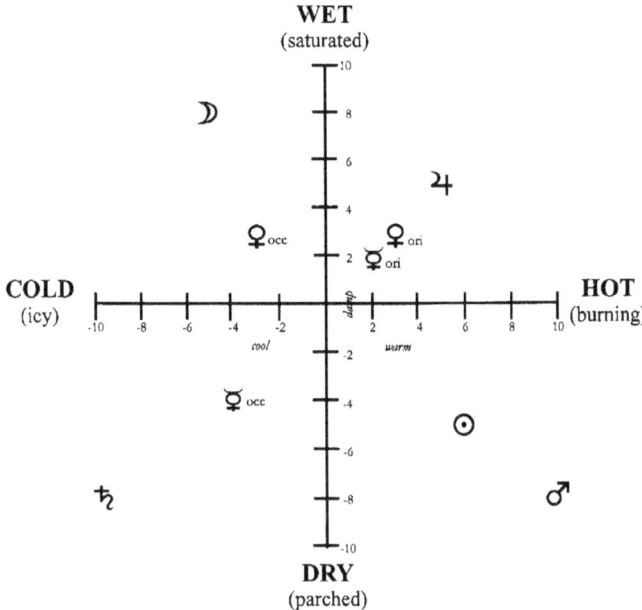

Figure 10. Qualities of the Planets (A Possible Schema)

not part of the planet's essence. Phase becomes an additional modification of a planet, but it is not part of that planet's essential nature. Even in the case of Mercury and Venus, when we are using the idea of a planet's position ahead of or behind the Sun as a factor to address definitions of its nature, we are, finally, still coming up with an assessment of intrinsic or essential quality, rather than accidental quality.

Ruling Planets and Almutens
Ruling planets (planets that are domicile rulers) are important because they are where the expression of the sign they rule finds an outlet. When a planet rules a point in the chart, like the Ascendant, the Ascendant will find part of its expression in the planet that rules it. When a planet rules a planet instead of a point – say Planet A rules Planet B – then Planet B's expression will be colored by the qualities of Planet A, its ruler, and the condition of Planet A will have an effect on the ease with which Planet B expresses itself. As co-significators of a planet or point, ruling planets must have a part/share in determining the qualities, and the humor, of that planet or point.

In the same way, almutens also color the expression of the sign or planet they rule. (An almuten is the planet that has the most counts of essential dignity in a particular sign and degree of the zodiac.) While we normally consider the ruler (domicile ruler) of a sign or planet to be the primary ruler, almutens cannot be ignored, because they are derived from examining all five of the essential dignities, not just one. Sometimes the almuten of a particular degree is the same as the domicile ruler of that degree, but not always. When using Ptolemaic (Lilly) triplicities and Ptolemaic terms,[10] in Scorpio, Aquarius, Sagittarius and Virgo, the sign ruler and almuten are the same. However, for certain degrees of Taurus, the Moon is the almuten rather than Venus. For certain degrees of Capricorn, Mars or Venus can be the almuten, while in Libra, Saturn can be the almuten as well as Venus. In a few degrees of Gemini Saturn will be co-almuten with Mercury. Jupiter can be the almuten of certain degrees of Cancer and co-almuten in Leo, Venus or Mars can be the almuten for certain degrees of Pisces, and the Sun can be the almuten of certain degrees of Aries. These variations in rulership can provide certain qualities/humors to temperament assessment that would otherwise not be realized. Since almutens derive from essential dignity, they are not accidental but essential.

The Sun

Modern astrology places great emphasis on the Sun sign. From newspaper horoscopes based on solar charts, to astrological 'cookbooks' that provide interpretation of the Sun by sign, our modern practice in a way is signophilic – we almost give more weight to the *sign* a planet is in than the planet itself.

While there is no question that the Sun is a linchpin of astrology, around which literally and symbolically the planets revolve, traditional astrology is not so quick to pile all of its interpretive eggs into the Sun-sign basket. The intrinsic qualities of the Sun as moderately hot and dry (in Western astrology, the Sun is not a malefic with an excessive quality) are considered in certain circumstances, and the sign of the Sun, especially as regards its standings in essential dignity, are considered. But in terms of temperament assessment, it is the *season* of the Sun that is the important factor. A person born in the winter will have indications of quite a different temperament than one born in the summer. (Of course, season is not the *only* indication of temperament.) We pointed out earlier in this book (on p. 57) that studies aligning seasons of birth to introversion or extraversion have shown some merit. With the exception of Ptolemy (who does not use either the Sun's sign or season to analyze the temperament), traditional methods of temperament analysis consistently favor the qualities of the season, not the sign, of the Sun. In fact, only Garcaeus appears to consider the sign of the Sun; but he also considers the season. So considering the Sun by season, we have the following assignments:

---

10. An ancillary question regarding almutens asks: which almuten system? There are four possible ways to calculate the almuten of a particular zodiac degree, based on which triplicity scheme and which term or bound scheme one chooses to use (thanks to Bernadette Brady for suggesting this line of inquiry). The possible systems are: Ptolemaic (Lilly) triplicities/Ptolemaic terms; Ptolemaic (Lilly) triplicities/Egyptian terms; Dorothean triplicities/Ptolemaic terms; and Dorothean triplicities/Egyptian terms. In the Ptolemaic (Lilly) triplicity scheme, Mars rules water both day and night. In the Dorothean triplicity scheme, Venus rules water in the day, Mars in the night. The different term schemes assign the planets differently to the 30 degrees of each sign. Egyptian terms are the oldest. Which systems did the ancient temperament writers prefer? We assume that Ptolemy uses his own triplicities and terms, though we cannot be sure because he gives no worked example (Ptolemy knew about the Egyptian terms, but created his own 'Ptolemaic' version). Montulmo, following the practice of Ptolemy, does not weight each dignity differently, but assigns them each one point. He works with the 4 dignities of domicile, exaltation, triplicity and term. He uses Ptolemaic terms. Bonatti uses Dorothean triplicities and what he thought were Ptolemaic terms (Bonatti thought he was using Ptolemaic

SEASON	SUN POSITION	QUALITIES
Spring	Sun in ♈,♉,♊	hot & wet
Summer	Sun in ♋,♌,♍	hot & dry
Autumn	Sun in ♎,♏,♐	cold & dry
Winter	Sun in ♑,♒,♓	cold & wet

Table 15. Qualities of the Sun by Season and Sign

Using the Sun's seasonal qualities proved to be very significant in the Waldorf Study as a predictor of temperament in the chart.

Regarding seasons in the Southern Hemisphere, more work needs to be done.[11] It may turn out that in Southern Hemisphere births, the seasons should be reversed – that is, spring births would be the signs Libra, Scorpio, Sagittarius; summer births would be Capricorn, Aquarius and Pisces; autumn births Aries, Taurus and Gemini; and Winter births Cancer, Leo, Virgo. There appear to be some overlaps in the hot/cold, wet/dry components of seasons both in the Northern and Southern Hemispheres. For instance, parts of Australia 'green up' in the autumn (Northern spring) – so both Northern and Southern Hemispheres appear to begin new growth at the same time, whether the season is called spring or autumn. So growth patterns could also be investigated in regard to seasons and temperament. It would also be useful to examine a large group of charts for people born in the Southern Hemisphere, to see whether the seasonal component in their temperament corresponds better to a northern or southern model. Along the same lines, those born in the tropics might be investigated in terms of a predominantly hot/wet or hot/dry model. While such a study is beyond the scope of this book at this time, it would be a worthwhile investigation, especially given the importance of season in the temperament model.

Moon Phases (Moon Quarters)

Since the Moon is a part of every temperament assessment, it makes no sense to evaluate it only in terms of intrinsic quality (cold and wet), for that would skew all temperaments toward the phlegmatic. We have explained the usefulness of using the sign of the Moon in analysis of the temperament. What about the phases, or to be more precise, quarters, of the Moon? At first glance, it might seem that, since phase is accidental, we ought not to consider it in temperament delineation, which leans toward the essential. Yet the Moon, like Mercury and Venus, is in part defined by its phase, since it moves so quickly. Therefore, it is not entirely inconsistent to use the Moon's phase (by quarter) quality as a factor in determining the temperament.

---

terms, but they are somewhat different from Ptolemy's actual terms. This is perhaps because of 1) scribal error and/or 2) the fact that Bonatti read Ptolemy in a Latin translation of an Arabic translation of the Greek original. See Bonatti, trans. Zoller, *Liber Astronomiae Part II*, pp. 7-8, esp. p. 8 note 1). Schoener uses Dorothean triplicities and Egyptian terms in the medieval weighted format. Lilly and the English school use the weighted format and Ptolemaic (Lilly) triplicities with Ptolemaic terms. In regard to determining a final formula for temperament, the difference in almuten systems will turn out not to be that critical. (See below, p. 87, especially note 26.)

11. Again, thanks is due to Bernadette Brady for suggesting this.

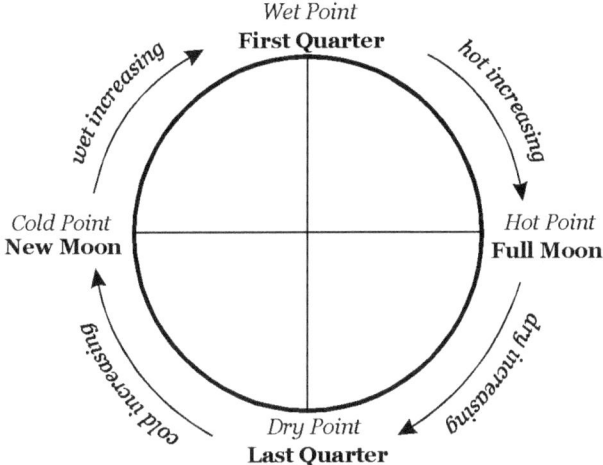

Figure 11. Ptolemy's Moon Phases

But which Moon-quarter qualities? We have seen, in the History section of this book, that Moon Quarters can be assessed as to quality by two methods – Ptolemy's, and the medieval (exemplified by Lilly, who followed the medieval tradition). In the Ptolemaic system, the New Moon is not hot and wet, as the medievals have it, but cold. It is only at the first visibility of the Moon, roughly 15° after the conjunction (what the Greeks called *anatolē*, or *Emergence*[12]), that wet increases. At the First Quarter is the wet point, but after that point in the cycle, hot increases until the Full Moon, the hot point. After that point, dry increases between the Full Moon and Last Quarter, while between the dry point of the Last Quarter and the cold point of the New Moon, cold increases.

While Ptolemy talks about increasing wetness between New Moon and First Quarter, he specifically does not say that the New Moon is wet; it is at the *Emergence* phase that wet begins to increase. Therefore, as Robert Hand points out in his note in the Schmidt translation of the *Tetrabiblos*,[13] the New Moon must be cold, not wet.[14]

Though Ptolemy characterizes the New Moon as cold, that does not necessarily mean that he considers the first of the waxing quarters of the Moon's cycle to be only cold and wet. As the Moon moves through the waxing quarters of the cycle it becomes increasingly wet, and then increasingly

---

12. Sometimes translated as "rising." See Greenbaum, *Late Classical Astrology: Paulus Alexandrinus and Olympiodorus*, p. 85, note 1 and p. 92, note 12 for an explanation of this word.
13. Book I, p. 19, note 1.
14. However, I am not sure I would characterize the entire New Moon to First Quarter phase as cold and wet, First Quarter to Full as hot and wet, Full to Last Quarter as hot and dry, and Last Quarter to New as cold and dry, as Hand says in his unpublished translation of Garcaeus. I think Ptolemy's intent was to show that the waxing phases were more wet and more hot, and the waning phases more dry and more cold. As Hand states in his note in the *Tetrabiblos*, Book I, p. 19, "We have here not four boxes containing qualities but four phases in the continuous ebb and flow of the four qualities."

hot, which fits with Ptolemy's characterization of the seasons, and planetary phases as well; while the beginning point of each quarter carries the dominant quality of the quarter before it, the progression of that quarter brings in the quality that will be dominant at the demarcation of the next quarter.[15] So the point of the Full Moon is the culmination of the hot that has been increasing throughout the quarter, after which dry increases (and heat decreases); and the Last Quarter point is the culmination of dry, after which cold increases (and dry decreases). It makes sense that the waxing quarters have increasing wet and hot, as waxing is associated with fertility and growth; and by the same token, the waning quarters have increasing dry and cold.

The Moon Phases used by Lilly and others start from a different premise. Whether because of a misunderstanding of Ptolemy, or a retooling of him, from New Moon to First Quarter is consistently characterized as hot and wet; First Quarter to Full Moon is hot and dry; Full to Last Quarter as cold and dry; and Last Quarter to New as cold and wet. Any formulae for temperament that use the qualities of the Moon Phases use these characterizations. We don't see the continuous ebbing and flowing of Ptolemy's phases, but a more static model. Thus, we have the following diagram:

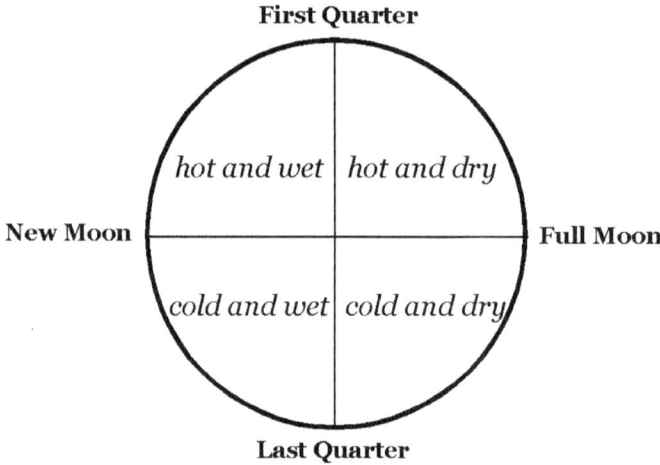

Figure 12. Lilly's Moon Phases

It is clear to see that applying one of the humors to each of these quarters would be easy: from New to First Quarter imparts the sanguine humor; from First Quarter to Full imparts choler; from Full to Last Quarter imparts melancholy; and from Last Quarter to New imparts phlegm. This scheme mimics both the seasonal and the day cycles: spring is considered hot and wet, summer hot and dry, autumn cold and dry; and winter cold and wet. At sunrise, the dew is still on the ground, but burns off as the heat of the day increases; at noon, heat has absorbed all the moisture and dryness increases; at sunset, cold begins to increase as the heat of the Sun can no longer warm; and at midnight, coldness brings

---

15. These ideas are reminiscent of those articulated by Ramon Lull, where he talks of a "proper" quality that is established but beginning to pass away, and an "appropriated" quality that is becoming stronger.

about the formation of dew (or frost, depending on the season). If we are using Moon Phase qualities to partially determine temperament, this arrangement of the qualities, which easily equate with humors, fits well into the medieval scheme.

But we still have not answered the original question: which phase qualities? Can we reconcile what Ptolemy says with how the medievals interpret? I believe we can to some degree, but I also have come to understand that Ptolemy is working very much from a 'qualities' model, while Lilly and the others are working from an 'elements/humors' model; putting the two together is a little like mixing apples with apple pie (it's nice to have lots of apples in the pie, but you need a crust, too, for it to be an apple pie and not, say, applesauce).

Let's think about each quarter of the Moon in regard to its qualities. Setting other criteria aside for a minute, is a person born between the New Moon and First Quarter going to be more hot or more cold? The answer is cold but becoming warmer, because light (and thus heat) is increasing during this quarter, even though it is cold at the New Moon. Is such a person going to be more wet or more dry? The answer is more wet, because the quarter is not sufficiently hot yet to burn off the moisture left from the previous quarter. Now, between the First Quarter and the Full Moon, is it going to be more hot or more cold? Clearly the answer here is more hot, because the light of the Moon is still increasing. More wet or more dry? More dry, because now the heat is sufficient to dry out the moisture left from the previous quarter. Next, between Full Moon and Last Quarter, will it be more hot or more cold? At this point the Moon's light is waning, and a waning Moon has less light and less heat, so even though it is warm, cold is increasing during this quarter. Is it more wet or more dry? It is still more dry, because the heat left from the previous quarter, coupled with the dry of that quarter, keeps it more dry than wet. Finally, between Last Quarter and New Moon, is it more hot or more cold? It is more cold: the Moon is still waning, and light and heat become less and less. It is more wet or more dry? It is more wet, because the cold in turn produces moisture, and the moisture is sufficiently more than the dryness at this quarter of the cycle.

So, for the purposes of temperament, between New Moon and First Quarter it is more wet, becoming hot (thus more sanguine); between First Quarter and Full Moon it is more hot, becoming dry (thus more choleric); between Full Moon and Last Quarter it is more dry, becoming cold (thus more melancholic); and between Last Quarter and New Moon it is more cold, becoming wet (thus more phlegmatic). This model appears to be useful as a component of temperament analysis.[16]

Aspects, and Planets in the 1st House
All traditional methods of temperament assessment look at the rulers of the significators, aspects to significators, and planets in the 1st house. Those planets in aspect to significators are defined by either their phase or the sign they are in. Is it useful to look at aspects to significators when assessing temperament? Are they enough on the 'essential' side that they should be considered a part of innate disposition?

---

16. For the purposes of temperament, I am using a more static model (which Lilly and the medievals use), even though the Moon's cycle in reality is more a continuum than a static state.

Certainly aspects to significators of temperament ought to be considered when looking at the 'manners' of the person. But they are already, in a way, two steps removed from the innate assessment. A first step uses the significator, such as the Ascendant or the Moon, itself. A second step looks at the ruler and/or almuten of the significator. To add aspects to these seems to dilute the strength of the two previous steps. Furthermore, aspects between planets are themselves accidental in nature, not essential.

What about planets in the 1st house? They too should certainly be considered when analyzing the 'manners' of the person – one's personality, for example, is clearly going to be affected by having, say, Saturn, or even Venus, close to the Ascendant. But in what house a planet falls in the chart is also accidental, and so it may be better to leave planets in the 1st house out of temperament assessment.

Fixed Stars

Not all writers use the fixed stars in their temperament delineations.[17] Like planets in the 1st house, but even, perhaps, more diluted, fixed stars fall onto the accidental side of the scale. Because of this, fixed stars seem better suited to be considered in delineation of manners, not temperament. In fact, Lilly even supports such a proposition, when he says, "The *Significator* of Manners joyned to fixed Starres of the first or second magnitude, being but little distant from the Ecliptick, have great signification in the Manners, and make those signified to be more apparent...."[18] In addition, Bernadette Brady's work with fixed stars suggests that they are even better suited to interpretations of a person's life path, rather than to temperament or even personality.[19] Thus it seems that the case for fixed stars to be used in temperament assessment is even more weakened.

The Lord of the Geniture

The Lord (or Lady) of the Geniture is the planet seen as the overall ruler of the chart. In modern astrology, the domicile ruler of the Ascendant is usually described as being the chart ruler, but in traditional astrology it's not quite so simple. First of all, there are a number of different formulae for determining the chart ruler, which complicates things if we intend to use the Lord of the Geniture as a component of temperament analysis. The ruler of the chart is called the *oikodespotēs* in Hellenistic astrology,[20] and the methods used in finding it usually involve dignified planets in strong houses. It is often used as what the Arabic astrologers would later call the hyleg, that is, a planet used in determining length of life. By medieval times, methods for finding the chart ruler included determining the planet with the most dignity in the places of the Sun, Moon, Ascendant, Part of Fortune and pre-natal syzygy (Schoener); the planet with the most essential dignity in the positions of the Sun, Moon, Ascendant, Part of Fortune and pre-natal syzygy, plus those planets' accidental dignity in houses and as the day or hour ruler (Ibn Ezra); and the planet with the most essential and accidental dignity overall, and placed well in the chart (usually angular), and not afflicted by malefics (Lilly and contemporaries).

---

17. While writers from Ptolemy to Garcaeus do take the fixed stars into account in determining temperament, Lilly, his contemporaries and successors do not.
18. William Lilly, op. cit., p. 536.
19. *Brady's Book of Fixed Stars* articulates the use of parans to link fixed stars with various stages of a person's life.
20. The term *oikodespotēs* is also used, in another context in Hellenistic astrology, as equivalent to almuten.

Not all writers use the Lord of the Geniture in temperament analysis. In fact, until Schoener, it was not considered to be a factor in temperament.[21] Is the Lord of the Geniture an essential component of temperament delineation? What are the problems associated with using it, and what might be some benefits?

One problem is figuring out which method works best for obtaining a Lord of the Geniture (the various methods above will, obviously, give different results). Another problem comes to light when we start to think about what the Lord of the Geniture really is. First, the Lord of the Geniture does not necessarily have any connection with the usual suspects of temperament analysis, namely the Ascendant, the Moon or the season of birth. Second, the Lord of the Geniture, as the overall ruler of the chart, would seem to have more to do with the life path, or destiny, of the individual, rather than with that person's innate disposition (though of course one's innate disposition can have an effect on the life path). John Frawley suggests that the importance of the Lord of the Geniture extends beyond just temperament when he talks about the Lord of the Geniture as the "pilot of the soul."[22] He calls the Lord of the Geniture our "internal king"[23] who becomes a beacon for our spiritual aspirations (and inspirations). Yes, the Lord of the Geniture is a most fundamental part of who we are and who we are striving to become, yet I am not sure that including it in temperament analysis contributes to the accuracy of that assessment (the Waldorf Study did not show strong correlations between the Lord of the Geniture and temperament). I think a more productive use of the Lord of the Geniture in chart analysis is to contemplate the relationship between the Lord of the Geniture and temperament, and how the two fit into our delineation of a whole person. As Frawley points out, the Lord of the Geniture can even "improve the temperament" (i.e. bring it more into balance) – a melancholic whose Lord of the Geniture is Jupiter can choose to bring more sanguine into his life.[24]

Qualities versus Temperaments
Should we assess temperament by using qualities, or by using temperament names? All traditional methods for determining temperament, whatever factors they consider, add up the qualities of each factor and decide the temperament from the qualities with the highest scores. When I began my work with temperament, I followed this practice and used it for my research in the Waldorf Study. However, I was somewhat troubled with the 'add-'em-up-and-get-an-answer' approach, because sometimes it really seemed to skew the end result. I was looking for something more integrative, but I wasn't sure how to do it. Through email conversations with Garry Phillipson, the idea of breaking each factor down by quality, adding them up and getting an answer was replaced by the idea of *not* breaking each factor down by quality, but using the temperament itself, and adding those up to get a distribution of temperaments that made up the complete assessment. This seems to me to be more organic, and more

---

21. Schoener lists the Lord of the Geniture in one of his two methods of temperament assessment. The other writers who use it are Garcaeus, Lilly, Coley and Partridge.
22. John Frawley, "The Pilot of the Soul," lecture given at the ISAR (International Society for Astrological Research) conference at Anaheim, California, Oct. 10, 2003.
23. John Frawley, *The Real Astrology Applied* (London: Apprentice Books, 2002), p. 142.
24. "The Pilot of the Soul," lecture at ISAR, Oct. 10, 2003.

philosophically in tune with astrological principles. Counting up each factor as a temperament, and then analyzing, keeps the integrity of the temperament concept as an intrinsic *combination* of qualities, rather than as discrete qualities added together at the end to produce a temperament. The feasibility of this idea was illustrated very well when Garry sent me his analysis of my own chart.

At that time (October of 2002), Garry was using a spreadsheet with fourteen different criteria for determining the temperament. He broke them down by quality, but then had a separate column where he totaled the factors up by temperament. Analyzing my chart in light of these 14 factors, he had come up with the following distribution: 7 points for hot, 7 for cold, 7 for wet and 7 for dry. A perfect balance. Assessing by temperament, however, showed 7 phlegmatic and 7 choleric. As Garry pointed out, "This has to be a key chart for evaluating whether it's better to total up hot/cold, dry/wet; or to count up the instances of each humour. Taking the former approach, there's complete balance; taking the latter, there is no melancholy or sanguine; phlegmatic and choleric are dominant, and equally strong. So which is more useful as a way of describing you?"[25]

As much as I would like to say I am perfectly balanced, I think, as Garry says, that the more "useful" description is that I am phlegmatic and choleric, with no melancholy or sanguine. I would describe myself as a primary phlegmatic with a large dose of choler. Sanguine does seem to me to be a rather alien concept, though I admire it greatly in others; and I've never considered myself to have many traits associated with melancholy. In addition, when I asked a Waldorf teacher to tell me what she thought my temperament was, she immediately said, "Phlegmatic." (I gave her no indication beforehand of what I thought my temperament was, or what the chart suggested it was.)

Of course, just because this idea works with one chart does not mean it will work with every chart. So I continued to experiment with using temperament names, rather than qualities, to describe the factors used in determining a temperament from the chart. On the whole, it worked rather well, as will be demonstrated in the example charts in the next chapter. There is one caveat, however: it is still useful to keep qualities in the back of your mind as you work with temperament assessment. Once the general temperament has been determined, I have found it fruitful to see which qualities are emphasized in a person's temperament. We can refine our temperament assessment further when we see if any qualities dominate in a temperament – for instance, a sanguine who has more hot versus a sanguine who has more wet. Both are still basically sanguine, but one embodies more wet, connective qualities (think Falstaff) and one is more interested in activity (think Curious George). And conversely, it is also useful to note when a quality is quite low or lacking – in the same way that it is important to note lack of a temperament in the temperamental makeup.

Which Factors?
And so finally we come to the $64,000 question: which factors best determine the temperament? After I did the Waldorf Study, I began to experiment with the 'top three' factors of Ascendant Sign by element, Moon Sign by element, and Season of Birth. I soon added in the other three factors that had

---

25. Garry Phillipson, email to Dorian Greenbaum, October 8, 2002

hit rates above 50%: Ascendant Ruler by Intrinsic Quality, Ascendant Almuten by Intrinsic Quality[26] and Moon Ruler by Sign (element). More experimentation and consultation with Garry Phillipson led to the addition of Moon Phase (using the Lilly system).[27]

As I explained in the "Qualities versus Temperaments" section above, I first added up the qualities, but then switched to adding up temperament names instead. The factors I chose (aside from being better at showing temperament in a chart in the Waldorf Study) are also factors that:

- have a strong relationship to the Ascendant and the Moon, which every writer agrees are important in determining the temperament
- incorporate the season of birth, which connects the person to earthly cycles but still is somewhat personal
- take into account more 'essential' components of the chart, rather than 'accidental' components

There still remained some issues: I was not using aspects to significators or planets in the 1st house, which many believed ought to be part of assessing the temperament. The reason for this was because I feel these are more accidental than essential, and because they seemed to muddy the waters in terms of finding a basic temperament. As Garry Phillipson commented,

> "It seems that there's a two-stage process here [looking at aspects after looking at rulers and elements]. ... If the aspects were integrated into the spreadsheet, I think that this perspective wouldn't come through. And it does seem to me to be plausible, at a theoretical level, that the aspects should constitute a stage which is subsequent to the qualities of the planets in their signs."[28]

For the same reason I decided not to use planets in the 1st house in the basic assessment of temperament. It also became clear that a decision needed to be made about the intrinsic qualities of Mercury and Venus. If I were going to use the intrinsic qualities of the Ascendant Ruler and Almuten, then I needed to be consistent in what qualities Mercury and Venus would have. At the end of October 2002 I began to experiment with calling Venus oriental intrinsically sanguine, Venus occidental intrinsically

---

26. I have chosen the almuten system that uses Ptolemaic (Lilly) triplicity rulers and Ptolemaic terms, the system used by Lilly and the English School. I have investigated the other systems and have come to the following conclusions, as regards temperament:
    1. The majority of almutens, in terms of their quality/temperament, will not change regardless of which system is used – only 153 degrees out of a possible 720 Day/Night degrees, or 21.25%, will change. Of those degrees, most almutens will change by less than one point (because they become co- or tri-almutens, or because their change is solely dependent on the phase of Mercury or Venus)
    2. Even if the almuten changes completely, it is only one point in the formula, or 10% of the total (see p. 89, *A New Formula for Temperament*), and thus is unlikely to significantly affect the determination of the temperament by using the birthchart.
27. As stated before, Lilly's system (and that of all the medieval and Renaissance astrologers) has the 1st Quarter as hot and wet, the 2nd Quarter as hot and dry, the 3rd Quarter as cold and dry, and the 4th Quarter as cold and wet.
28. Garry Phillipson, email to Dorian Greenbaum, October 8, 2002.

ANALYSIS OF TEMPERAMENT IN THE NATAL CHART

	SANGUINE (hot & wet)	CHOLERIC (hot & dry)	MELANCHOLIC (cold & dry)	PHLEGMATIC (cold & wet)
BY ELEMENT	Air	Fire	Earth	Water
BY SEASON	Spring	Summer	Autumn	Winter
BY SIGN (element of the sign)	♊ ♎ ♒	♈ ♌ ♐	♉ ♍ ♑	♋ ♏ ♓
BY PLANET*	♃; ♀ (oriental); ☿ (oriental)	☉; ♂	♄; ☿ (occidental)	☽; ♀ (occidental)
BY MOON PHASE	New to 1st Quarter	1st Quarter to Full	Full to Last Quarter	Last Quarter to New
BY HUMORS	Blood	Yellow Bile	Black Bile	Phlegm
BY AGES OF MAN	Childhood	Early Adulthood	Middle Age	Old Age

* **Oriental** refers to a planet rising before the Sun; an **Occidental** planet rises after the Sun

Table 16

Chart Design by Peter Standaart

phlegmatic, Mercury oriental intrinsically sanguine and Mercury occidental intrinsically melancholic. This worked surprisingly well (i.e., the phase of Mercury or Venus when they were a ruler or almuten of the Ascendant did seem to correlate with the temperament). Things were beginning to fall into place.

Weighting Factors

The final piece of the puzzle was to weight certain factors, namely, the Ascendant sign, the Moon sign and the Season of birth. These were the 'big three' in the Waldorf Study, and it seemed reasonable to give them more weight in temperament assessment than the other factors involved. So those factors were given double the weight of the other factors.

A New Formula for Temperament

The final formula, which I have been working with for the past 2 years, is this:

> Ascendant Sign (by element) = 2 points
> Ascendant Ruler (by intrinsic quality) = 1 point
> Ascendant Almuten (by intrinsic quality) = 1 point
> Moon Sign (by element) = 2 points
> Moon Ruler (by sign) = 1 point
> Moon Phase (Lilly) = 1 point
> Season of Birth = 2 points

So, does it work? Let's take a look, again, at Lilly's worked example on page 742 of *Christian Astrology*, (see over the page), this time using my formula. You'll recall that Lilly's method showed the man to be sanguine/choleric, though further analysis by Lilly concludes that the testimonies are actually balanced: "I cannot perceive any superabundance in any of the four Humours…."[29] Yet Lilly's direct observations of the man lead him to conclude that he is, in fact, "Sanguine, Melancholly Sanguine….";[30] and he finds justification for that assessment not in his own method, but in noticing that the Sun, Moon, Mercury and Venus are in air signs, and the Ascendant and its Lord, Saturn, are in earth signs. Shall we see what my formula shows for the man's temperament?

> ASC Capricorn, earth = 2 Melancholic
> ASC ruler Saturn, intrinsically cold and dry, thus = 1 Melancholic
> ASC almuten also Saturn, intrinsically cold and dry, thus = 1 Melancholic
> Moon Gemini, air = 2 Sanguine
> Moon Ruler by Sign Mercury in Libra, air = 1 Sanguine
> Moon Phase 3rd Quarter = 1 Melancholic
> Season Autumn = 2 Melancholic
> Totals: 7 Melancholic, 3 Sanguine

---

29. William Lilly, op. cit., p. 743. The table accompanying the analysis shows 7 hot, 6 moist, 6 cold and 7 dry.
30. Ibid., p. 744.

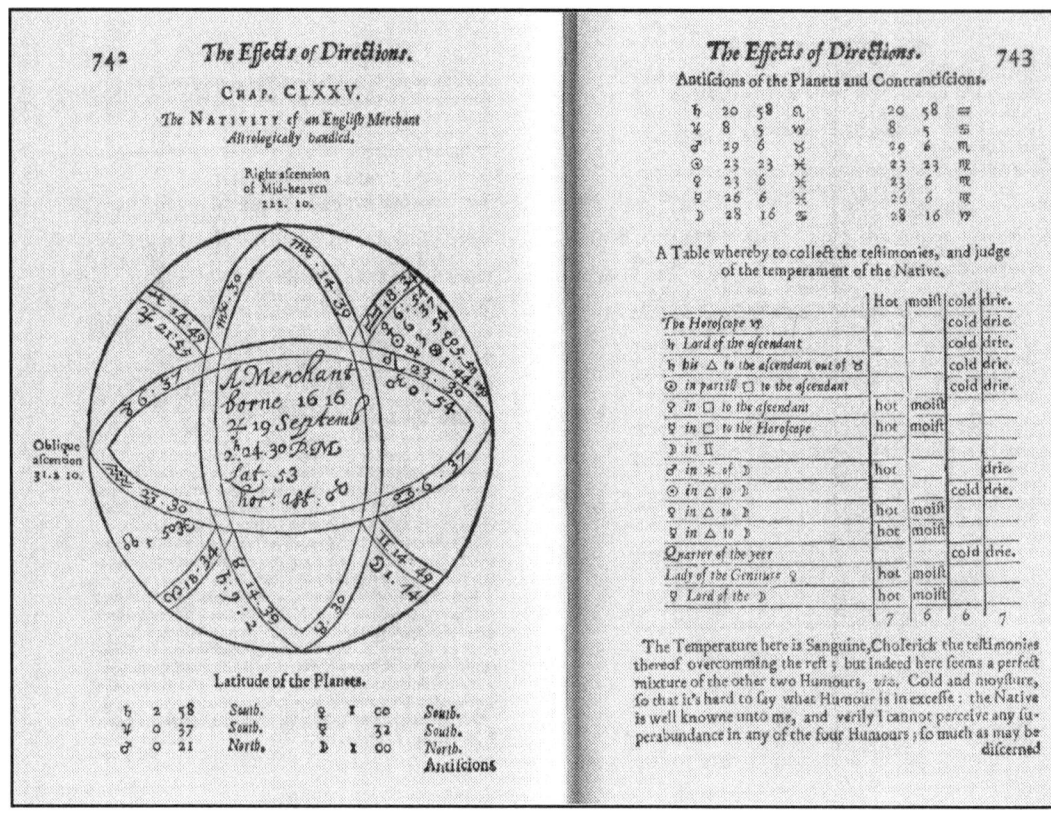

This agrees with Lilly's observational assessment (which he backed up, not by his method, but by highlighting the personal planets in air signs, and the Ascendant and Ascendant ruler in earth signs). It would seem that this new formula can indeed be used profitably to assess a temperament, even according to Lilly's lights.

Although the formula is not perfect (is anything?), it does seem, after much testing, to correlate with a person's temperament to a surprisingly high degree, and with much less analysis than a 'traditional' assessment of temperament would take. Once an initial analysis of the temperament has been made, one can then look at the 'manners' or personality of the individual by looking at other chart factors. The two combined give a fairly complete picture. The next sections of this book will discuss the varieties of temperament (both pure and mixed types), look at a number of example charts of those with the various temperaments (using the present formula), and give a short introduction into combining temperament and manners to give an impression of a 'whole' person.

Varieties of Temperament

Not many people, relatively speaking, have a 'pure' temperament. Most of us are a mixture – with, usually, one temperament dominant, and another temperament secondary to that. (By the same token, not many people are perfectly balanced, either.) This section, however, will describe *both* the pure and the mixed types (or what Culpeper called the 'Commixtures'). The reason for this is because pure types become a good baseline for comparison. Regarding the mixed types, Culpeper disregarded 'commixtures' which consisted of two active temperaments or two passive temperaments (e.g. Sanguine/Choleric or Melancholic/Phlegmatic). His reasoning for this, as stated in his book *Galen's Art of Physick*, was that the order of the signs precluded such mixtures.[31] This reasoning seems rather weak. Graeme Tobyn, in his book *Culpeper's Medicine*, ascribes a better reason for Culpeper's decision: that since an active quality was twice occurring in these mixtures, the heat in, say, Sanguine/Choleric and the cold in, say, Melancholic/Phlegmatic would resolve the former into choleric and the latter into phlegmatic.[32] However, in reality, I have seen people whom I would describe as Sanguine/Choleric (or the reverse) and Melancholic/Phlegmatic (or the reverse). So I will include these types in the following descriptions.

The Pure Temperaments

Each temperament will be followed by an example chart illustrating the principles of the pure temperament. The analysis of the example charts is not meant to be complete, but to focus on the temperament as it plays out in the life.

Choleric

Key words:	will, inexhaustible, optimistic, aggressive, assertive, take-charge, impatient, hates details
Favorite Book:	Machiavelli, *The Prince*
Favorite Songs:	"Climb Ev'ry Mountain"
	"I Can Do Anything (Better than You Can)"
Favorite Music:	Wagner, "Ride of the Valkyries"

- Demands much and gives much
- Easy to see the world as black & white, as absolutes
- Puts best foot forward, and can't understand those who don't
- If I'm not noticed, I'm nothing
- Activity, more activity – hard to sit still
- Truly can't understand that their arrogant behavior might be off-putting
- Believes in hierarchy, with them at the top

---

31. Nicholas Culpeper, *Galen's Art of Physick* (London:Peter Cole, 1652), p. 58.
32. Graeme Tobyn, op. cit., p. 58. See p. 42 for additional discussion.

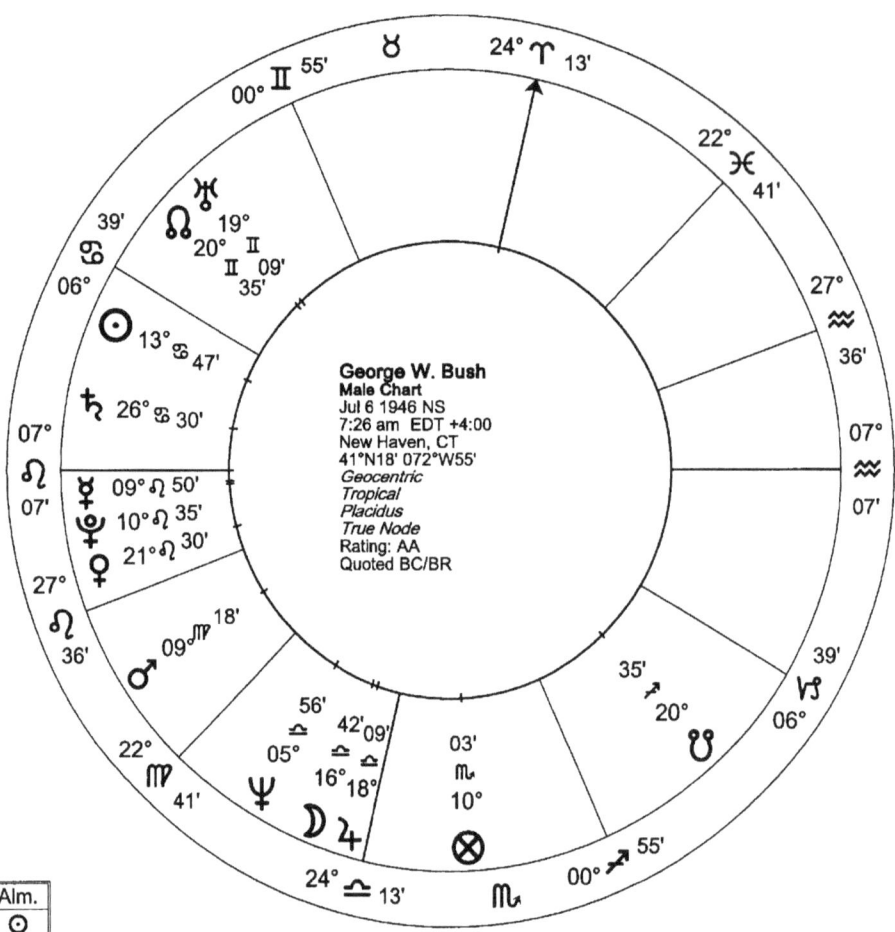

- My opinion is the only one that matters
- President of the Student Council
- Noblesse oblige
- Happiest when running a project
- Can-do attitude
- Quick on the uptake
- High expectations
- Life is a series of challenges to be overcome – triumphantly!
- Q: Why did you climb the mountain? A: Because it's there.

Cholerics get along with: sanguines (who say: happy to help with your project; it sounds like fun!)
phlegmatics (easily dominated)
Cholerics can't stand: other cholerics (competition!)
melancholics (too negative)

Example Chart: George Bush

It's no surprise that George W. Bush has a choleric temperament. In fact, he could be the poster boy for cholerics. Born to a life of privilege, he coasted in his youth (perhaps the influence of his sanguine Libra Moon), but his true choleric colors blazed forth when he became governor of Texas. With his lack of attention to details, and with a noblesse oblige that is more like ignorance of obligation, Bush was surprised to discover in 1999 that Texas was near the top in the Agriculture Department's annual statistics on hunger. When he ran for President in 2000, he was perhaps still seen as an amiable drifter whose 'compassionate conservatism' would improve the country; his sanguine Moon masked the choleric's burning ambition and steadfastness of purpose. After 9/11, of course, Americans were hoping for a strong leader, which Bush seemed to be, and his responses in the early days after the attack seemed to be just what the country needed.

Yet the choleric temperament can be prone to excess. Bush's chart is excessively hot (in addition to the 8 points of choler he has, giving 8 points of hot, he also has more hot in the Libra Moon) and

George W. Bush	Temperament			
	S	C	M	P
Birth Season	2	2		
Asc Sign	2	2		
Asc Ruler	1	1		
Asc Almuten	1	1		
Moon Sign	2	2			
Moon Phase	1	1		
Sign of Moon Ruler	1		1		
Totals		2	8	0	0

(scoring table designed by Anne Lathrop)

the extreme circumstances brought this heat to the fore. For cholerics especially, it is easy to see the world as black and white, and a can-do attitude combined with activity (without thinking necessarily about the consequences of that activity) is embraced as the solution to any problem. A willingness to fight for what he believes in coupled with a reluctance to change his positions with changing events has probably contributed to the less successful outcomes of his policies in Iraq.

What others would call faults, the choleric must ignore or trumpet as virtues: Bush's difficulty in putting an articulate sentence together is touted as being in touch with the sensibilities of the common folk (though his life has been lived in anything but the common circumstances of most people). It's hard for the choleric to admit he's wrong; Bush cannot recall ever making a mistake since becoming President. Hyperarrogance marks the excessive choleric; Bush is sure he is making the world safe for democracy even though many have the opposite opinion.

When one reads the temperament descriptions of John Gadbury, they seem almost like comic exaggerations. Yet with George W. Bush, extreme circumstances seem to have brought out an extreme manifestation of his already extremely choleric temperament:

> "The cholerique person is imperious, tyrannical, full of revenge, quarrelsome, apt to anger, importunate, hardy, rash, involving himself in many unnecessary troubles and vexations; a seditious Fellow, yet in many things ingenious and wittily apprehensive; but a very *Proteus* in his Opinion....of a rugged, surly and tyrannical disposition."[33]

This is what one sees in a temperament taken to negative excess. With the choleric, at least, it's not a pretty sight.

Other Cholerics: Cherie Blair, Martha Stewart, Andrew Lloyd-Webber, Ingrid Bergman, Luciano Pavarotti, Johannes Brahms, Michael Milken, Lena Horne, Barbra Streisand, Martina Navratilova, Donald Trump.

Sanguine

Key Words:	friendly, social, shallow, unfocussed, cheerful, dilettante, lucky
Favorite Book:	Peale, *The Power of Positive Thinking*
Favorite Songs:	"You're Never Fully Dressed Without a Smile"
	"Consider Yourself"
	"Life is a Cabaret"
Favorite Music:	Joplin, *The Entertainer*

- Hail fellow well met
- Never met a party they didn't like
- Tuned in, as if by magic, to the latest trends
- Networking is an art form

---

33. John Gadbury, *Doctrine of Nativities* (1658; Ballantrae Reprint, no date), Chapter XII, secs. 5 & 7, pp. 94, 97.

- Doesn't hold a grudge
- A finger in every pie
- Invented the game "Six Degrees of Separation"
- Disaster is not having a date on a Saturday night
- Sally Field in Oscar speech: "You like me, you *really like* me!"
- New places are wonderful – never want to travel to the same place twice
- Speak first – think afterwards
- Secretary of the Student Council
- Miss Congeniality
- Life is a popularity contest
- Q: Why did you climb the mountain? A: I climbed a mountain? I thought I was just going uphill!

Sanguines get along with: cholerics (you help with my project, I'll help with yours)
phlegmatics (who don't mind sanguine chatter; it saves them from having to think of something to say)
other sanguines (let's have a party!)

Sanguines can't stand: melancholics (downer, dude)

Example Chart: Tony Blair

Sociable, affable Tony Blair became the youngest Prime Minister in nearly 200 years when he was elected in 1997. He won a landslide victory in 2001, showing his massive popularity at that time. He had always been gregarious, easily making friends at school and singing lead in a rock band called Ugly Rumours. Though not an outstanding student, he attended Oxford and graduated from its law school.

He met his wife, Cherie, while both were in law school (interestingly, she is as choleric as Blair is sanguine – is this why Tony gets on so well with George W. Bush?). After a political campaign in which both ran for office, Cherie lost and Tony won, and his political rise could be described as meteoric. Politically, Blair has been influenced by John MacMurray, the Scottish theologian whose books "combine Christian thought and psychology with 'community' politics."[34] He was awarded the Charlemagne Prize in 1999 for his peacemaking efforts in Northern Ireland (a sanguine's dream come true).

Articulate, intelligent, sincere and genuinely interested in consensus, Blair was riding on a wave of popularity when President Bush decided to invade Iraq. Whether because of the sanguine's desire to support a friend, a belief in the sincerity and probity of Bush's motives, or his own conviction that it was the right thing to do, Blair supported Bush's endeavors even though much of the country and even members of his own cabinet were against it. Never let it be said that a sanguine desert his friend! In spite of the country's opposition, Blair managed to survive as Prime Minister, though with

---

34. Lois Rodden, *AstroDatabank Biography for Tony Blair*.

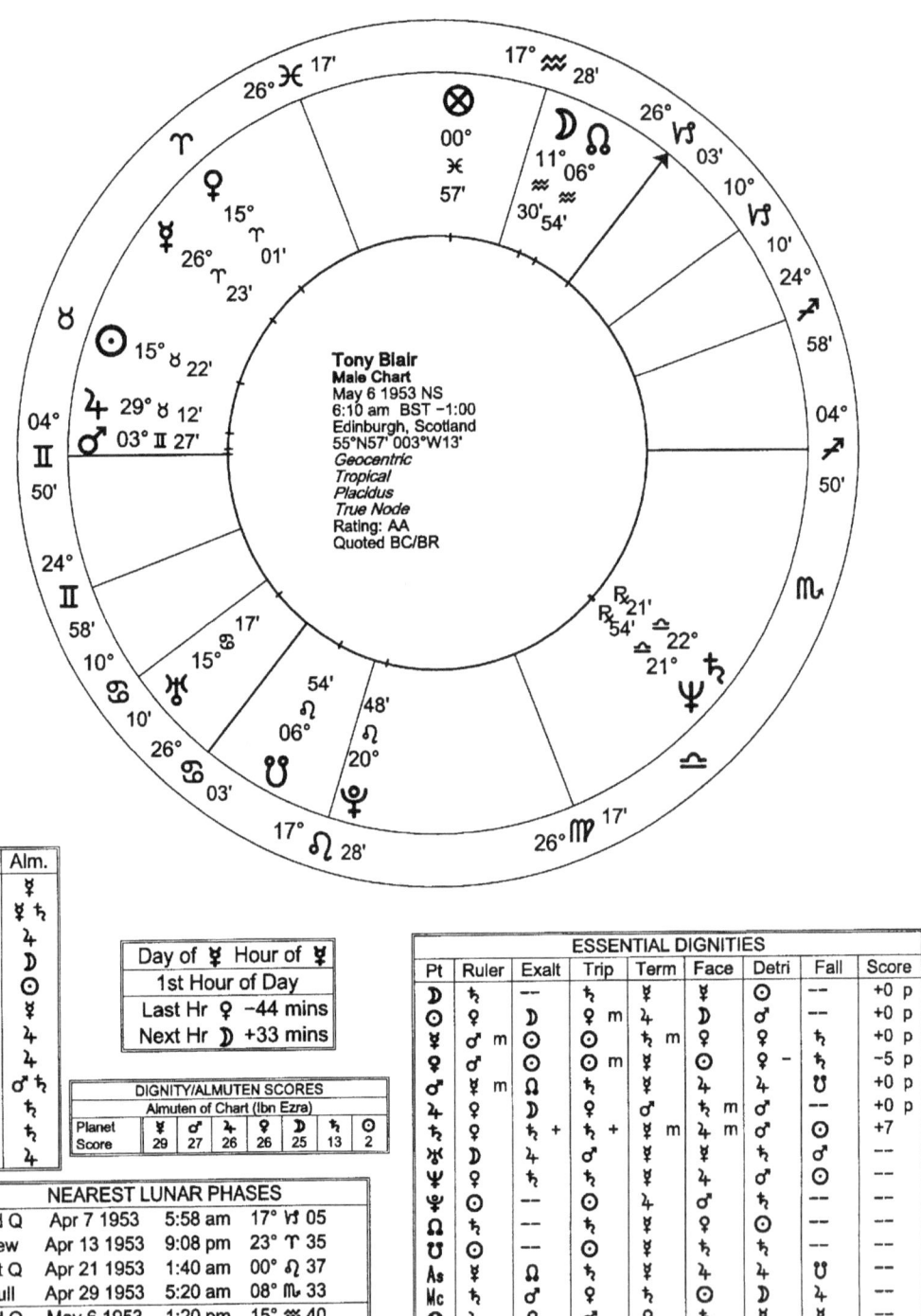

Tony Blair	Temperament			
	S	C	M	P
Birth Season	2	2		
Asc Sign	2	2		
Asc Ruler	1	1		
Asc Almuten	1	1		
Moon Sign	2	2		
Moon Phase	1		1	
Sign of Moon Ruler	1	1		
Totals	9	0	1	0

greatly reduced popularity. This is perhaps testimony to the pure sanguine temperaments' ability to keep their allies even when they have disagreements. From an American perspective, one seldom has the sense with Tony Blair that he dissembles for political gain – he seems genuinely committed to following a course he feels is best for the whole country, regardless of the personal toll on him. Despite his unsupported policies, it remains difficult not to like him – perhaps the mark of a true sanguine.

Other Sanguines: Richard Simmons, Steffi Graf, Ewan McGregor, Alois Alzheimer, Madalyn Murray O'Hair, Cary Grant, Gregory Peck, Pope John Paul II, Venus Williams, Omar Sharif, Lord Alfred Douglas, Britney Spears

Melancholic

Key Words: anti-social, analytical, pessimistic, connoisseur, studious
Favorite Books: Kant, *Critique of Pure Reason*
   Dostoevsky, *Crime and Punishment*
Favorite Songs: "I Am a Rock"
   "Send in the Clowns"
   "It's a Hard-Knock Life"
   "This Nearly was Mine"
Favorite Music: Beethoven, *Pathétique Sonata*
   Albinoni, *Adagio in g minor*

- Succeeds through hard work and persistence
- Don't get your hopes up
- Nothing is ever good enough
- Really good at analyzing and organizing
- The light at the end of the tunnel is an oncoming train
- Idea of a fun time is reading the dictionary
- Likes to play the blame game
- Lost to the sanguine in the Student Council election

- Was appointed to the sanguine's job after the sanguine missed too many meetings (due to partying the night before)
- Believes in hierarchy, and they will be near the bottom – undeservedly
- Don't jump to conclusions – weigh the evidence
- Are often alone, but don't like it much
- Can't bear the idea of superficial knowledge
- Life is not fair
- Life is a series of disappointments
- Q: Why didn't you climb the mountain? A: Because I never would have gotten to the top

Melancholics get along with: phlegmatics (they're like them, but not so negative)
Melancholics can't stand: other melancholics (pity party)
cholerics (too bossy)
sanguines (they have all the luck)

Example Chart: Paul Simon

If there were any doubt as to the basically melancholic nature of Paul Simon's temperament, a selection of his song titles would suffice: "The Sound of Silence" ("Hello darkness, my old friend…."), "I am a Rock" ("I am shielded in my armor"), "Wednesday Morning 3 AM," "Bridge Over Troubled Water," "Think Too Much" ("Maybe I think too much for my own good"), "Learn How to Fall." Even his more upbeat songs have a melancholic tinge: "The 59th Street Bridge Song" begins with "Slow down, you move too fast;" "Me and Julio Down by the Schoolyard" contains the line "if I get that boy I'm gonna stick him in the house of detention."

Undoubtedly the creative force behind Simon & Garfunkel, Paul Simon and Art Garfunkel met in the 6th grade and were performing together by the age of 15. Their first commercial success was "The Sound of Silence" in 1964 – they had tapped into teenage melancholy (which would turn to activism later in the decade). Simon provided the music, gritty lyrics and a raw but arresting tenor, and Garfunkel supplied the angelic voice and pop suaveness. "The Sound of Silence," part of the album *Wednesday Morning 3 AM*, was followed by a succession of hit albums *Sounds of Silence*; *Parsley,*

Paul Simon	Temperament			
	S	C	M	P
Birth Season	2		2	
Asc Sign	2		2	
Asc Ruler	1		1	
Asc Almuten	1		1	
Moon Sign	2			2
Moon Phase	1		1	
Sign of Moon Ruler	1			1
Totals	0	0	7	3

Using Temperament in Modern Astrological Practice   99

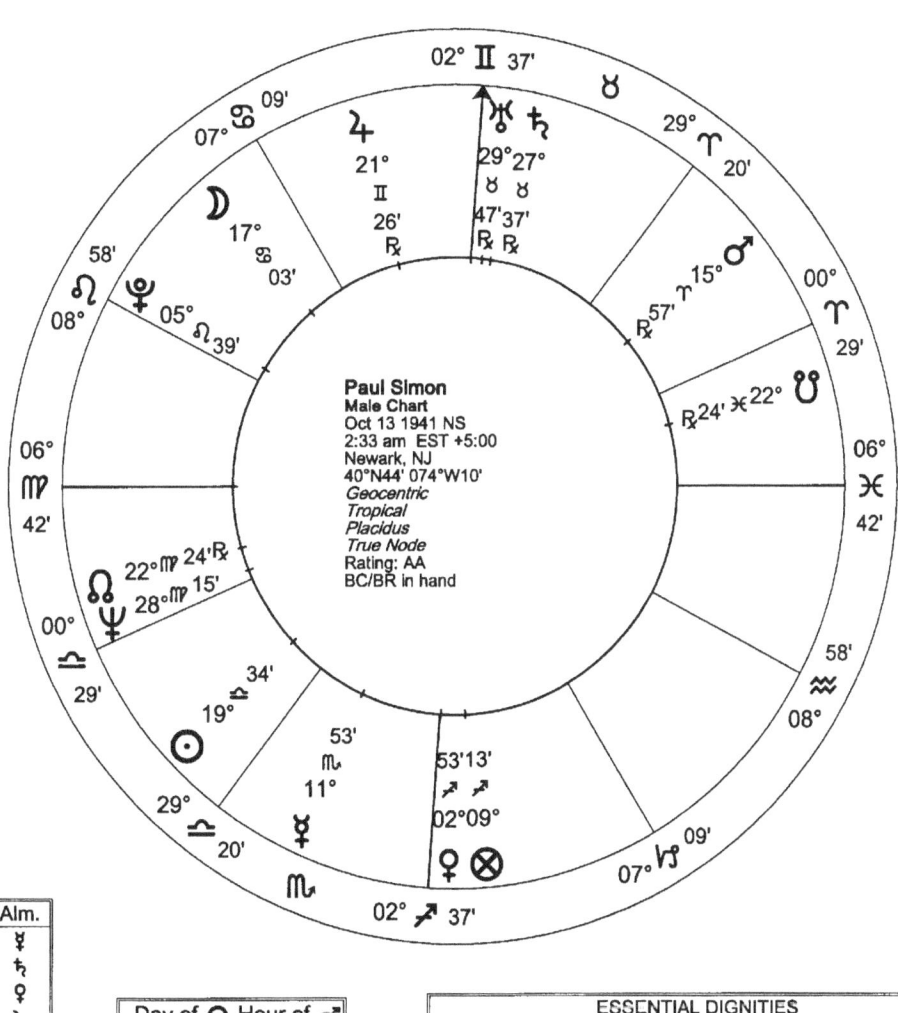

Sage, Rosemary and Thyme; *Bookends*; and 1970's *Bridge Over Troubled Water*, which ironically or prophetically was their final album as a team (not counting "greatest hits" and live concert albums). The reason for the breakup was supposedly their clearly diverging tastes in music and Garfunkel's growing career as an actor; it's not hard to imagine the intensely creative and perfectionistic Simon feeling stifled by what he perceived as Garfunkel's cloying sweetness and blandness. He said at the time, "I wouldn't say that my ideas were bigger than Simon & Garfunkel, but I would say that my ideas were different from Simon & Garfunkel. And I didn't want to go in that direction of a duo."[35] Here is melancholic deprecation, coupled with a certainty that he can do a better (or a more true to his talent) job on his own.

And of course Simon was gloriously vindicated in his choice with the superb albums following the breakup, which cemented his reputation as a brilliant composer: *Paul Simon* – containing 11 autobiographical (in emotion if not events) songs exploring the angst and frustration of realizing or not realizing your dreams. This album was followed by *There Goes Rhymin' Simon*, *Still Crazy After All These Years*, *One Trick Pony*, *Hearts and Bones*, *Graceland* and *The Rhythm of the Saints* – some more brilliant than others, but all infused with a melancholic sensibility combined with a persistent glimmer of hope that is the hallmark of Paul Simon.

Other Melancholics: Carrie Fisher, Howard Pinter, Erwin Rommel, Susan Sarandon, Dick Cavett, Elizabeth I, Nicholas Culpeper, Yehudi Menuhin, Montgomery Clift, Sean Connery, Matt Damon, Derek Jacobi

Phlegmatic

Key Words: contemplative, reserved, shy, slow-moving, resigned
Favorite Book: Burnett, *The Secret Garden*
Favorite Songs: "Wouldn't It Be Loverly"
                  "Mellow Yellow"
                  "In My Own Little Corner"
Favorite Music: Debussy, *La Mer*
                  Beethoven, *Moonlight Sonata,* 1st movement

- Slow and steady wins the race – does winning even matter?
- I'll make up my mind when I'm good and ready
- If I ignore it, it will go away
- Aim for the status quo
- Don't do today what you can put off 'til tomorrow
- Inertia is wonderful

---

35. Quote taken from the Art Garfunkel.com website, http://www.artgarfunkel.com/chrono/1970-1974.htm (accessed April 2004).

- Enjoys food and chews slowly and carefully
- There's no place like home
- Likes to ponder
- Would rather study one thing in depth than a lot of things superficially
- Visits the same places over and over, becoming more comfortable each time
- Greta Garbo: "I want to be alone."
- Would never dream of running for the Student Council
- Life is best lived at a slow pace
- Q: Why didn't you climb the mountain? A: That's way too much work.

Phlegmatics get along with: sanguines (they don't notice the phlegmatic's silence)
melancholics (they understand where they're coming from)
cholerics (it's a relief to be told what to do)

Phlegmatics can't stand: other phlegmatics (too much awkward silence because no one can think of anything to say)

Example Chart: George Harrison

Known as 'The Quiet Beatle,' George Harrison always seemed to be in the shadows of the more flamboyant and charismatic Lennon and McCartney, and was even eclipsed by the zany antics of Ringo Starr. Yet he continued on, playing his guitar with a slowly and continuously refined skill, seemingly unperturbed at not being in the spotlight (or as much not in the spotlight as any Beatle could be).

He was a school friend of McCartney's and was encouraged by Paul to improve his guitar playing. He spent several years slowly developing his style by listening to other guitarists such as Chet Atkins and Buddy Holly – a true phlegmatic's approach to learning (imitation and slow deliberation brings you where you want to be).

Even though the songwriting of Lennon and McCartney dominated the Beatles' work, Harrison left his mark on the group with his songs "While My Guitar Gently Weeps" (a phlegmatic lament if there ever was one) and "Here Comes the Sun" – the long cold lonely (phlegmatic) winter leading to the

George Harrison	Temperament			
	S	C	M	P
Birth Season	2			2
Asc Sign	2	2		
Asc Ruler	1			1
Asc Almuten	1			1
Moon Sign	2			2
Moon Phase	1		1	
Sign of Moon Ruler	1		1	
Totals	2	0	2	6

102   Temperament: Astrology's Forgotten Key

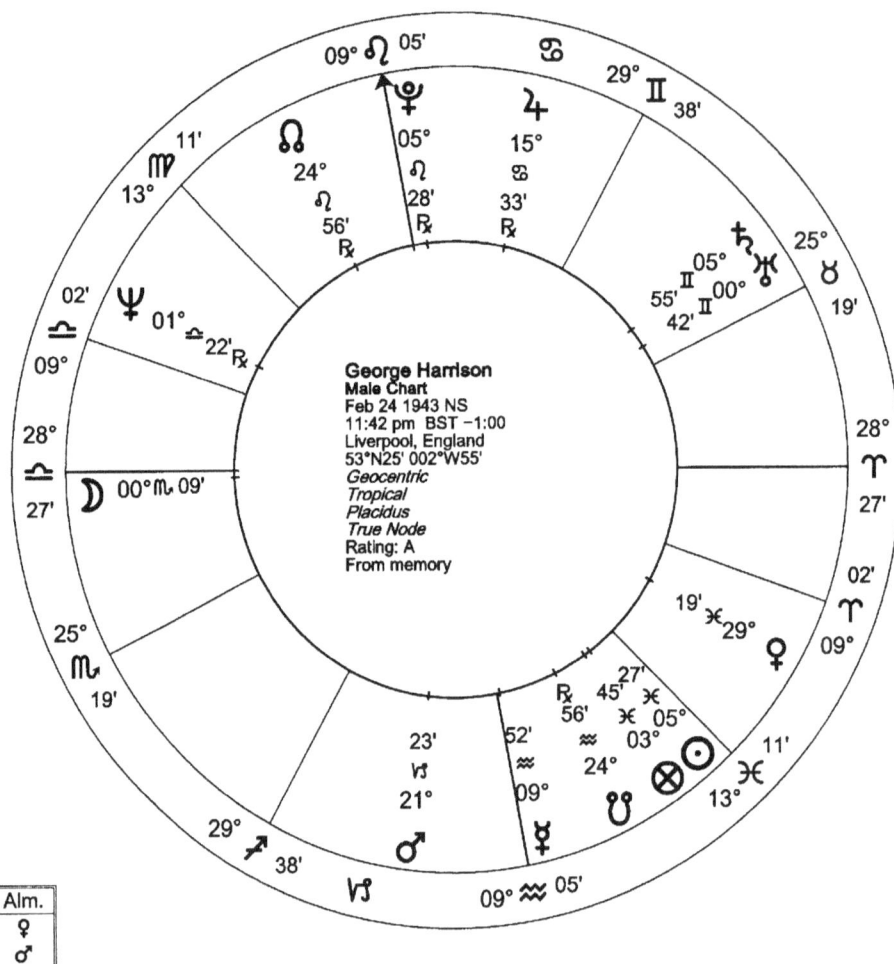

sun that makes everything all right. He also introduced the Beatles to Transcendental Meditation (another phlegmatic title!) and was greatly influenced both by Ravi Shankar and Maharishi Mahesh Yogi.

After the Beatles' breakup, Harrison went on to write his own experimental music and to produce solo albums like *All Things Must Pass* and *Dark Horse*. Lennon's assassination in 1980 upset him deeply, and he spent a dozen years as a recluse, rarely appearing in public and refusing to grant any interviews. It was easy and comfortable for him, as a primary phlegmatic, to do this. As his friend Michael Palin commented, "I think in some ways he is just recovering from being a Beatle."[36] He was happiest as a homebody, living with his wife Olivia and son Dhani in their English mansion. The following quote aptly describes his phlegmatic temperament: "I'm really quite simple. I don't want to be in the business full-time, because I'm a gardener. I plant flowers and watch them grow. I don't go out to clubs and partying. I stay at home and watch the river flow."[37]

Other Phlegmatics: Franz Schubert, Frank Sinatra Jr., Francis Poulenc, Lady Antonia Fraser, Nathan Lane, Hector Berlioz, Liza Minnelli, Johnny Cash, Elvis Stojko, Jerry Lewis, Joni Mitchell, Sybil Leek, Paul Cezanne

The Compound Temperaments

As I did for the pure temperaments, I will give descriptions of each compound temperament, and then follow with a worked example of each temperament type. Again, the worked example is not meant to be a complete analysis of the chart, but one that points out the salient features of the temperament as it relates to the chart and to the life.

Choleric/Melancholic and Melancholic/Choleric Temperaments

These compound temperaments are united by the *dry* quality. Thus there will be a lack of moisture in the temperament, which will have an effect on its expression; someone in whom these temperaments predominate will be more structured or more rigid; will tend toward the analytical rather than the synthesizing, the discrete rather than the encompassing.

Choleric/Melancholic

- Can counter any argument with facts and logic
- Does not suffer fools gladly
- Not as willful as the pure choleric; can see consequences
- Quick-witted; thinks on his feet
- Witty – a quip for every occasion, often *le mot juste*
- Wants to win the spelling bee

---

36. Quoted in Lois Rodden's biography of George Harrison on *AstroDatabank*.
37. Quote taken from the "Beatles on Abbey Road" website: http://webhome.idirect.com/~faab/AbbeyRoad/george2.htm (accessed April 2004).

- Leads because has a plan worked out in all details
- Decide in haste, repent at leisure
- Holds grudges and may take revenge (good at biding time)
- More impulsive than reflective, and may regret impulsivity

Example Chart: Antoine de Saint-Exupéry

The author of *Le Petit Prince* was born into an aristocratic family. After his father's death, when Antoine was only 4 years old, the family moved to a chateau owned by his mother's aunt. St.-Exupéry spent a happy childhood there, nicknamed, as befits one with a good amount of choler, "le Roi Soleil" (King Sun). At the age of 9, he was sent away to a series of boarding schools, where his constant disorderliness and lack of interest in studying led to discipline and punishment. With his choler still in the foreground, these punishments seem to have had no effect in making the young St.-Exupéry buckle down; on the contrary, his willfulness became all the more apparent. Instead of studying, he spent his teenage years reading and writing poetry. It's rather difficult to see the melancholic side of his nature in these descriptions, yet he was described thus by a fellow student: "A shy youth, wild, inclined to sudden changes of mood, at one time full of energy and life, at another, taciturn, shut up seemingly in anger, all of it a clue to his musing activity. He was little sociable, and that made him suffer, because he wanted to be loved."[38] Is this not a perfect description of a choleric/melancholic?

In fact, throughout his life, St.-Exupéry seemed to seesaw between the choleric and melancholic sides of his temperament. When he developed a passion for flying, he was single-minded in attaining his goal of becoming a pilot. Yet setbacks plunged him into melancholy, vociferously articulated to friends and family. Finally successful as a pilot, he also developed a talent for writing that was poetic and often autobiographical. He wrote *Le Petit Prince* after crashing his plane and spending five days in the desert before being rescued by Bedouins. Writing poetry and mystical prose like that in *Le Petit*

Antoine de Saint-Exupéry		Temperament		
	S	C	M	P
Birth Season	2	2		
Asc Sign	2		2	
Asc Ruler	1		1	
Asc Almuten	1		1	
Moon Sign	2		2	
Moon Phase	1	1		
Sign of Moon Ruler	1			1
Totals	1	4	4	1

---

38. Quote found in a biography of St.-Exupéry by Joelle Eyheramonno at the website http://www.members.lycos.nl/tlp/antoine.htm (accessed April 2004).

Using Temperament in Modern Astrological Practice 105

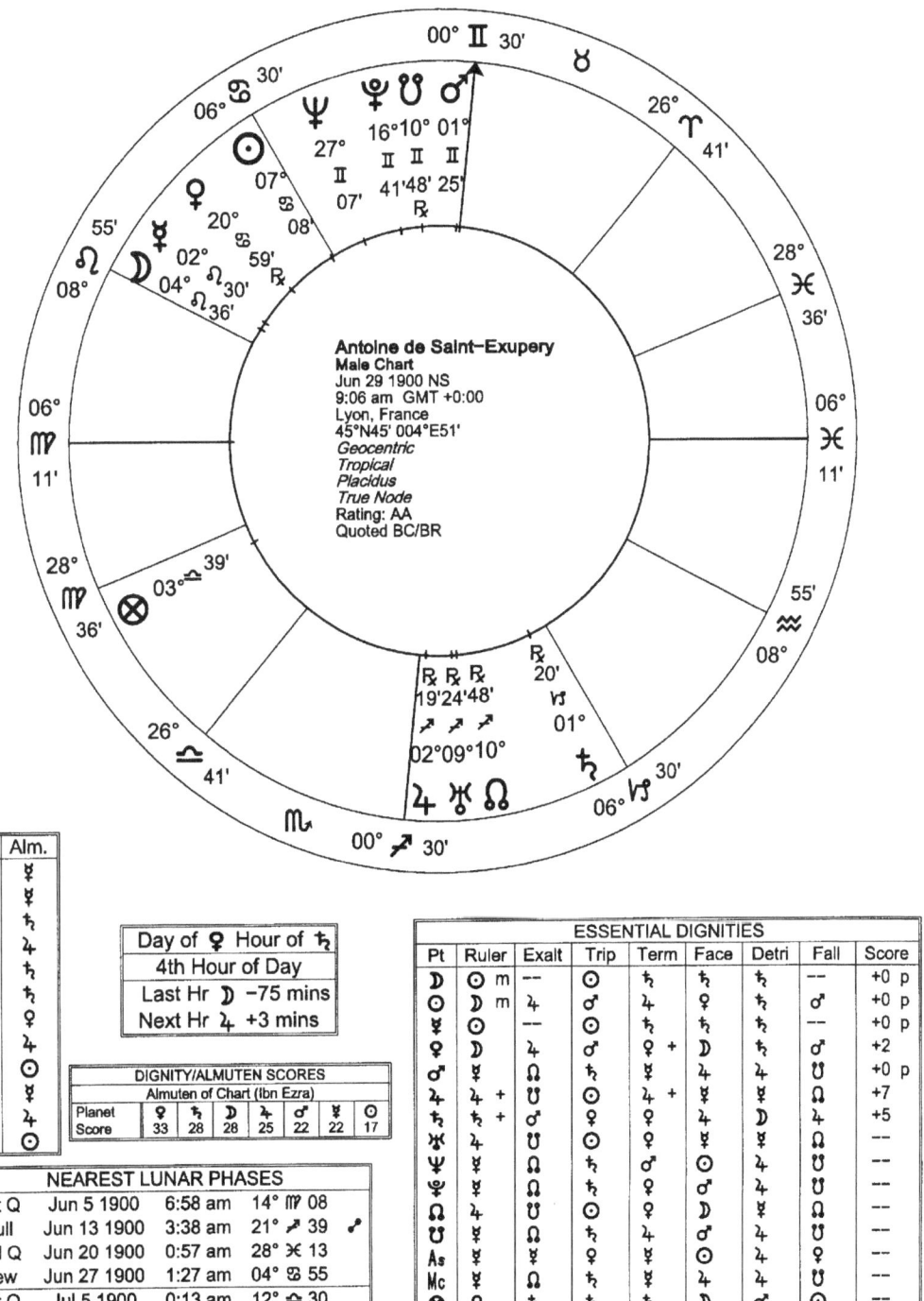

Prince might not seem to fit a choleric/melancholic temperament, yet St.-Exupéry had a knack for saying the profound and mysterious in a few perfectly chosen words.

Other Choleric/Melancholics: Prince Charles, Andrea Bocelli, Pablo Picasso, Michel Gauquelin, David Crosby, Jean Anouilh, Gene Simmons, Heather Locklear, John Lennon

Melancholic/Choleric

- Would rather stay in the background, but can take the spotlight if necessary; not overly ambitious
- Not as pessimistic as the pure melancholic – able to see the positive more easily
- Not as focused on achievement as the pure choleric
- Deliberative thinking with flashes of inspiration
- Dry wit; master of puns
- Wants to coach the winner of the spelling bee
- The power behind the throne
- Can take too long to make a decision, and the momentum is lost
- Strikes only when the iron is hot
- More reflective than impulsive; may regret too much reflection

Example Chart: John Cleese
At the age of 13, John Cleese began to collect and organize jokes he liked – a melancholic premonition (the penchant for categorization) of his later comedic career. He began to write humor while studying law at Cambridge; his first televised successes were with David Frost's *The Frost Report*. He came to international fame, however, with Monty Python's Flying Circus, in which he had major roles as both writer (for 4 seasons) and performer (for 3). His "Dead Parrot" and "Ministry of Silly Walks" are classics. Python humor has been described as having "a general air of silliness combined with obscure intellectualism."[39] Much in his humor is dry, as befits a melancholic/choleric temperament where dry is the dominant quality. Garry Phillipson characterizes him as having "a strong tension…between coiled energy and control, and he emerges as basically melancholic with a choleric Moon."[40] A "biography" written by Cleese at the Python on Line website pokes fun at his melancholic side: "Mr. Cleese is happily unmarried and is the President of the Holland Park Schadenfreude Society."[41]

---

39. Steve Bryant, biography of John Cleese at http://www.museum.tv/archives/etv/C/htmlC/cleesejohn/cleesejohn.htm (accessed April 2004).
40. Garry Phillipson, email to Dorian Greenbaum, October 7, 2002
41. John Cleese, biography online at http://www.pythonline.com/plugs/cleese/index.shtml (accessed April 2004).

Using Temperament in Modern Astrological Practice   107

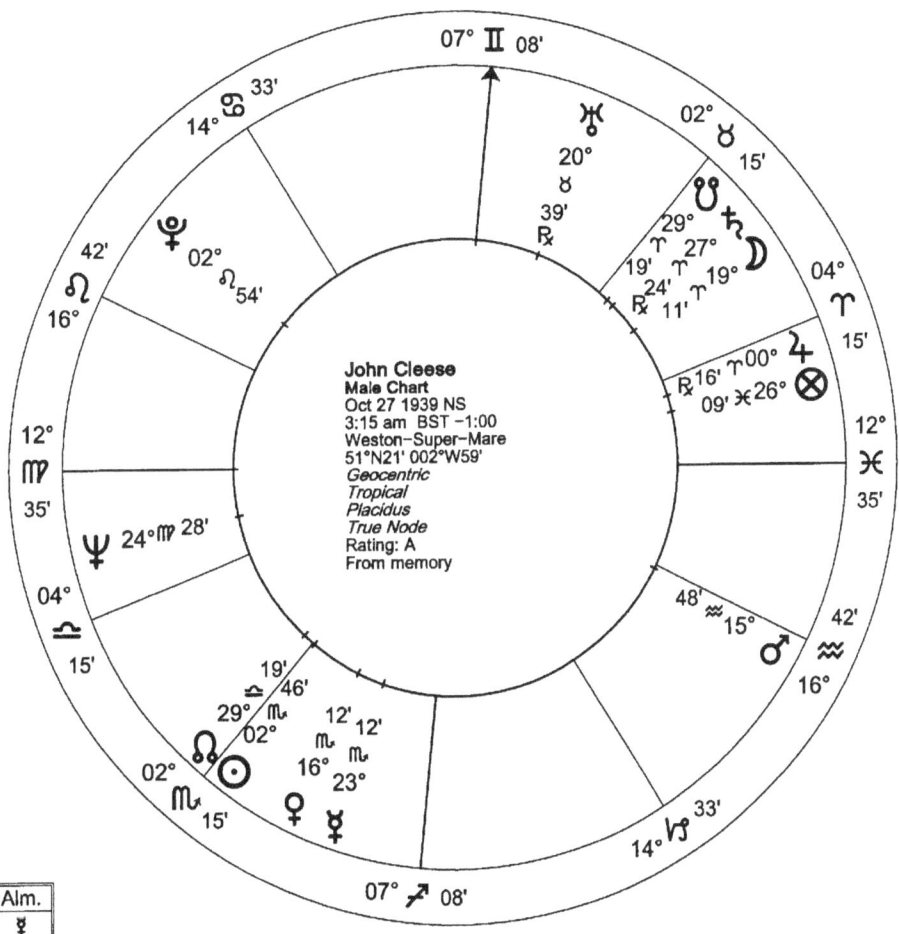

John Cleese	Temperament			
	S	C	M	P
Birth Season	2		2	
Asc Sign	2		2	
Asc Ruler	1		1	
Asc Almuten	1		1	
Moon Sign	2	2		
Moon Phase	1	1		
Sign of Moon Ruler	1	1		
Totals	1	3	6	0

The peak of this brand of humor founded on perfectionistic endeavors gone awry came when Cleese teamed up with his then-wife Connie Booth in the brilliant *Fawlty Towers*. Basil Fawlty's earnestness and pedantry combined with arrogance and stubbornness seems a perfect blend of melancholy with choler. Cleese has since made a fortune in business training videos (choleric drive coupled with melancholic efficiency).

Other Melancholic/Cholerics: Queen Elizabeth II, Dustin Hoffman, Meg Ryan, Lucille Ball, Vanessa Redgrave, Ernest Hemingway, Michael Crichton, Copernicus

Choleric/Sanguine and Sanguine/Choleric Temperaments

These compound temperaments are united by the *hot* quality. So there is abundant energy in these temperaments, and a desire for activity. Both these compound temperaments are also basically optimistic, and can't let go of looking on the bright side. They are also quick and full of vitality.

Choleric/Sanguine

- Quick to anger but doesn't hold a grudge
- Loves to lead and finds it easy to get followers because of social skills
- Makes goals and assumes luck, not skill, will accomplish them
- Can flame out easily by being overloaded or distracted from the goal
- Gung-ho at the beginning of a project but then gets bored with it
- Comes up with a plan and cajoles people into accepting it
- Sting like a bee, float like a butterfly
- Keep moving

Example Chart: Anne Frank

Anyone who has read Anne Frank's diary will recall Anne's headstrong willfulness coupled with youthful exuberance and ebullience. Not even forced seclusion and the horrific circumstances under which she lived when she wrote the diary could keep her choleric/sanguine temperament from shining through. Though some of the choleric or sanguine qualities she displays could be the temperamental overlays associated with childhood (sanguine) and young adulthood (choleric), the preponderance of these two temperaments, despite depressing circumstances which might surely elicit more melancholic or phlegmatic responses, clearly shows (and her chart confirms) that Anne's temperament was truly a choleric/sanguine one.

Anne writes candidly of her disposition and her faults, so we see much evidence of both the sanguine and the choleric. She has abundant energy (arranging, with her father, the "Secret Annexe" when they first move in, while her mother and sister lie exhausted). She often writes of her need to be independent: "I am my own skipper and later on I shall see where I come to land."[42] She also acknowledges that she is sometimes conceited, headstrong and pushing, even though she feels her family exaggerates the severity of these faults. She admits that she is sometimes too self-centered: "…my pride has been shaken a bit [the Leo Moon!], for I was becoming much too taken up with myself again."[43] She is also a great talker (she once had to write a series of essays as a school punishment on being an "incurable chatterbox." She describes herself as "quicksilver Anne" [the Ascendant ruler, the Sun, in Gemini]. Before they went into hiding, she had lots of friends, and her sociable and cheerful nature attracted "strings of boyfriends."

Anne Frank	Temperament			
	S	C	M	P
Birth Season	2	2		
Asc Sign	2	2		
Asc Ruler	1	1		
Asc Almuten	1	1		
Moon Sign	2	2		
Moon Phase	1	1		
Sign of Moon Ruler	1	1		
Totals	4	6	0	0

---

42. Anne Frank, *The Diary of a Young Girl*, p. 40.
43. Ibid., p. 201. Other quotes in this and the next paragraph come from pp. 6, 33, 2, 233.

110 *Temperament: Astrology's Forgotten Key*

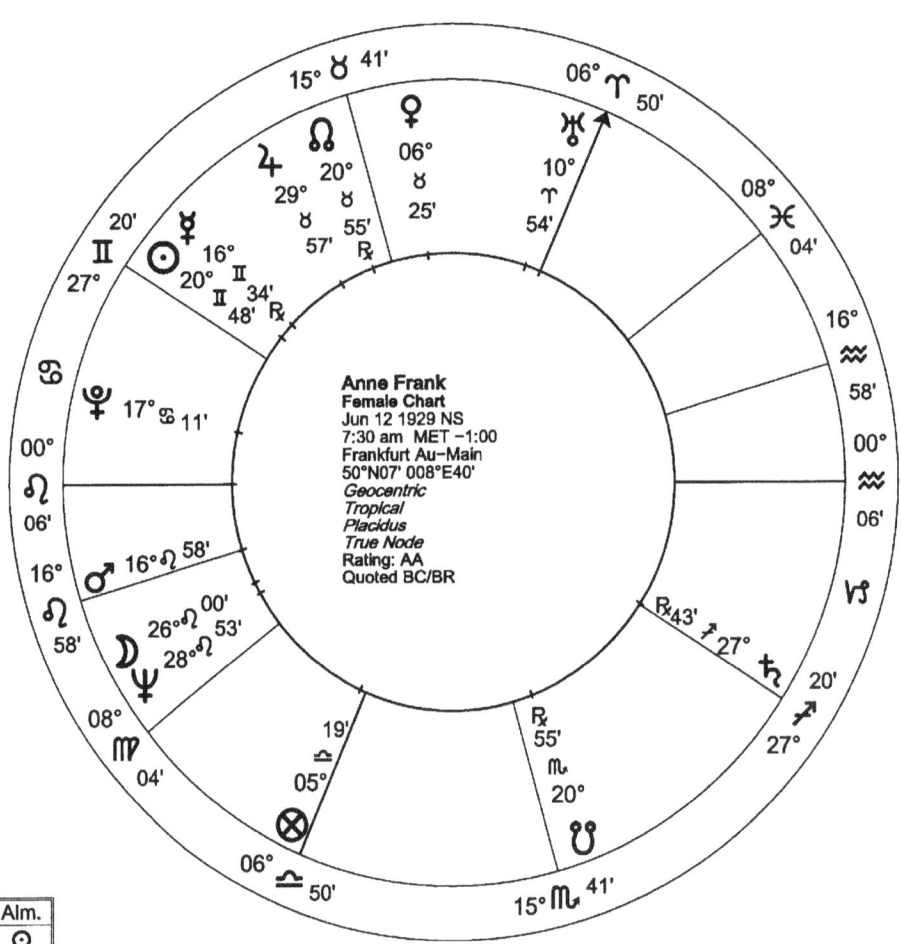

Both the choleric and sanguine temperaments are optimistic, and Anne is no exception. Though she does not look at the world through rose-colored glasses, she cannot embrace her mother's melancholy pessimism, but believes ultimately in the goodness of people: "It's really a wonder that I haven't dropped all my ideals, because they seem so absurd and impossible to carry out. Yet I keep them, because in spite of everything I still believe that people are really good at heart."

Other Choleric/Sanguines: Donald Rumsfeld, Judy Collins, Walt Whitman, Sylvester Stallone, Eva Peron, Celine Dion, Alan Dershowitz, Mary Baker Eddy, Jessica Lange

Sanguine/Choleric

- Fighting is a game to be forgotten when it's over
- Loves to be with a group of friends and will lead if so inclined
- Doesn't enjoy working hard unless there is a personal goal to be achieved
- Finds it difficult sometimes to focus on a goal and achieve it
- May think a whole project is too hard, but able to embrace one part and achieve it
- Thinks consensus is good as long as people agree with him/her
- Float like a butterfly, sting like a bee
- Don't sit down

Example Chart: Fred Astaire

A perfect physical type for a sanguine/choleric (short, thin, lively and well-proportioned), Fred Astaire was the son of an immigrant and got his first taste of fame as part of a dancing duo with his sister, Adele. He and his sister were dancing superstars for 16 years, until Adele married in 1932 and quit the act. When Astaire first took a Hollywood screen test, the famous assessment of one of the world's best

Example Chart: Fred Astaire

	Temperament			
	S	C	M	P
Birth Season	2	2		
Asc Sign	2		2	
Asc Ruler	1	1		
Asc Almuten	1	1		
Moon Sign	2	2		
Moon Phase	1	1		
Sign of Moon Ruler	1		1	
Totals	7	3	0	0

112   *Temperament: Astrology's Forgotten Key*

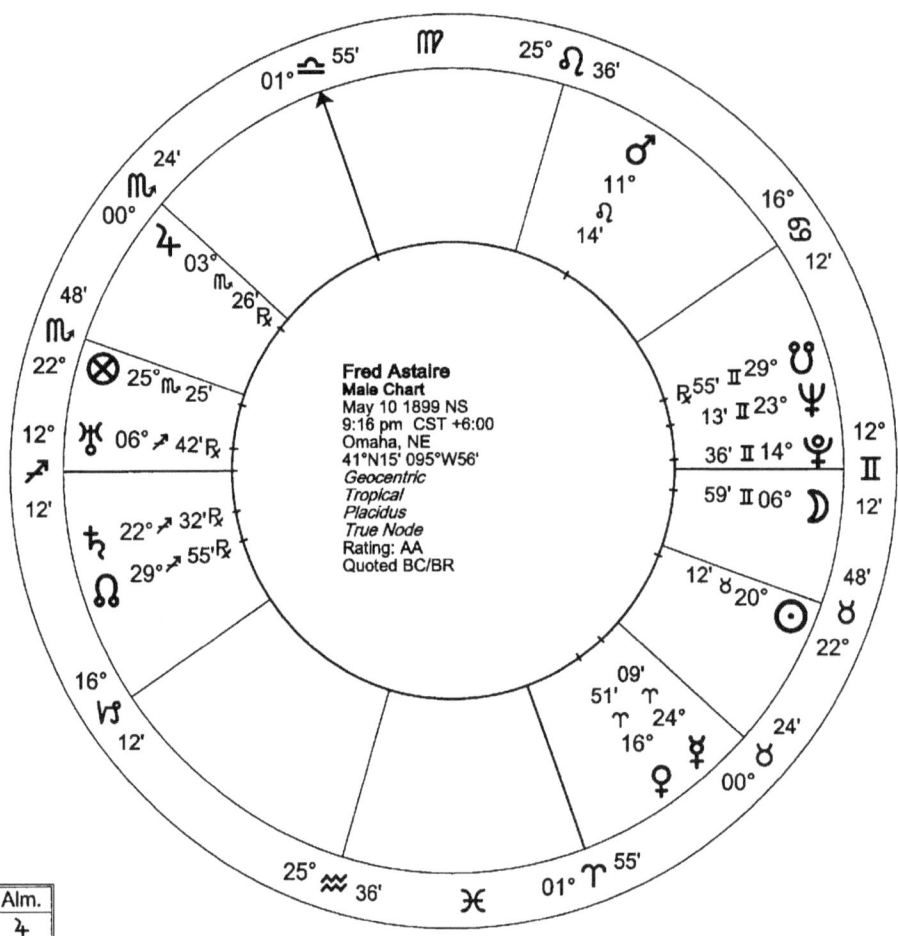

entertainers was made: "Can't act. Slightly bald. Also dances."[44] In spite of this comment, Astaire went on to a phenomenally successful career in films, where his elan, debonair attitude, grace and ability to make even the most difficult dances look effortless showed a perfect combination of sanguine and choleric – the grace, style and sociability of the sanguine combined with the stamina and drive of the choleric. He was universally admired and liked – another sign of the quantity of sanguine in his temperament.

Astaire's well-known perfectionism (he was known to spend as much as 18 hours a day rehearsing to achieve that effortless look) might seem at odds with the sanguine part of his nature. Yet the choleric in him gives a fear of looking foolish or inadequate, plus drive and ambition, and Saturn in the 1st house, though not perhaps a part of his innate disposition, would certainly contribute to his perfectionism. Even for a sanguine, though, if you love what you do (as Astaire obviously did), working is no drudgery but a joyous adventure.

The sanguine quality of Astaire's dancing – smooth, lighter-than-air, downright happy – is recognized in the following quotes from various reviews. "There is an inspired puckishness about his dancing...."[45] "...the young man combines eccentric agility with humor."[46] "Mr. Astaire is an urbane delight...."[47]

Other Sanguine/Cholerics: Muhammad Ali, Ethel Kennedy, Kathie Lee Gifford, Zara Phillips, Joel Grey, Jimmy Connors, Shirley Temple Black

Choleric/Phlegmatic and Phlegmatic/Choleric Temperaments

These compound temperaments have no quality in common, so there is a certain disjointedness when they are combined – a one now, then the other effect. These two temperaments are also natural opposites, which are sometimes difficult to reconcile. Yet since there is also no lack of a quality, when they find a way to work together, they can be exceedingly productive, creative and energetic.

Choleric/Phlegmatic

- Enjoys being in the limelight but needs time alone to recharge batteries
- Urge toward activity, whether useful or not, tempered by restraint
- Productive and lazy days equally important
- Rather than seizing on instant solutions to problems, will benefit from reflection and calm deliberation

---

44. Attributed to an RKO studio head, found in a biography of Fred Astaire at http://www.fredastaire.net/biography/broadway.htm (accessed April 2004).
45. Review in *Punch*, found in a biography of Fred Astaire at http://www.fredastaire.net/biography/rko.htm (accessed April 2004).
46. Louis Sherwin in *The New York Globe*, found in a biography of Fred Astaire at http://www.fredastaire.net/biography/broadway.htm (accessed April 2004).
47. Andre Sennwald in *The New York Times*, found in a biography of Fred Astaire at http://www.fredastaire.net/biography/rko.htm (accessed April 2004).

- Secretly enjoys a good fight (or *thinks* it's a secret that they enjoy a good fight)
- Fights for what they believe in with tenacity
- All or nothing – there is no middle ground

Example chart: Princess Margaret
Four years younger than her sister, Queen Elizabeth II, Margaret was always seen as the rebellious one, with a feistiness that would certainly fit someone with a great deal of choler. With a personality in complete contrast to her sister's sober and dutiful one, Margaret always appeared to be trying to compensate for being born second. (In temperament, though both have choleric, Elizabeth is a melancholic/choleric.) Before Margaret married the "acceptable" Anthony Armstrong-Jones, she had a romance with Peter Townsend, a divorcé whom she gave up in a "duty before love" speech in 1955. Her marriage to Armstrong-Jones produced two children and ended in divorce in 1978.

Margaret always moved with a fast crowd (perhaps she was even the epitome of the "jet-setter"). After her divorce she was often seen in the company of the much younger Roddy Llewellyn. She spent many winters in her house on the island of Mustique in the Caribbean – her phlegmatic side recharging her batteries. In spite of what could be seen as an idle and frivolous life, she had a strong sense of duty to pull her weight performing the necessary royal obligations – she was involved with numerous charities and especially loved music and the ballet. As befits one with Mars as the ruler and almuten of the Ascendant, she could be strong-willed, even headstrong – both in ways that benefited her and her reputation (giving up Townsend, her arts patronships) and hurt her (her liaison with Llewellyn, her persistence in living a hard-drinking, hard-smoking life). In her last days the effects of her lifestyle proved too much for her constitution. Two choleric-themed illnesses became her downfall – a series of strokes beginning in 1998, and a serious scalding of her feet in 1999 curtailed her activities and forced her to become a recluse (the phlegmatic side asserting itself). She died after a last stroke on February 9, 2002.

Other Choleric/Phlegmatics: Lily Tomlin, Umberto Eco, Claude Debussy, Leonard Bernstein, Maria Montessori, Camilla Parker-Bowles, Zelda Fitzgerald, Ringo Starr

Princess Margaret	Temperament			
	S	C	M	P
Birth Season	2	2		
Asc Sign	2	2		
Asc Ruler	1	1		
Asc Almuten	1	1		
Moon Sign	2			2
Moon Phase	1			1
Sign of Moon Ruler	1			1
Totals	0	6	0	4

Using Temperament in Modern Astrological Practice   115

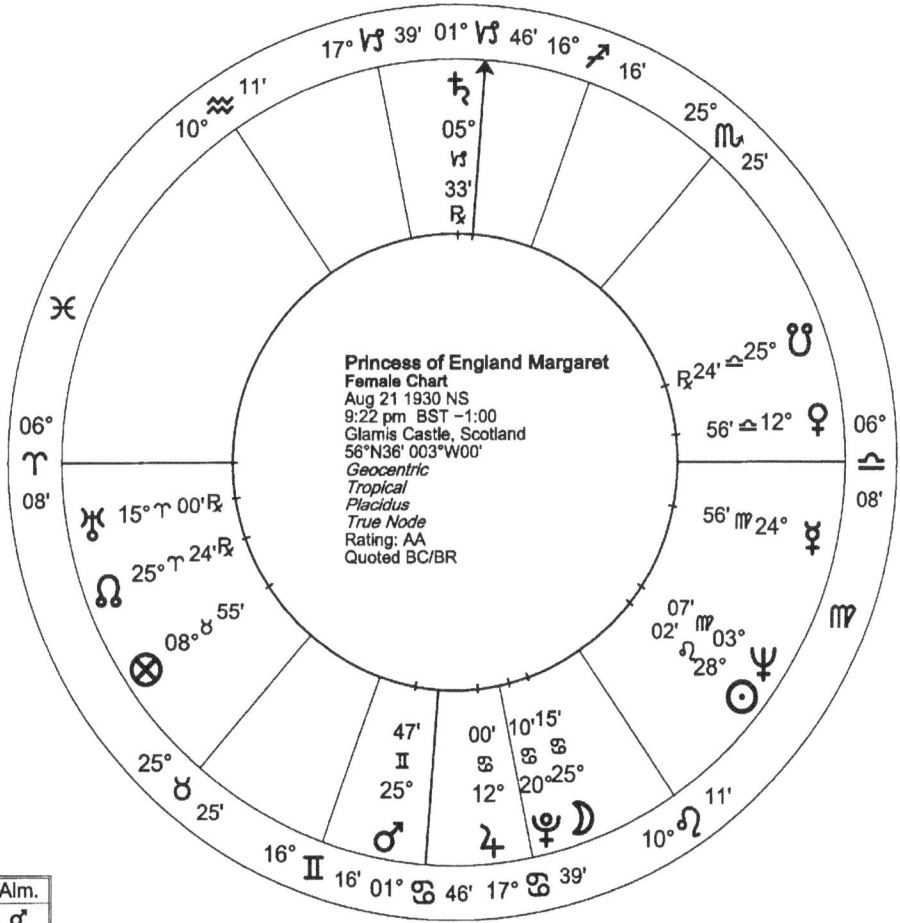

Phlegmatic/Choleric

- Would prefer to stay home, but can go into "performance mode" when required
- Tendency to lethargy counterbalanced by urge for accomplishment
- Lazy and productive days equally important
- Gestation of ideas will lead to creative solutions to problems
- Will try to avoid fights, but will defend themselves if necessary
- Slow to anger, but don't cross them when finally aroused
- Nothing or all – there is no middle ground

Example Chart: Charles Lindergh
With the steady single-mindedness of the phlegmatic added to the ambition of the choleric, Charles Lindbergh became the first media celebrity of the American public. Born in Detroit, Michigan, an only child of a lawyer and a teacher, Lindbergh gave up his engineering studies at the University of Wisconsin to pursue his passion of aviation. He was a barnstormer for two years and then decided to try for the Orteig Prize for crossing the Atlantic in a plane alone. This seems a perfect combination of the phlegmatic and choleric – a daring, dangerous flight performed utterly alone. When he landed at Le Bourget Field in Paris, he became an instant star.

He married Anne Morrow in 1929, after only a few dates kept secret from the press. Lindbergh's biographer A. Scott Berg describes the couple as "extremely modest and shy people."[48] As if he were alternately living out the two sides of his temperament, the rest of his life was spent either in the glare of the public spotlight (the kidnapping and murder of his first-born son) or an escape from that glare (he lived in Europe for a while after the kidnapping, trying to escape relentless publicity in the U.S.). His extreme isolationist views may also be a reflection of the phlegmatic side of his temperament. In

Charles Lindbergh	Temperament			
	S	C	M	P
Birth Season	2			2
Asc Sign	2			2
Asc Ruler	1	1		
Asc Almuten	1	1		
Moon Sign	2	2		
Moon Phase	1			1
Sign of Moon Ruler	1		1	
Totals	0	4	1	5

---

48. A. Scott Berg, interview with Elizabeth Farnsworth on PBS Newshour with Jim Lehrer, April 23, 1999, found at http://www.pbs.org/newshour/bb/entertainment/jan-june99/pulitzer_4-23.html (accessed April 2004).

Using Temperament in Modern Astrological Practice   117

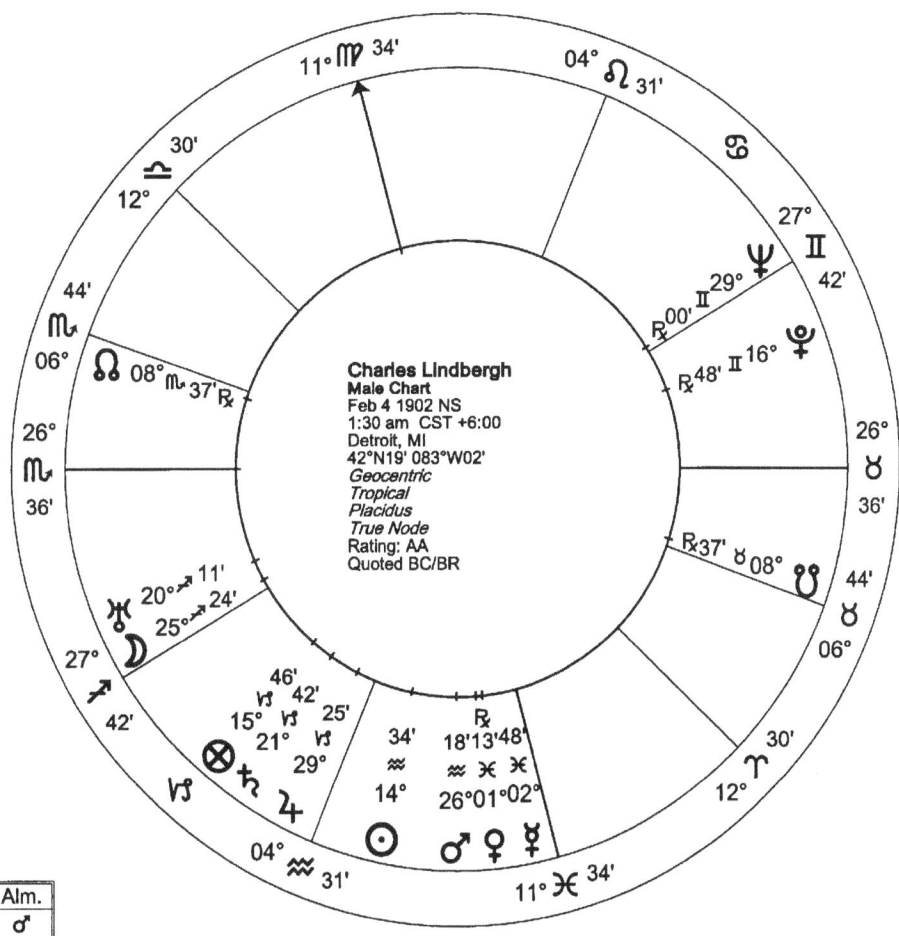

addition, he apparently carried on a secret affair with a German woman for over 20 years, producing two children – all the while living with his wife and having six children with her. His nickname, "The Lone Eagle," seems particularly apt for a phlegmatic/choleric. The inscription on his tombstone reads, "If I take the wings of the morning, and dwell in the uttermost parts of the sea."[49]

Other Phlegmatic/Cholerics: A.J. Cronin, Robert DeNiro, Bernadette Peters, Simone de Beauvoir, Nostradamus, Chelsea Clinton, Jessye Norman, James Levine, Stephen King

Sanguine/Melancholic and Melancholic/Sanguine Temperaments

These compound temperaments again have no quality in common, so these people also tend to alternate between temperaments. The disjunction combined with the fact that sanguine and melancholic are natural opposites often makes it difficult for the two sides to integrate. Yet they have a unique perspective: they can see and relate to the viewpoints of both the young and the old, which gives them a certain timelessness.

Sanguine/Melancholic

- Good social skills, but may be standoffish when faced with deep intimacy
- Space cadets can be serious, too
- Intellectual friendships
- Good at creating rapport in interviews, creating a feeling of ease that allows them to broach thoughtful or hard questions without alienating their subjects
- Attracted to things such as online games, first by the social factor, but then drawn in by the detailed systems of the games
- Laughing on the outside, crying on the inside

Example Chart: Woody Allen

Woody Allen has made a career out of neurosis. A pessimist at heart, he has turned his melancholic outlook on life into a comedic riff many can relate to. He first found he could be funny in high school, and he began writing one-liners for columnists and journalists. He uses a mournful, deadpan delivery when doing his own material in front of an audience. His movies almost always contain an autobiographical character, often played by Allen himself, who is full of angst.

Even when young, he was a *puer* in an old man's body. His first romantic liaisons were age-appropriate, but his relationship with Mia Farrow, 10 years his junior and with a juvenile, waiflike look, may have been the first indication that his attractions were not necessarily in the normal range. Because of this, his personal life has been problematic, to say the least, especially the rancorous breakup with Farrow under accusations of child molestation, and his marriage to one of Mia's adopted daughters 35 years Allen's junior (is this an attempt to integrate the child-like sanguine with the melancholic

---

49. Biography of Charles Lindbergh, found at http://www.charleslindbergh.com/history/index.asp (accessed April 2004).

Using Temperament in Modern Astrological Practice   119

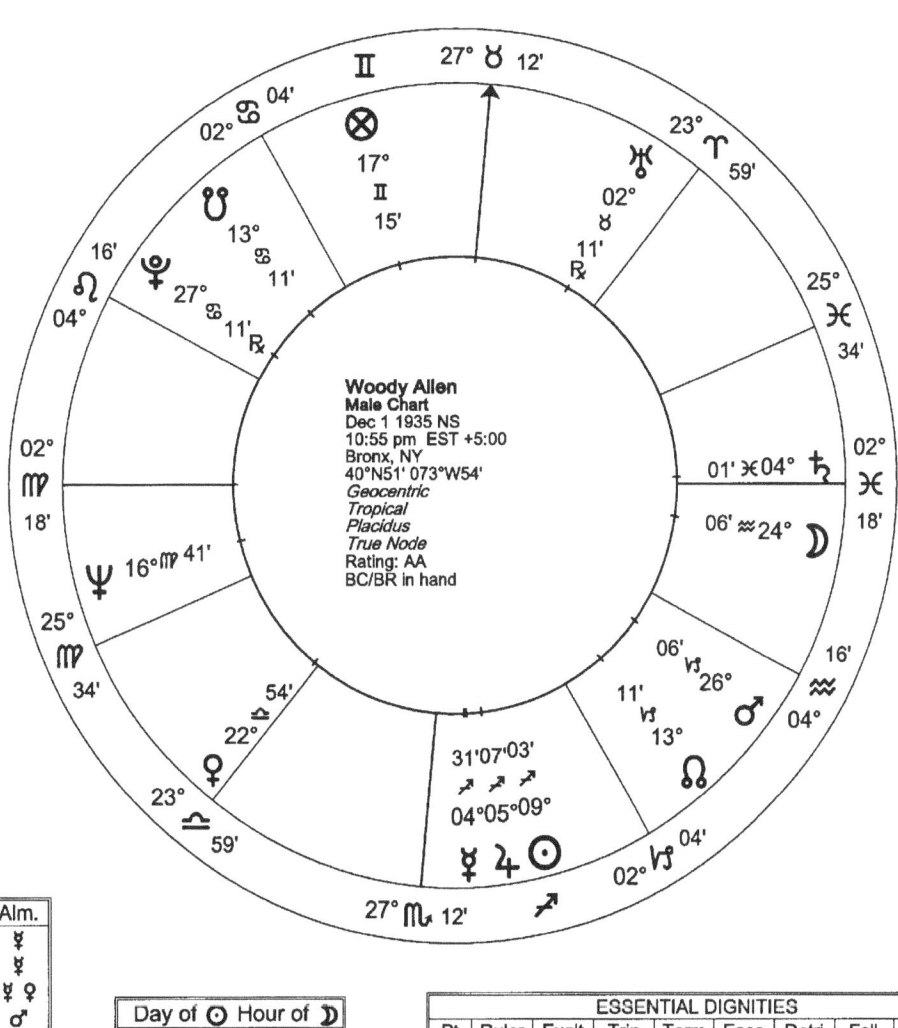

Woody Allen	Temperament			
	S	C	M	P
Birth Season	2		2	
Asc Sign	2		2	
Asc Ruler	1	1		
Asc Almuten	1	1		
Moon Sign	2	2		
Moon Phase	1	1		
Sign of Moon Ruler	1			1
Totals	**5**	**0**	**4**	**1**

old man?). It seems that, in Allen's case, this compound temperament shows at its worst in his personal life, where the two temperaments demonstrate their lack of similarity. In his professional life, he has been able to compensate better, using the sanguine's humor (excuse the pun) to make light of the depressing realities of the human condition. Even his jazz-clarinet playing seems symbolically appropriate for a sanguine/melancholic temperament.

Other Sanguine/Melancholics: Barbara Walters, Rainer Maria Rilke, William Shatner, Chevy Chase, Sir Laurence Olivier, Vivien Leigh, Edward Lear, William Butler Yeats, Conan O'Brien, Bruce Springsteen

Melancholic/Sanguine

- Able to make detailed and thoughtful plans; not reluctant to delegate to achieve a goal
- Nerds just want to have fun
- Social intellectual
- Good interviewing skills – able to bring out the best in interviews by asking thoughtful questions
- Natural standoffishness in socializing counterbalanced by need for and enjoyment of social interaction
- Fantasy games like Dungeons and Dragons fill need for detailed (alternate) universe and being social with like-minded people

Example Chart: Agatha Christie
Probably one of the most famous and prolific mystery writers in the world, Agatha Christie's life shows periods of public exposure matched with periods of total privacy. A painfully shy child, she kept her reticence in adulthood and rarely gave interviews, but her books made her universally famous. She started writing as a teenager, "stories of unrelieved gloom."[50] Her first detective novel, featuring her

---

50.   Lois Rodden, Biography of Agatha Christie in *AstroDatabank*.

Using Temperament in Modern Astrological Practice   121

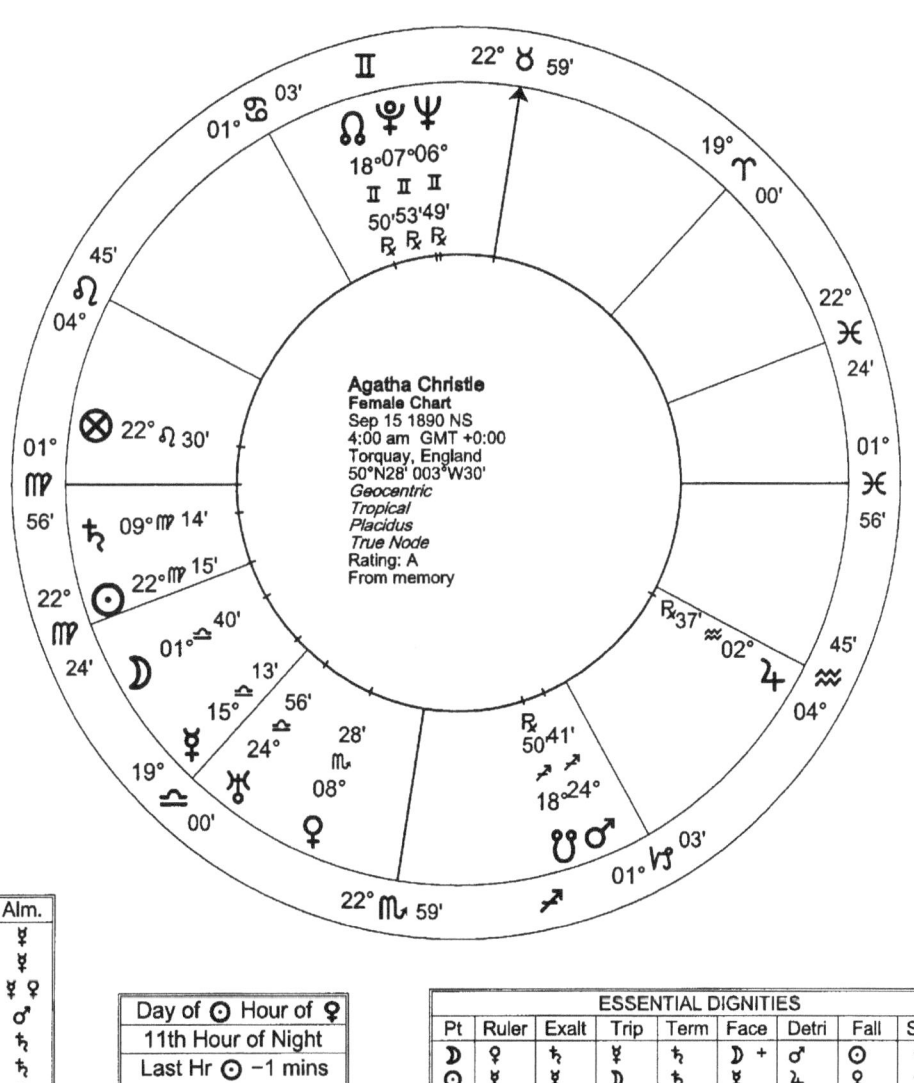

Agatha Christie	Temperament			
	S	C	M	P
Birth Season	2		2	
Asc Sign	2		2	
Asc Ruler	1		1	
Asc Almuten	1		1	
Moon Sign	2	2		
Moon Phase	1	1		
Sign of Moon Ruler	1			1
Totals	3	2	4	1

Belgian detective Hercule Poirot, was written on a dare from her sister. Once published, the book gained instant popularity (Christie had an uncanny knowledge of human nature and always created characters people could enjoy and/or relate to). Thirty-three more books featured the vain and egotistical Poirot as detective. Her other well-known detective, Miss Marple, was probably more like Christie herself – a quiet spinster in a country village, uninterested in the latest trends, whose knowledge of human nature allows her to solve crimes. Christie's plots are intelligent and detailed, often with unexpected endings. *The Murder of Roger Ackroyd* was the first detective novel narrated in the first person by the murderer.

Christie was married twice, first to Archibald Christie, whose unfaithfulness in 1926 precipitated Agatha's unexplained disappearance for several weeks. Her second husband was archaeologist Max Mallowan, who adored her even though he was 14 years her junior (unequal love relationships seem to try to integrate the sanguine and the melancholic). She spent years with Mallowan on his digs in Iraq, cataloguing artifacts in the desert heat.

We can see both her primary melancholic traits (the reticence, the intricate plots, her powers of observation) and secondary sanguine ones (her extensive knowledge of human nature, ability to create believably human characters whom her audience could easily relate to) in the elements of her life.

Other Melancholic/Sanguines: Simone Signoret, Louisa May Alcott, Marsilio Ficino, Albert Camus, Jane Fonda, F. Scott Fitzgerald, Ursula LeGuin, Moshe Dayan, Walt Disney, Stephen Sondheim

Sanguine/Phlegmatic and Phlegmatic/Sanguine Temperaments
These temperaments are united by the *wet* quality. So people with these compound temperaments may be fluid or hard to pin down, and easily able to make connections (even where none may exist). There is an almost chameleon-like quality to these temperaments; they can take on the form of their surroundings (psychological or emotional) with ease. There is also a laziness that is hard to shake when these two temperaments combine.

Sanguine/Phlegmatic

- Finds it easy to argue both sides in a debate
- Can understand alternative points of view and sees no inconsistency in espousing more than one
- Jack of all trades and master of a few
- Would be bored with just one career or project
- Easy to make friends and has the staying power to cultivate lasting ones among all his/her acquaintances
- A cause is fine as long as there's not too much invested in it
- Looks for the easy solution first

Example Chart: Leonardo da Vinci

As one of the most multi-faceted people who ever lived, Leonardo da Vinci seems to be an almost perfect embodiment of the sanguine/phlegmatic temperament (and he escapes the laziness of that compound temperament by having a choleric Ascendant). Born of a wealthy notary and a peasant woman, his illegitimate birth kept a number of doors closed to him. However, his inability to have a conventional career led him to the mastery of a number of different trades: painting, sculpture, architecture and engineering among them. With his patron Ludovico Sforza he was both architect and military engineer; while working for Cesare Borgia, Leonardo worked on fortresses in the papal territories. He was Court painter to Louis XII of France. He also conducted scientific experiments for Pope Leo X.

The phlegmatic side of his temperament shows in his physical appearance, and allowed him the persistence to attain the kind of mastery that could create paintings such as the *Mona Lisa* (is that perhaps a phlegmatic smile?) and the *Last Supper*, as well as such engineering and architectural works as his studies in hydraulic engineering (he had an obsession with water and how it could be used) and the map of Imola he prepared for Borgia. However, his sanguine side shows through in his insatiable curiosity in many disciplines, and his many inventions which were never realized even though copious designs for them were produced. He left drawings for a myriad of things ranging from the bicycle,

Leonardo da Vinci Temperament

	S	C	M	P
Birth Season	2	2		
Asc Sign	2		2	
Asc Ruler	1	1		
Asc Almuten	1	1		
Moon Sign	2			2
Moon Phase	1			1
Sign of Moon Ruler	1			1
Totals	4	2	0	4

Leonardo da Vinci
Male Chart
Apr 23 1452 NS
9:40 pm LMT −0:44
Vinci, Italy
43°N47' 010°E55'
Geocentric
Tropical
Placidus
True Node
Rating: AA
Quoted BC/BR

Hs	Alm.
1	♃
2	♄
3	♄
4	♃
5	♂
6	☽
7	☿
8	♃
9	♃
10	☿
11	♀
12	♂

Day of ♀	Hour of ☿
4th Hour of Night	
Last Hr ♀ −17 mins	
Next Hr ☽ +35 mins	

DIGNITY/ALMUTEN SCORES
Almuten of Chart (Ibn Ezra)

Planet	♀	♄	♃	☽	♂	☉
Score	37	30	25	23	13	12	10

NEAREST LUNAR PHASES
New	Mar 21 1452	11:06 am	09° ♈ 48
1st Q	Mar 28 1452	1:18 pm	16° ♋ 45
Full	Apr 4 1452	9:54 am	23° ♎ 27
3rd Q	Apr 12 1452	5:28 am	01° ♒ 03
New	Apr 19 1452	10:53 pm	08° ♉ 32

ESSENTIAL DIGNITIES
Pt	Ruler	Exalt	Trip	Term	Face	Detri	Fall	Score
☽	♃	♀ m	♂	♀	♄	☿	☿	+0 p
☉	♀	☽	♀	☿	♂	♂	---	+0 p
☿	♂	☉	♃	♀	♂ m	♀	♄	+0 p
♀	♀ +	☽ m	☽	♄	♄	♂	---	+5
♂	♄	---	☿	♀	☿ m	☉	---	+0 p
♃	♃ +	♀	♂	♀	♄	☿	☿	+5
♄	♀	♄ +	☿	♃	♄ +	♂	☉	+5
♆	☽	♃	♂	♀	☽	♄	♂	---
♅	♀	♄	☿	♄	♂	♀	☉	---
♇	☉	---	♃	☿	♃	♄	---	---
☊	♄	♂	☽	☿	♃	☽	♃	---
As	♃	☊	♃	♃	♀	☿	☊	---
Mc	☿	☿	☽	♂	☿	♃	♀	---
⊗	♄	---	☿	☿	♀	☉	---	---

airplane, submarine and tank, to thousands of studies in human anatomy. Like a true sanguine, often the idea was enough – finishing it was not important. He was also known as a trickster – there is speculation that he created the Shroud of Turin. On the other hand, his practice of mirror writing seems more attuned to the secretive and phlegmatic side of his nature. The wet characteristics of both these temperaments suggest an image of the mind of Leonardo flowing widely over many subjects and sinking in enough to absorb and create works of genius from them.

Other Sanguine/Phlegmatics: John Edwards, Billy Joel, Roberta Flack, Cybill Shepherd, Maria von Trapp, Gabriel Fauré, Garth Brooks, Anthony Armstrong-Jones, Rosemary Clooney, Roger Daltry

Phlegmatic/Sanguine

- Has both a rich interior life and an exterior one – not difficult to move between them
- Can see both points of view in a debate, so wonders why even have a debate? Or may have a debate just for the fun of it
- Master of a few subjects and acquaintance with many others
- One career or project is enough as long as it has sufficient variety in it
- Can be social on a superficial level, but doesn't really understand or care about its intricacies
- Can't understand why people get so worked up about things
- Can get stuck in one position through inertia
- Prone to take the easy way out

Example Chart: Rush Limbaugh
Where we see creative works of genius in Leonardo, in Rush Limbaugh we have more the sense of the needle stuck in the groove of the broken record. Limbaugh's fame rests on his ability to beat the same ultra-conservative rhythm on his drum, aided by his skill in knowing what buttons to push in his audience. Described as "a fat, powerless, lonely little boy,"[51] by all accounts Limbaugh had a gift for oratory but lacked the staying power to obtain a college degree: he "flunked out of speech in college."[52] It was only after he discovered a talent for making provocative and controversial pronouncements on the air (after being fired from several radio jobs) that he was given a talk show in New York that soon reached a national audience.

---

51. Lois Rodden, Biography of Rush Limbaugh in *AstroDatabank*.
52. Ibid.

126 *Temperament: Astrology's Forgotten Key*

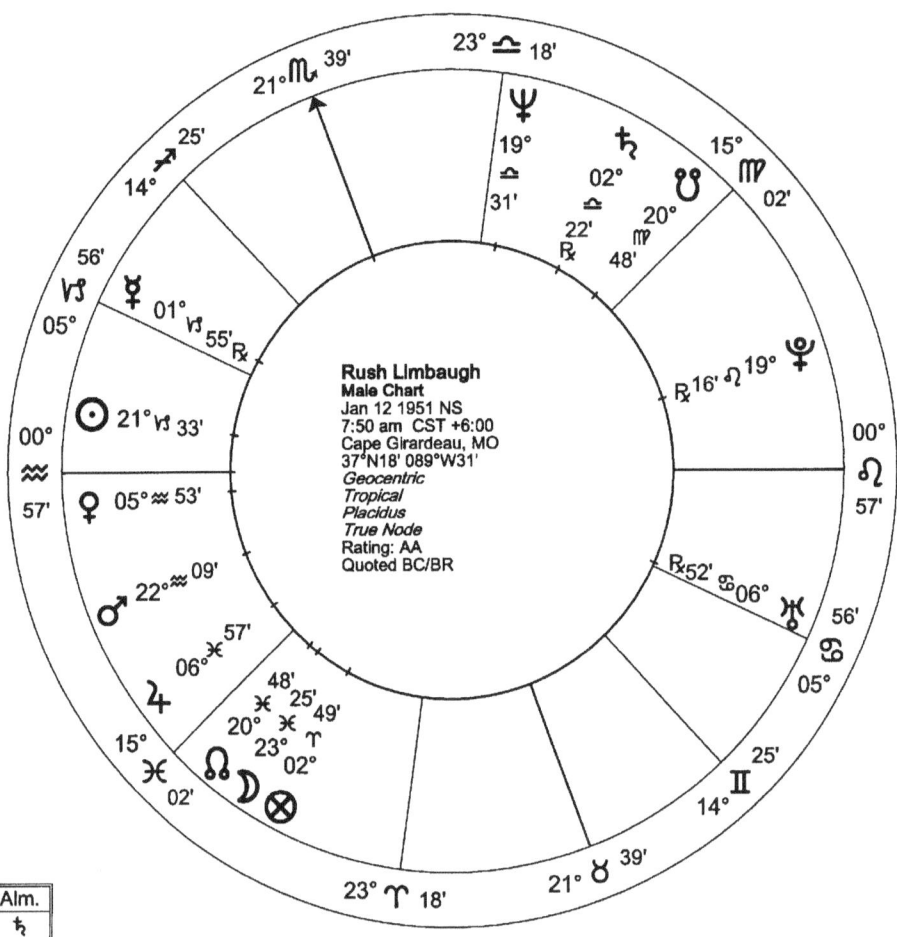

Rush Limbaugh	Temperament			
	S	C	M	P
Birth Season	2			2
Asc Sign	2	2		
Asc Ruler	1		1	
Asc Almuten	1		1	
Moon Sign	2			2
Moon Phase	1	1		
Sign of Moon Ruler	1			1
Totals	3	0	2	5

There is no denying that Limbaugh has a way with words and is easily able to come up with outrageously witty though often truth-deprived monologues that continuously bash the objects of his contempt: liberals, women, gays and other minorities. This is surely the sanguine part of his temperament – the quick quip and ability to think on his feet. However, his constant habit of playing fast and loose with the truth confirms a fundamental laziness that can be the negative side of both the sanguine and the phlegmatic temperaments. Whether he has no interest in the truth because it does not support his personal views, or because finding actual facts to support his positions would be too much like work, Limbaugh has been caught in misstatements hundreds of times – and resorting to the sanguine claim, "What I do is just entertainment" – seems disingenuous at best.

It is interesting to note that Limbaugh's fans are known as "dittoheads" – they take pride in the lazy way of not thinking for themselves and rubber-stamping whatever their god Rush says. This is the negative epitome of the phlegmatic. Note also that Limbaugh's physique is a perfect embodiment of both the phlegmatic and the Falstaffian sanguine – fat and fleshy.

Other Phlegmatic/Sanguines: Vaslav Nijinski, Mel Gibson, Drew Barrymore, Sidney Poitier, Jim Bakker, John Partridge, John Belushi, Elvis Presley, Burl Ives

Melancholic/Phlegmatic and Phlegmatic/Melancholic Temperaments
These temperaments have the *cold* quality in common. So those with these compound temperaments will tend to act and think slowly and deliberately, always taking their time in whatever they do. You just can't hurry them. This is the quintessential "slow-to-warm-up" person. But their deliberation can pay off in unusual insights that would be missed had they not taken their own sweet time.

Melancholic/Phlegmatic

- The world is a dangerous place – it's better to stay inside where it's safe and secure
- Ability to create intricate systems for their own amusement – no interest in sharing such a private thing with others
- May feel aggrieved but no energy to do anything about it

128 *Temperament: Astrology's Forgotten Key*

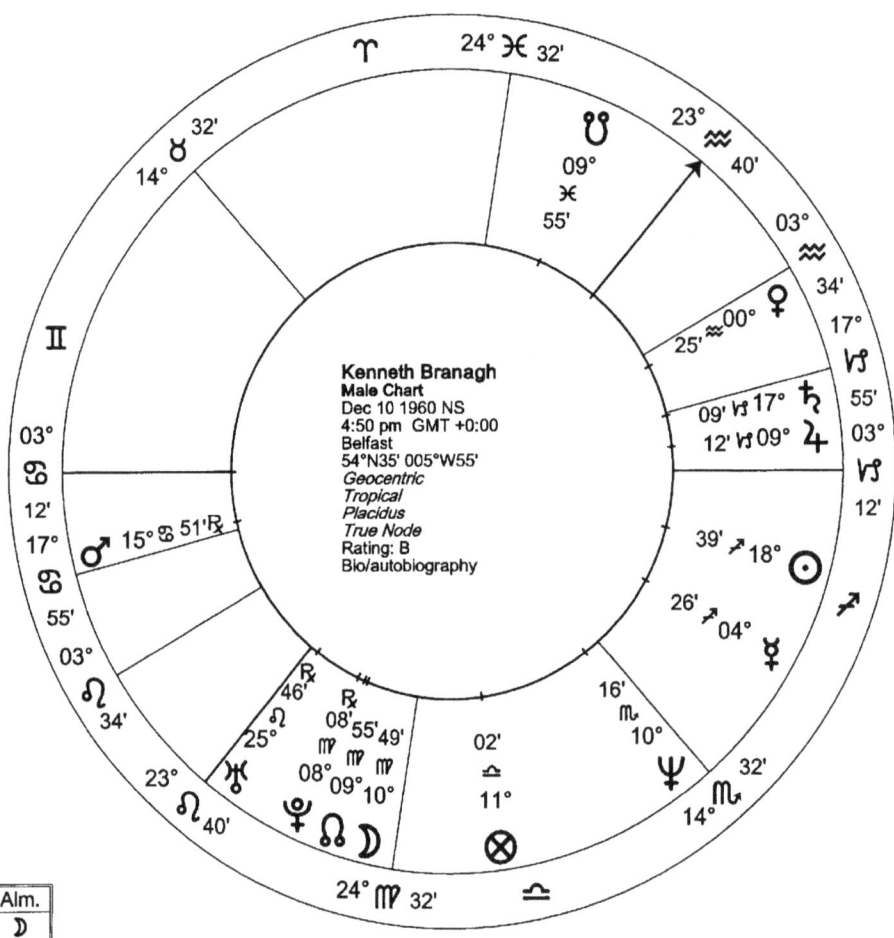

- A nagging feeling that the world is not on their side
- Feel out of step with the world around them
- Monastic

Example Chart: Kenneth Branagh

The actor Kenneth Branagh grew up in a poor Protestant family in Belfast, Northern Ireland. He moved to London at the age of 10, lost his heavy Irish accent through much hard work, and determined to become an actor. His chosen goals and life path were foreign to his relations in Belfast, and he experienced a sense of "belonging nowhere."[53] He is known for immersing himself in the character he plays; he also directs in addition to acting. He secretly married his second wife in 2003. While his Ascendant, Ascendant almuten and Ascendant ruler are all phlegmatic (submerging into the character; secret plans), his Moon, Moon phase and season of birth are all melancholic, showing his determination and ability to work steadily toward a goal. We would not normally think that someone as ambitious as Branagh would be temperamentally a melancholic/phlegmatic – but it seems that his goals for himself just *happen* to involve putting himself before the public; his is not a temperament that craves the spotlight for its own sake.

Kenneth Branagh	Temperament			
	S	C	M	P
Birth Season	2		2	
Asc Sign	2			2
Asc Ruler	1			1
Asc Almuten	1			1
Moon Sign	2		2	
Moon Phase	1		1	
Sign of Moon Ruler	1	1		
Totals	0	1	5	4

Other Melancholic/Phlegmatics: August Strindberg, J. Paul Getty, Charles Munch, Paul Newman, Dick Cheney, Sigourney Weaver, Olivia Newton-John, H.R. Haldeman

Phlegmatic/Melancholic

- Reserved and content to live in their own little world – outside is an uncomfortable place
- Great ability to create systems/alternate worlds/universes down to the last detail (think Tolkien's Middle-earth)
- A recluse with a chip on his/her shoulder

---

53. Lois Rodden, Biography of Kenneth Branagh in *AstroDatabank*.

- Marching to a different drummer and doesn't care what anyone else thinks
- Understands and embraces an interior life
- A hermit

Example Chart: Arthur Schopenhauer

Schopenhauer was a 19th century German philosopher, influenced by Kant, who was known for his pessimism and misogyny. He was an atheist, but quite attracted by Eastern thought (primarily Buddhist and Hindu). He believed that there was no individual will, but only a pervasive single will that was a source of endless suffering. His major work, *The World as Will and Idea*, was published before he was thirty, but did not sell well. Schopenhauer lived a solitary life, disdaining friendships and unable to get along even with members of his own family; he never married. (He did have a pet poodle, however.) His is an extreme example of a phlegmatic/melancholic temperament, living alone in a world view steeped in negativity. Both his Ascendant (Cancer) and season of birth (winter) are phlegmatic, while his Moon (Virgo) and its phase (3rd Quarter) show his melancholic side, further emphasized by the Sun conjunct Saturn.

Arthur Schopenhauer	Temperament			
	S	C	M	P
Birth Season	2			2
Asc Sign	2			2
Asc Ruler	1			1
Asc Almuten	1	1		
Moon Sign	2		2	
Moon Phase	1		1	
Sign of Moon Ruler	1			1
Totals	1	0	3	6

Quote: "There is no more mistaken path to happiness than worldliness, revelry, high life."[54]

Other Phlegmatic/Melancholics: William Blake, Mia Farrow, Martin Luther King, Enrico Caruso, Benjamin Britten, Placido Domingo, John Travolta, Laura Bush

---

54. Arthur Schopenhauer, from *Essays. Personality; or, What a Man Is. Our Relation to Others*, sec. 24; quoted in Justin Kaplan, ed., *Bartlett's Familiar Quotations* (Boston:Little, Brown, 1992), p. 404.

Using Temperament in Modern Astrological Practice   131

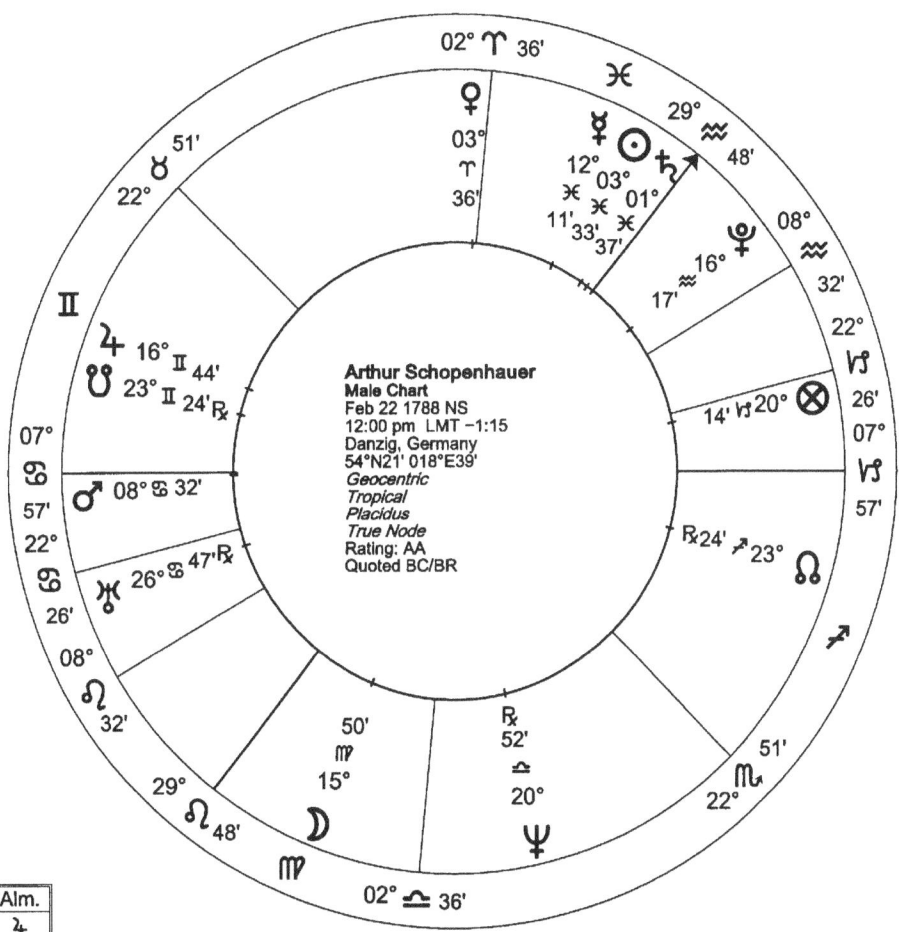

Fictional Characters: What Temperament?

Though it may not have been in the minds of their authors as they wrote, a number of characters in works of popular fiction seem to be archetypes of the various temperaments (that this should be so gives credibility to the universality of the temperamental model). I've gathered some of the most popular fictional characters and typed them by temperament.

The Wizard of Oz
Dorothy: sanguine
Scarecrow: phlegmatic/sanguine
Tin Man: melancholic
Lion: choleric (or choleric wannabe?)

Harry Potter
Harry: melancholic/choleric
Hermione: choleric
Ron: sanguine
Neville: phlegmatic

Peanuts
Lucy: choleric
Charlie Brown: melancholic
Snoopy: phlegmatic/sanguine
Linus: melancholic/sanguine
Schroeder: phlegmatic

The Lord of the Rings
Bilbo: sanguine
Frodo: melancholic
Merry and Pippin: sanguine/phlegmatic
Sam: phlegmatic/choleric

Gone With the Wind
Scarlett O'Hara: choleric
Rhett Butler: phlegmatic
Melanie Wilkes: sanguine
Ashley Wilkes: melancholic

The Simpsons
Bart: sanguine
Lisa: melancholic/choleric
Homer: phlegmatic
Marge: sanguine/melancholic

Winnie the Pooh
Pooh: phlegmatic/sanguine
Tigger: choleric/sanguine
Eeyore: melancholic
Roo: sanguine
Rabbit: melancholic/sanguine

Temperament and Manners

In researching and writing this book on temperament I have been constantly amazed at how well temperament works and how useful it is in chart analysis. Now, I would no more leave a temperament assessment out of a consultation than I would forget to look at the aspects between planets. In fact, temperament is now the first thing I look at when I start to analyze a chart. However, I have also come to realize that temperament analysis, while a vital first step, is still a *first* step in delving into the chart. Yes, temperament shows the innate disposition, but once we are born and begin to have experiences in our interactions with the world, the external or accidental factors which influence personality (or "manners" as Lilly would say) need also to be considered if we are to create a true portrait of the person. Garcaeus articulates this sentiment well when he says: "Furthermore, once the temperament is recognized, one can judge more correctly and certainly with regard to manners, erudition, illnesses and similar matters."[55]

So I feel that this book will not be complete without a small "what next?" section that explains in brief how to continue a chart analysis by finding the "manners" in the chart. All the astrologers who wrote on temperament considered this, from Ptolemy's, Montulmo's and Schoener's "quality of soul" to Lilly's "manners." Here is where we put meat on the sturdy bones of temperament.

For Ptolemy, Montulmo and Schoener, the quality of soul was an adjunct to the Temperament. Where Temperament was primarily physical and concerned with the body, the Quality of Soul was concerned with the more intangible mind as well as soul. For ancient, medieval and Renaissance astrologers, the mind was considered as a part of the Soul. The Soul (following the ideas of Aristotle) had three parts: vegetative, sensitive or non-rational, and rational or intellective. It is the latter part that we today would call mind. So we see Ptolemy and Montulmo talking about the different forms of soul in their astrology. The sensitive (and Montulmo's vegetative) soul is ruled by the Moon, while the rational or intellective is formed by Mercury and sometimes the Moon. I pointed out earlier in this book (p. 20) that the Moon is always a common thread in determining both temperament and quality of soul, showing its inextricable bond with body, mind and soul. The Moon links the physical with the non-physical. It connects and binds the vital and essential parts of ourselves, whether physical or not.

All the astrologers consider both the sign of the Moon and Mercury, their rulers and/or almutens, and planets aspecting the Moon and Mercury in their delineation of soul/manners. In addition, Montulmo, Schoener and Lilly consider the Ascendant sign, the Lord or almuten of the Ascendant, and planets in the 1st house.[56] We can see by these lists the strong connection that delineation of soul or manners has to the temperament, as many of the same factors are used for both.

In my modern work, following the clear association of temperament with both physical and psychological qualities, I have treated temperament not only as physical, but as a combination of both the physical and psychological. My differentiation between temperament and personality/manners

---

55. Johannes Garcaeus, "On the Temperament Type," unpublished handout from Robert Hand, p. 2.
56. Montulmo and Schoener also look at various triplicity lords: Montulmo the triplicity lord of the 1st; Schoener, somewhat obscurely, the triplicity lords of the 7th and 12th.

focuses on what I believe are mostly essential indications in the birthchart for temperament, opposed to (or better, adjoined to) mostly accidental indications for personality or manners, which can be externally influenced. After all, we learn our manners, and they can change. I will borrow from Ptolemy, Montulmo, Schoener and Lilly[57] in my assessment of soul or manners and arrive, I hope, at a technique that will give us a strong indication of both what a person is and wants or chooses to become. So once we have ascertained the temperament, we should then take a look at the following:

Planets in the 1st house, their sign and aspects to them. If there is more than one planet in the first, consider all of them but, as Lilly points out, though all planets in the 1st will contribute to the personality, the strongest will have the greatest effect – will corral the others into following its lead, as it were. If there are no planets in the 1st, look at the almuten of the Ascendant, its sign, house placement and aspects. Consider first the nature of the planet itself. Then the sign of the ruler of the 1st, or the planet in the 1st, will be an additional "layer" of extra meaning to interpret the personality. Adding house placement and aspects, which are more accidental, will add more layers and character to the personality. A planet in the 1st will color the expression of the temperament. Someone with Saturn in the 1st will come across differently than someone with, say, Venus in the 1st, even if they both have the same temperament. If the planet in the 1st also rules the Ascendant, that too will emphasize its qualities in the personality. Planets aspecting a planet in the 1st or ruling the 1st will provide yet another layer, another mode of expression of that planet and its characteristics.

The Moon, its ruler and aspects to the Moon. The Moon is not only the body, but the non-rational mind as well. We considered the sign of the Moon, its ruler by sign and its phase in assessing temperament. Now, for manners or personality, we pay more attention to the Moon's ruler and aspects to the Moon. Consider both the planet or planets aspecting (most important) and the kind of aspect (less important but still worthwhile). Tighter aspects will have a greater effect. If no planets aspect the Moon, consider the ruler and almuten of the Moon, its sign, house placement and aspects.

Mercury. As the significator of the rational mind, it's important to consider Mercury in delineation of personality, because how we think surely has an effect on how we express ourselves. Consider Mercury's sign, its essential and accidental dignity, its rulers, house placement and aspects. Retrogradation and combustion will also affect Mercury's expression, though I (having a retrograde and combust Mercury myself) would not necessarily interpret these as negatively as in the past. What we are trying to discover here is how Mercury operates and with whom, not judge how authentically "Mercurial" it is.

The Lord of the Geniture. In spite of the difficulty in deciding which method to use to find the Lord of the Geniture, we should still consider it in an analysis of the quality of soul or manners in the chart. It is after all, as John Frawley so poetically put it (quoting Plato's *Phaedrus* 247c), the Pilot of the Soul. Our purpose is to discover how the Lord of the Geniture interacts with the qualities of the temperament, with the rulers of the temperament or with the planets influencing the personality. An aspect between the Lord of the Geniture and these planets will facilitate its expression in the person's

---

57. For descriptions of Quality of Soul or Manners by these authors, see Appendix A.

life, even if the aspect is difficult. In addition we can consciously choose to integrate the Lord of the Geniture into the way we live and express ourselves. Thus it ought to be considered in our expansion of the chart delineation.

Fixed Stars. Though I would not consider the fixed stars to be as important for the indication of manners as the items listed above, one should still pay attention to them if they fall close to the Ascendant or tightly conjunct (1 degree orb) the Moon – especially, as Lilly says, those 1st or 2nd magnitude stars close to the ecliptic.

We'll close this section by looking at one more chart, this time examining both temperament and "manners."

Significators of Manners:

Neptune in the 1st house, square the Sun	
Ascendant ruler and almuten:	Mercury
Moon in Leo:	Moon ruler is the Sun in Gemini conjunct the MC, widely conjunct Mercury, very wide sextile to the Moon. Moon itself square Venus, sextile Mercury
Mercury in Gemini:	retrograde, under the beams, conjunct the MC, sextile the Moon, widely conjunct the Sun
Lady of the Geniture:	Venus, with Mercury and Jupiter participating
Fixed stars:	McCartney has no fixed stars close to the Ascendant or conjunct the Moon

With his Ascendant ruler and almuten, Mercury, oriental (thus sanguine) his Moon phase 1st quarter (sanguine), his Moon ruler by sign the Sun in Gemini (sanguine) and his season of birth spring (sanguine), McCartney's basic temperament is sanguine. That will be the underlying stuff which clothes his responses to the circumstances and events of his life. Physically he has the boyish look of the sanguine; psychologically, his general outlook will be optimistic, he will be basically cheerful, and

Paul McCartney — Temperament

	S	C	M	P
Birth Season	2	2		
Asc Sign	2		2	
Asc Ruler	1	1		
Asc Almuten	1	1		
Moon Sign	2		2	
Moon Phase	1	1		
Sign of Moon Ruler	1	1		
Totals	6	2	2	0

136 *Temperament: Astrology's Forgotten Key*

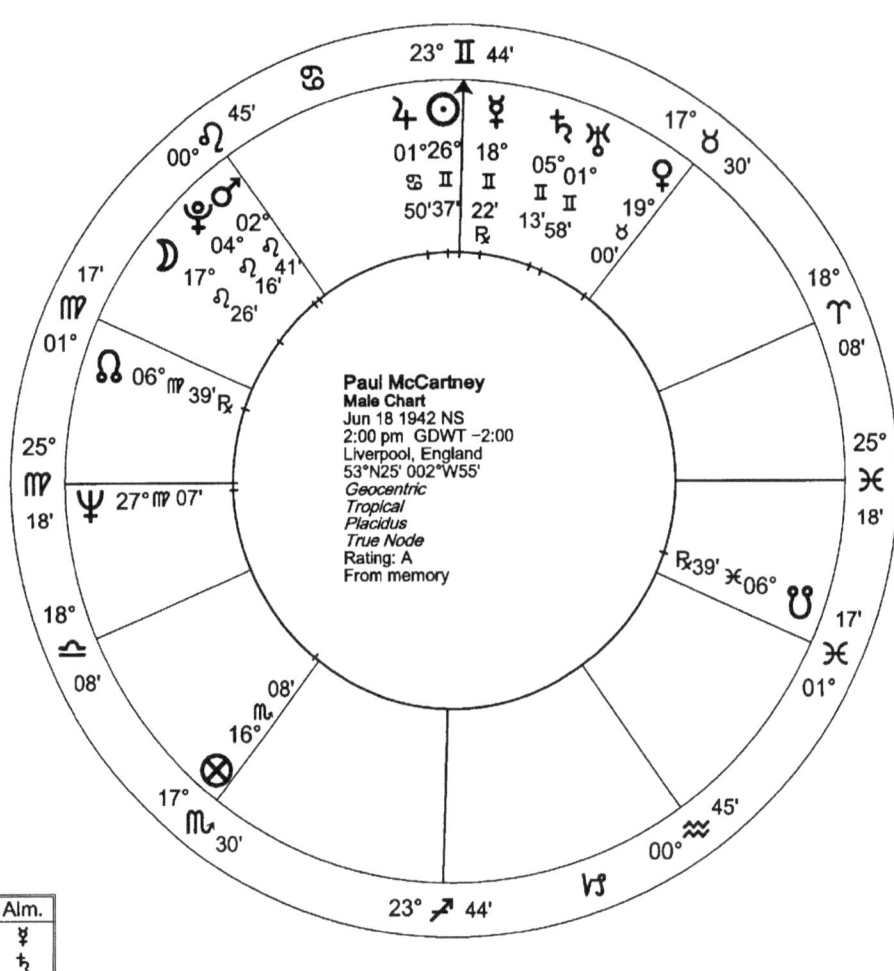

happiest when he is able to be social. His manners, or his personality, will be built and expressed on this sanguine foundation. We should also look at the parts of his temperament that are not sanguine, his Ascendant and his Moon.

McCartney's Ascendant, Virgo, provides some much needed melancholy amongst all the warmth of his choleric Moon and the other sanguine factors of his temperament. He is able to ground himself, to work for what he wants to achieve, to not lose his path in an excess of exhilaration. That might be tempting given the Moon, his emotional nature among other things, in Leo. He could express himself cholerically with this Moon, but he is not likely to hold a grudge for too long. Even though peregrine (without essential dignity), the Moon sits in the 11th house of friends, showing how important they are to his emotional well-being. The Moon's ruler is the Sun, in Gemini and conjunct the Midheaven. So McCartney has an emotional need to express himself to the world. The two luminaries are linked in his chart; they form an important part of his temperament and personality. There is a need for him to make a blazing statement, a burst of creativity, reflecting the bond of the two lights. The Beatles' rise was meteoric and McCartney had a lot to do with that.[58]

Let's take a look now at his manners. The significators of his manners are Mercury, ruler and almuten of his Ascendant; and we should also look at Venus, which is in an applying square to his Moon, ruler of the sensitive soul. With the influence of this beautifully dignified Venus in Taurus, McCartney's songs were romantic ballads ("Yesterday" and "Michelle" for example). Venus is also oriental, so it is able to work well with his sanguine temperament and make him someone quite pleasant to get along with, as a general rule. When Mercury and Venus are the significators of manners, Ptolemy says:

> "[Venus] joined with Mercury, in honorable positions Venus makes them artistic, philosophical, gifted with understanding, talented, poetic, lovers of the muses, lovers of beauty, of worthy character, seekers after enjoyment, luxurious, happy, fond of friends, pious, sagacious, resourceful, intellectual, intelligent, successful, quick to learn, self-taught, seekers after the best, imitators of beauty, eloquent and pleasing in speech, commanding affection, of well-ordered character, earnest, fond of athletics, upright, of good judgment, magnanimous; in affairs of love, restrained in their relationships with women but more passionate with boys, and jealous."[59]

Until women came along, being the Beatles was the passion of John, Paul, George and Ringo. But – the aspect of Venus to the Moon is a square, not a trine, and this will create some trouble in paradise, and the trouble will be female. Moon square Venus shows some difficulty with females, or females somehow altering your own personal plans or feelings (Moon in Leo). One of the main reasons the Beatles broke up was because of their relationships with women — Paul's with Linda Eastman, and John's with Yoko Ono. Linda told Paul he could "be his own man." Paul pushed to have Linda's father

---

58. Lennon also, of course, was probably as important as McCartney in assuring the blazing fame of the Beatles; interestingly, his Ascendant is 19 Aries 54, conjunct the exaltation degree of the Sun (it also trines McCartney's Moon).
59. Ptolemy, *Tetrabiblos*, Book III, Ch. 13, pp. 357, 359 (Loeb edition).

made the Beatles' financial manager, while the other Beatles wanted Allen Klein. When Klein was appointed to the post while McCartney was on vacation, that was the final straw for Paul, and the group broke up shortly thereafter. Venus doesn't figure in McCartney's temperament assessment, but we can see how pivotal it is in the expression of his manners. This Venus-Moon square also symbolizes the tragedy he has had with women: both his mother and his first wife died of breast cancer, and his second wife had an accident in which she lost a leg.

However Mercury, the ruler and almuten of his Ascendant (a sanguine Mercury both by sign and by phase) is also very important both to his personality and to his career. This is a Mercury in high dignity (its own ruler), one of the most elevated planets in the chart, conjunct the Sun and the Midheaven. He finds himself through Mercurial pursuits, through writing and playing music, and sharing that music with the world. Mercury is also in a tight sextile with the Moon (it is the Moon's next aspect). His rational mind and sensitive soul connect in an aspect that makes it easy for him to integrate these parts of himself, and articulate his emotions in a clear expression of what he is feeling. The Moon, which provides the choleric streak in his basically sanguine temperament, also rules his non-rational soul – it gives his intuition, his inspiration – and it's a Moon in the kingly sign of Leo. Allied with Mercury, here is the ability to take his own experiences, his own emotions, and turn them into songs the whole world can identify with.

As modern astrologers, we also cannot ignore the planet Neptune only 2 degrees away from the Ascendant. It is, I think, an added testimony to McCartney's ability to tap into the cultural feeling of the Sixties, and it emphasizes the universal compassion and peace for which he has campaigned much of his life. It is in Virgo, which will provide him with the ability in his personal life to discriminate, to be precise in spite of the Neptunian fog, or to use that fog to his advantage.[60] It is square to the Sun, which is conjunct the Midheaven – McCartney is seen as a carrier of the zeitgeist.

Now, what about the Lord of the Geniture? McCartney's chart is a perfect example of confusion about which planet to use as his "pilot of the soul." The planet with the most essential dignity is Venus in Taurus, which it rules both by domicile and by triplicity; it is in the 9th house, cadent, but of the cadent houses, the 9th is one of the best, being the house of the Sun God. Another candidate is Mercury, also dignified by domicile rulership, and very close to the 10th house cusp – but it is also retrograde and combust (though leaving combustion very shortly). Or we could pick Jupiter, which is in the sign of its exaltation, Cancer, and also angular in the 10th house, but intercepted in Cancer. Perhaps it is not surprising that we have 3 dignified contenders vying for Lord of the Geniture in Paul McCartney's chart. Which will do best as his Pilot of the Soul? By Ibn Ezra's system, Mercury, in spite of its accidental debilities, is Lord of the Geniture, with Jupiter in second place. Lilly, however, would probably pick Venus. It has the most points of essential dignity, and Lilly would give it 2 points of

---

60. Of course a whole generation of people was born with Neptune in Virgo, and I do not mean to imply that they will use Neptune in the same way that McCartney does, or even that this is what Neptune in Virgo means on a collective or mundane level. It is because it is so close to McCartney's Ascendant and square his Sun that he can use it in a more personal way.

accidental dignity for being in the 9th. Mercury clearly has been a prime factor in his creativity and fame. Jupiter, that planet of faith, of generosity of spirit, may have something to do with McCartney's character — how Paul McCartney operates at his highest potential, and finds underlying strength in his life even in tragedy. Yet Venus shows in all his work: the romantic ballads, the importance of relationships in his life and above all, the power of love to transform the world. "And in the end, the love you take is equal to the love you make."[61]

Some Final Thoughts

> "Nature that framed us of four elements,
> Warring within our breasts for regiment,
> Doth teach us all to have aspiring minds:
> Our souls, whose faculties can comprehend
> The wondrous Architecture of the world:
> And measure every wandering planet's course,
> Still climbing after knowledge infinite,
> And always moving as the restless Spheres,
> Will us to wear ourselves and never rest,
> Until we reach the ripest fruit of all,
> That perfect bliss and sole felicity,
> The sweet fruition of an earthly crown."
>
> –Christopher Marlowe

Last night on the news, I watched a reporter announce with excitement that scientists had surprisingly discovered that cholesterol levels drop in the spring and summer – because the volume of blood in the body is greater during those seasons. My question is: Why didn't they read Hippocrates?

It seems that much of the time in this oh-so-up-to-date and sophisticated world of ours we "discover" something that the ancients knew all along. It's been my goal in this book to re-illuminate some of the truths of our world that have been lost or discarded as fusty relics of the past. Of course no clear-thinking scientists use temperament today – but maybe if they did, we wouldn't need them to discover what Hippocrates[62] already knew. Astrologers are in both the fortunate and unenviable position of being outside the mainstream – so for us to embrace a technique ignored by modern science isn't so strange and may even be quite enlightening. If what I had to say about temperament has piqued your interest, if you decide to try it for yourself, if you tell your friend about it, or share it with your class – if you find yourself thinking a little differently about those old, dead astrologers and their ideas – then I am content that I've achieved what I set out to do.

Duxbury, Massachusetts
April 2004

---

61. The last words McCartney sang as a Beatle; from "The End," *Abbey Road*.
62. And Galen, and Ptolemy, and Montulmo, and Schoener, and Lilly, and Steiner!

APPENDIX A
DETERMINING TEMPERAMENT ETC. THROUGH THE AGES: A SYNOPSIS

Ptolemy (*Tetrabiblos*, Book III, Ch. 11, Ch. 13; translation by Dorian Greenbaum)

Bodily Form and Mixture

And so generally one must observe carefully the *rising horizon* and those *planets that are* either *upon it or those that are its ruler* [*oikodespotēs*; the almuten] in the way we said before; and in the same way look particularly at *the Moon*. For the true disposition of the body is observed through the formative nature of both these places and of their rulers, and through the commixture according to each form [*eidos*]; and in addition through the *figure-descriptions* [aspects] *of the fixed stars co-rising with these*. The stars [planets] having rulership are first in power, but the distinctive character of their places also contributes.

The Quality of Soul

Of the qualities of soul, those concerning the *rational and noetic part* are comprehended on each occasion through observing the condition of the star of *Hermes*; those concerning the *sensitive and non-rational* from the more corporeal of the two lights (that is, the Moon), and from the *stars configured with her both by application and separation*. But since the form [*eidos*] of the soul's impulses is so extremely varied, it is reasonable that we make such an investigation neither simply nor haphazardly, but through many complex observations. For the differences in those *zôidia* [signs] *containing Hermes and the Moon or those who have predomination* [*epikratēsis*] *over them* can contribute much in regard to the unique features of the soul; and also *the solar and pivotal figures* [that is, solar phase and angularity] of those stars having a relationship to the aforementioned form; and in addition *the distinctive character, according to the nature itself, of the stars* which relate to the movements of the soul.

Antonius de Montulmo (*On the Judgment of Nativities*, Part 2, Ch. VIII; trans. Hand)

Again Concerning the Form and Complexion

The *Ascendant* of the nativity is the factor which always signifies the body of the native; wherefore consider *first* what it may signify concerning forms and complexion. *Second*, consider the *Almuten of the Ascendant* and the *sign in which it is*, and what each may signify concerning forms. *Third*, you will consider the *place of the Moon* because the Moon [also] signifies the body of the native. Also see whether there is any *planet in the degree of the Ascendant especially if it should have any dignity in these places*, and if it should not be there according to the center [of its orb], at least *let it project rays according to the moiety of its orb*, because if it should be thus, it will be a principal significator of the form of the native. [The effect will be obtained] by mixing together the form of the Almuten in the sign in which it is with the form of the place of the Moon, [with the form] of every planet which aspects said places, increasing or diminishing [the influence] as is fitting. But *if there is no planet in the Ascendant of the native, consider according to the figure of the Almuten* in the place in which it is, and *principally the ascending sign especially if the Almuten aspects the Ascendant*; and you shall judge the form of that Ascendant according to that which predominates, mixing together the form of the Moon and of the other planets which aspect said places. *Consider also* which *forms of the images of the fixed stars may be in the Ascendant or in the place of the Almuten of the Ascendant, and of the Ascendant [itself] with the sign in which it is, also according to the aforesaid's state of being with respect to latitude, retrogradation or directness.* [With all of this] you will be able to judge concerning the complexion of the native.

Indeed consider the *time of the nativity, whether it may be day or night*, and in which *quarter of the year* he may have been born because these times have an increase or remission of the forms of the principal significators. ...

... And see also the *principal significators*, especially whether they are *in luminous, smokey, or dark degrees*...

...... Indeed, know that the Ascendant signifies the body, and that the Almuten of the Ascendant chiefly signifies the face of the native according to its state of being, etc.

Quality of Soul

The principal significators of the *vegetative soul* first are the *Ascendant*, *Moon* and the *Almuten of the Ascendant*, [any] *planet which is in the Ascendant*, especially if it should have any dignity here, the *triplicity lord of the Ascendant*, and the place which has been chosen as the *Hyleg*.

However, the principal significators of the *sensitive power* are the *Moon*, the *Almuten of the Ascendant*, and [that] *planet which is in the Ascendant*, and the *luminary whose is the authority*.

The principal significators of the *intellective power* are *Mercury*, the *Almuten of the Ascendant*, and the *Moon*.

Johannes Schoener (*Three Books on the Judgment of Nativities,* Book I, Chapter 5, pp. 81 and 88, Chapter 7, p. 122; translation by Robert Hand)

For the form of the body consider the following:

1. The Ascendant.
2. The Almuten of the Ascendant.
3. The place of the Moon. [i.e., the sign]
4. A planet or the rays of one [that fall] on the Ascendant.
5. The image of the heavens. [This seems to relate to the constellations and fixed stars that are on the Ascendant or with the Almuten of the Ascendant.]
6. The quarter of the year.
7. The Part of Stability. [Formulae: Day = Asc + Spirit − Fortune; Night = Asc + Fortune − Spirit]

8. The Part of Future Things [Also called the Part of Spirit: Day = Asc + Sun – Moon, Night = Asc + Moon – Sun]

Others draw the constitution of complexion of the body from the following:
1. The sign of the Ascendant.
2. The Almuten of the Ascendant.
3. The sign of the Almuten of the Ascendant.
4. A planet or its rays in the Ascendant.
5. Planets that aspect the Ascendant.
6. The quarter of the lunar month.
7. The sign of the Moon.
8. A planet aspecting the Moon.
9. The quarter of the year of the Sun.
10. The Almuten of the Geniture.

You will gather the complexion from the four qualities of these points.

Concerning the Qualities of the Soul

For the qualities of the soul consider the following:
1. Mercury
2. The Almuten of the place of Mercury.
3. The Moon.
4. The Almuten of the place of the Moon.
5. The Ascendant.
6. The Almuten of the Ascendant.
7. The second triplicity lord of the twelfth house.
8. The third triplicity lord of the twelfth house.
9. The third triplicity lord of the seventh house.

Johannes Garcaeus (*Astrologiae Methodus...*, Concerning Temperament and Complexion; translation by Robert Hand)

These are the significators of complexion:
1. The Horoscope and its lord.
2. The planet or planets which are located in the Horoscope, or which aspect the planet by a partile aspect or which fall into the sign which is intercepted between the first and second [cusps].
3. Planets which aspect the degree of the Horoscope among which ☊ and ☋ are counted.
4. The Moon.

5. Planets which aspect the Moon by the moiety of their orbs.
6. The quarter of the year or the sign of the Sun at the time of the birth.
7. The Lord of the Geniture.
8. Any planet which shares rulership with the preceding.
9. Fixed stars.

William Lilly (*Christian Astrology*, Book III, Chapter CVI)

Significators of the Complexion are:

> First, *the Signe ascending, and Lord thereof.*
> Secondly, *The Planet or Planets placed in the ascendant, or the ☊ or ☋ or the Planets partilly aspecting the ascendant.*
> Thirdly, *The ☽ and Planet or Planets beholding her within Mediety of their Orbs.*
> Fourthly, *The quarter of the yeer or Signe the ☉ is in.*
> Fiftly, *The Lord of the Geniture.*

…Consider the qualities of the *Significators* and Signes, and collect the testimonies of every of the four qualities, *viz.* Hot, Moyst, Cold, Dry, according to the major testimonies, so judge of the Complexion.

If Heat and Moysture overcome, the Native is of Sanguine Complexion: if Cold and Moysture, then he is Phlegmatick: if Heat and Drinesse, then cholerick: if Cold and Drinesse, then Melancholly.

You must deale warily in the collection of the testimonies of the four Humours, of *Heat*, *Humidity*, *Cold* and *Drinesse*; for it may come to passe, that the qualities of the Planet and Sign may obtain the same equall number of testimonies, and the one have as many testimonies of Heat, as the other of Cold, these being repugnant qualities, the one takes off the other, and they are not numbered or accounted: where there is no contradiction, those testimonies are accepted, when one Planet is Lord of the Geniture and Horoscope, you shall allow him in collection of testimonies a three-fold vertue or influence in the Complexion: the ☽ being in the ascendant, her testimonies shall be twice exhibited.

Manners According to William Lilly
Christian Astrology, Chapter 107, pp. 535-6

The general rules of discovering the qualities of the mind by a Nativity, are these:

> First, if any Planet do occupy the Sign ascending, or which is intercepted, he shall be principall *Significator* of Manners; but he shall also participate in the same signification, whatsoever Planet he is, that hath dignity in the place of the *Significator* of Manners.

> Secondly, consider that Planet who is the *Significator*, and his *Dispositor*; for if he be a benevolent Planet, or in aspect with such, and strong, he denotes laudable or compleat Manners, according to his nature: if he prove a malevolent Planet, or is infested with the hostile beames of one, and be impotent besides, he renders evill and corrupt Manners, such as naturally that Planet signifies. If a good Planet by nature be *Significator*, or configurated with good, but exist weak, he shewes good and wholesome

Manners in shew, yet inwardly they are somewhat obscure, muddy, or very simple: The *Infortunes* potent, argue good, pretty conditions, but ever mixed with a tincture of poyson, or with the remaines of some crabbed condition or other; which I have ever found true.

☿ affords manners according to the nature of that Planet whose nature he assumes; and this he doth in a two-fold way.

1. When joyned to any Planet by ☌, but if he be joyned to many, he assumes the nature of that Planet with whom he is neerest in ☌, and who is the most fortified or dignified.
2. If he be not in ☌ with any Planet, he assumes his nature in whose essentiall dignity he is placed: ☊ is equivalent to ♃, ☋ to ♄ and ♂.

The *Luminaries* in the *Horoscope*, effect no great matters, but in a generall way, unlesse they be wonderfully strongly fortified.

If many Planets occupy the Horoscope, all shall be *Significators*, and they breed variety of manners: but the most powerfull Planet amongst them, shall give the most durable, and such as will continue; the other not so permanent. How long they shall continue, you may know by directions; for when the ☽ is directed to the termes or aspect of the most potent Planet then the Native is almost wholy participant of his Manners, and shall most manifest them to the world in his actions; when the ☽ varies her Terme or aspect, and doth meet with another of another quality, then doe his Manners very, and he assumes the condition of that Planet to whose termes or aspect she is directed, *viz*. if the ☽ comes to the Terms or aspect of ♀, the Native is Cheerfull; to the Termes or aspect of ♃, Discreet, Modest, Religious; to the Termes or ♂, Angry, Cholerick, Quarrelsome; to Terms or aspect of ♄, Grave, Melancholly, Sullen, full of Fears, Laborious, &c.

No Planet posited in the ascendant, observe what Planet is joyned to ☽ or ☿, judge the manners of the Native to assimilate with the nature of that Planet.

If the Planet be joyned to ☽ and ☿ both, it's as much as if there were many Planets in the Horoscope, for they signifie discrepancy in manners; but yet those signified by the most powerfull Planet shall continue longest, &c.

No Planet in the ascendant, or joyned to *Mercury* or *Luna*, then take the Lord of the ascendant, according to his nature, be it good or ill, and so judge of the manners; but so, as his *Dispositor* behold him with some aspect. If no Planet aspect him, have recourse to that Planet who forciby aspect *Luna* and *Mercury* with a partill aspect.

If none have a partill aspect to *Mercury* or *Luna*, then he shall signifie the manners, who in the place of *Mercury* and *Luna* hath the most essentiall dignities.

The *Significator* of Manners joyned to fixed Starres of the first or second magnitude, being but a little distant from the Ecliptick, have great signification in the Manners, and make those signified to be more apparent....

Henry Coley (*Clavis Astrologiae, or a Key to the whole Art of Astrology. New Filed and Polished in Three Parts.* pp. 534-5)

I. Consider what Sign possesseth the Horoscope (or Ascends at Birth) and Judge according to the Nature of that Sign, as if *Gemini* Ascend an Aireal Sign, the Native is Sanguine; if *Cancer* a Watry Sign, Phlegmatique; if *Leo* a Fiery Sign, Cholerique; if *Virgo* an Earthy Sign, Melancholy, &c. If two Signs are concerned in the Ascendant, mix their significations.

II. You are also to consider the Lord of the Ascendant, the Planet or Planets therein, or in Aspect (partile) thereunto.

III. The *Moon*, and those planets she is in Aspect with.

IV. The Lord of the Geniture, and Sign of the *Sun* is in (*viz.* the Quarter of the Year).

V. Lastly, Consider the qualities of the Several Significators, and Collect their Testimonies, *viz.* Hot, Moist, Cold, Dry; and Judge according to the Major Testimonies [*The qualities of the Signs, and Planets, you will find in the first part.*]

If Heat and Moisture Predominate, the Native is Sanguine; if Cold and Moisture, Phlegmatique; If Heat, and Dryness, Cholerique; if Cold, and Dryness, Melancholy. [*Note that if one Planet be Almuten of the Geniture, and Lord of the Horoscope, allow him a threefold Vertue in the Complexion of the Native, or the Moon in the Ascendant, you are to double her Testimonies.*]

John Partridge (*Mikropanastron*)

Significators of Complexion:

1. The Ascendant and its lord.
2. The planet or planets place in the Ascendant, or beholding the same with a partile aspect; among which the North Node and the South Node are also numbered.
3. The Moon.
4. The planet holding the Moon within orbs.
5. The quarter of the heavens, or the sign the Sun possesseth.
6. The lord of the nativity.

(The North Node is the nature of Jupiter and Venus; the South Node is the nature of Saturn and Mars.)

Planetary Qualities: A Synopsis

Ptolemy (Book I Chapter 4 and Book III Chapter 12 of the *Tetrabiblos*)

- Saturn: Intrinsic quality cold and slightly drying; Oriental cold and wet, Occidental cold and dry
- Jupiter: Intrinsic quality warms and moistens, temperate; Oriental hot and wet, Occidental wet
- Mars: Intrinsic quality dry and hot; Oriental hot and dry, Occidental dry
- Venus: Intrinsic quality slightly warms, and moistens; Oriental hot and wet, Occidental wet
- Mercury: Intrinsic quality sometimes dry, sometimes wet; Oriental hot, Occidental dry
- Moon: Intrinsic quality wet and slightly heats; from New to 1st Quarter, wet increases; from 1st Quarter to full, heat increases; from full to last Quarter dryness increases; from last Quarter to New, coldness increases
- Sun: Intrinsic quality heating and slightly drying

Abu Mashar (Chapter 5 of *The Abbreviation of the Introduction to Astrology*)

- Saturn: Intrinsic quality cold and dry
- Jupiter: Intrinsic quality hot and wet
- Mars: Intrinsic quality hot and dry
- Sun: Intrinsic quality hot and dry
- Venus: Intrinsic quality cold and wet
- Mercury: Intrinsic quality changes
- Moon: Intrinsic quality cold and wet

Al Biruni (Sections 396-401, *The Book of Instruction in the Elements of the Art of Astrology*)

- Saturn: Intrinsic quality extremely cold and dry
- Jupiter: Intrinsic quality moderately hot and wet
- Mars: Intrinsic quality extremely hot and dry
- Sun: Intrinsic quality predominantly hot; dry
- Venus: Intrinsic quality moderately cold and wet
- Mercury: Intrinsic quality moderately cold and dry
- Moon: Intrinsic quality cold and wet, sometimes moderate

Bonatti (Tractate 3, Chapters 1-7 of *Liber Astronomiae*; Book 9, Ch. 3-11)

Saturn: Intrinsic quality cold and distemperate dryness; Oriental cold and wet, Occidental dry

Jupiter: Intrinsic quality heat and moisture; Oriental hot and wet, Occidental wet

Mars: Intrinsic quality heat and distemperate dryness; Oriental hot and dry, Occidental dry

Sun: Intrinsic quality heat and dryness

Venus: Intrinsic quality cold and moisture; Oriental like Jupiter, Occidental cold

Mercury: "signifies things of the earth;" Oriental hot, Occidental dry

Moon: Intrinsic quality cold and moisture

Montulmo (Part 2, Chapter 8 of *On the Judgment of Nativities*)

Saturn: Oriental cold and moist; Occidental cold and dry

Jupiter: Oriental hot and moist; Occidental moist

Mars: Oriental hot and dry; Occidental dry

Sun: Oriental (above the horizon) "of good color" (no quality given)

Venus: Oriental wet; Occidental cold

Mercury: Oriental hot; Occidental dry

Moon: Intrinsic quality "temperateness and moisture"

Schoener (Canon II, 2nd Part of *Opusculum Astrologicum*; Chapter 5 of Book 1, *Three Books on the Judgment of Nativities*)

Saturn: Intrinsic quality cold and dry; Oriental cold and wet, Occidental dry (in Chapter 5 of Book 1, *Three Books...*, Schoener says Saturn occidental is cold and dry)

Jupiter: Intrinsic quality hot and wet; Oriental hot and wet, Occidental wet

Mars: Intrinsic quality hot and dry; Oriental hot and dry, Occidental dry

Sun: Intrinsic quality hot and dry; spring hot and wet, summer hot and dry, autumn cold and dry, winter cold and wet

Venus: Intrinsic quality cold and wet; Oriental hot and wet, Occidental wet

Mercury: Intrinsic quality dry but can change; Oriental hot, Occidental dry

Moon: Intrinsic quality cold and wet; from ♂ to □ hot and wet, from □ to ☍ hot and dry, from ☍ to □ cold and dry, from □ to ♂ cold and wet

Garcaeus (*Astrologiae Methodus...*)

Saturn: Oriental cold and wet, Occidental dry

Jupiter: Oriental hot and wet, Occidental wet

Mars: Oriental hot and dry, Occidental dry

Sun:	Spring hot and wet, Summer hot and dry, Autumn cold and dry, Winter cold and wet
Venus:	Oriental hot and wet, Occidental wet
Mercury:	Oriental hot, Occidental dry
Moon:	from ☌ to first □ hot and wet, from first □ to ☍ hot and dry, from ☍ to second □ cold and dry, from second □ to ☌ cold and wet

Lilly (Book I, Chapters 8-14, Book III, Chapter 106 of *Christian Astrology*)

Saturn:	Intrinsic quality cold and dry; Oriental cold and wet, Occidental dry
Jupiter:	Intrinsic quality temperately hot and wet; Oriental hot and wet, Occidental wet
Mars:	Intrinsic quality hot and dry; Oriental hot and dry, Occidental dry
Sun:	Intrinsic quality hot and dry but more temperate than Mars; in spring hot and wet, in summer hot and dry, in autumn cold and dry, in winter cold and wet
Venus:	Intrinsic quality temperately cold and wet; Oriental hot and wet, Occidental wet
Mercury:	Intrinsic quality cold and dry; Oriental hot, Occidental dry
Moon:	Intrinsic quality cold and wet; from ☌ to 1st Quarter hot and wet, from 1st Quarter to full hot and dry, from full to last Quarter cold and dry, from last Quarter to New cold and wet

Culpeper (from Tobyn, *Culpeper's Medicine*)

Saturn:	Intrinsic quality cold and dry
Jupiter:	Intrinsic quality hot and wet
Mars:	Intrinsic quality hot and dry
Sun:	Intrinsic quality hot and dry
Venus:	Intrinsic quality cold and wet
Mercury:	Intrinsic quality cold and dry
Moon:	Intrinsic quality cold and wet

APPENDIX B

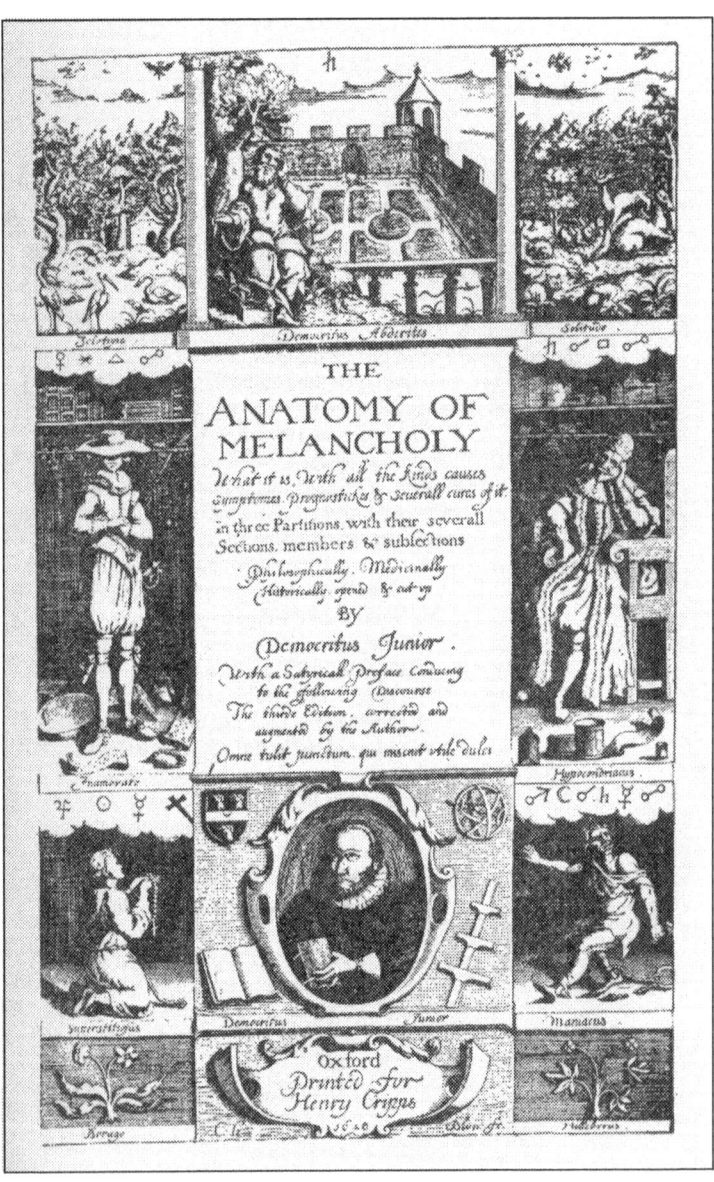

Frontispiece for Burton's *The Anatomy of Melancholy*, 1621

The Argument of the Frontispiece

TEN distinct Squares here seen apart.
Are joined in one by Cutter's art.

I

Old *Democritus* under a tree,
Sits on a stone with book on knee;
About him hang there many features,
Of Cats, Dogs, and such like creatures,
Of which he makes Anatomy,
The seat of Black Choler to see.
Over his head appears the sky,
And Saturn, Lord of Melancholy.

II

To th' left a landscape of *Jealousy*,
Presents itself unto thine eye.
A Kingfisher, a Swan, an Hern,
Two fighting-Cocks you may discern;
Two roaring Bulls each other hie,
To assault concerning Venery.
Symbols are these; I say no more,
Conceive the rest by that's afore.

III

The next of *Solitariness*
A portraiture doth well express,
By sleeping Dog, Cat: Buck and Doe,
Hares, Conies in the desart go:
Bats, Owls the shady bowers over,
In melancholy darkness hover.
Mark well: If't be not as't should be,
Blame the bad Cutter, and not me.

IV

I' th' under Column there doth stand
Inamorato with folded hand;
Down hangs his head, terse and polite,
Some ditty sure he doth indite.
His lute and books about him lie,
As symptoms of his vanity.
If this do not enough disclose,
To paint him, take thyself by th' nose.

V

Hypochondriacus leans on his arm,
Wind in his side doth him much harm,
And troubles him full sore, God knows,
Much pain he hath and many woes.
About him pots and glasses lie,
Newly bought from's Apothecary.
This Saturn's aspects signify,
You see them portray'd in the sky.

VI

Beneath them kneeling on his knee,
A *Superstitious* man you see:
He fasts, he prays, on his Idol fixt,
Tormented hope and fear betwixt:
For hell perhaps he takes more pain,
Than thou dost heaven itself to gain.
Alas, poor Soul, I pity thee,
What stars incline thee so to be?

VII

But see the *Madman* rage down right
With furious looks, a ghastly sight.
Naked in chains bound doth he lie,
And roars amain he knows not why!
Observe him; for as in a glass,
Thine angry portraiture it was.
His picture keeps still in thy presence;
'Twixt him and thee, there's no difference.

VIII-IX

Borage and *Hellebore* fill two scenes,
Sovereign plants to purge the veins
Of Melancholy, and cheer the heart,
Of those black fumes which make it smart;
To clear the Brain of misty fogs,
Which dull our senses, and Soul clogs.
The best medicine that e'er God made
For this malady, if well assay'd.

X

Now last of all to fill a place,
Presented is the Author's face;
And in that habit which he wears,
His image to the world appears.
His mind no art can well express,
That by his writings you may guess.
It was not pride, nor yet vain glory,
(Though others do it commonly,)
Made him do this; if you must know,
The Printer would needs have it so.

Then do not frown or scoff at it,
Deride it not, or detract a whit.
For surely as thou dost by him,
He will do the same again.
Then look upon't, behold and see,
As thou like'st it, so it likes thee.
And I for it will stand in view,
Thine to command, Reader, Adieu!

Burton's Criteria for Melancholy, from other Authors

Jovianus Pontanus:
1. Mercury in Virgo or Pisces in the Ascendant, square Saturn or Mars
2. Saturn or Mars in the 4th or 10th house, opposed; cured if Mercury aspects
3. Moon conjunct or opposed the Sun, Saturn or Mars, or in square to them

Cardan adds to #3:
      or begotten during a lunar quarter, eclipse or earthquake

Garcaeus and *Leovitius*:
      Look at the Lord of the Geniture; or
      Aspect between the Moon and Mercury, but neither aspect the Ascendant; or
      Saturn or Mars lord of present conjunction or opposition in Sagittarius or Pisces (either the Sun or Moon in those signs)

Onset of Melancholy:
Significators of a geniture (Ascendant, Moon, hyleg, etc.) directed to "hostile beams or terms" of Saturn and Mars; or fixed star of the nature of Saturn or Mars; or Saturn by transit or revolution aspects significators.

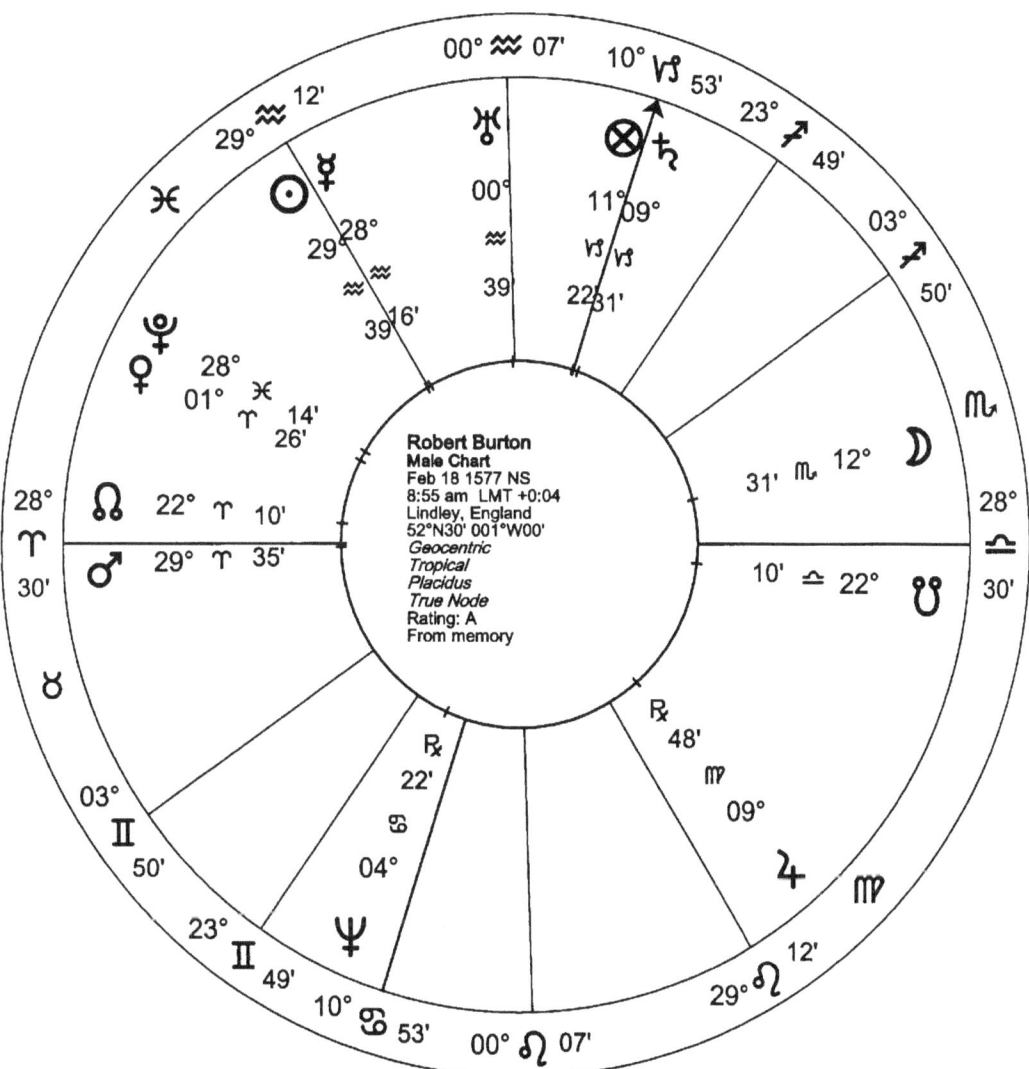

APPENDIX C
RAMON LULL'S DESCRIPTIONS OF TEMPERAMENT
From Ramon Lull, *Treatise on Astronomy*, pp. 10-21
(translation by Kristina Shapar)

Melancholy
Men who are born in its [Saturn's] constellation are melancholy and heavy through the ponderousness that they have from earth and water, which are naturally heavy. Through the nature of the weight they are constant and firm in their appetites and enterprises and naturally look toward the earth. They have a good memory because water is restrictive and is greedy and receptive, and they love imaginative and mathematical forms, while the earth is the dense subject in which the impression of the recollected forms endures. Therefore, melancholy men are disposed to have great knowledge through the multiplication of many forms. By nature melancholy men are suspicious and see the future from far away through their imagination, which has more in accord with melancholy than with another constitution. The reason that melancholy has more of a relation and accord with the imagination is that the imagination conceives measures, lines, figures, and colors, which can often be impressed in water and earth because they have denser matter than fire and air.

Sanguine
The men born under Jupiter should be happy, because the life of men subsists principally through moistness and heat; and they should be generous, just as fire is generous inasmuch as it diffuses and divides the parts, and the air is that which is filling and more convertible than any other element. And therefore, sanguine men do not fear poverty or need and are naturally vainglorious and love honoring more than other men, just as they have a more noble constitution. And through the greater appetite that they have for the good, they naturally have more desire for infants, whom they love and want to have more than other men, whereby they multiply the human species.

Sanguine men are naturally more faithful than others and more trusting in all men, and are neither calumniators nor maledictors. They are more willing to show what they know than other men, because they think more than other men by reason of the liberality of fire and of the abundance of air. And for this reason sanguine men collect thick forms in the imagination, as the choleric collects lean and meager ones, for as water restricts them and fire extends them, so earth dries them and air fills and vivifies them. ... And therefore the scientific habit that the men of Jupiter have, that is to say, those born under it, is a faithful and tangible science, easy to understand, for sanguine men do not naturally hold secrets. But the subject of their habit of knowing is not so stable as with that of the men of Saturn, and this is because the subject of the imagination of the sanguine is soft in comparison to that of the choleric, which is hard and dry. And therefore, it is said that the men of Jupiter learn and understand more easily than the men of Saturn; but they forget sooner than the melancholics. ... And so sanguine men are, more than other men, founders of new ways of doing, while melancholics stand more firmly in ancient customs than in new ones.

Choleric

Therefore they say that men born in its [Mars'] constellation are evil and combative, and make quarrels through the choler that they have, and are light men, because fire is light and consumes the gross matter of the earth, which is dense and adheres to the form of the earth. And for this reason they say that choleric men do not live long, for the nature of the earth is scanty and dried out, and heat does not have anything by which it can be sustained, such as charcoal, the material of which is consumed and makes ash. However, if the choleric man survives his youth, he lives long by nature, for the matter of the earth thickens by the accord that it has with water, which gives it cold against the heat of fire. And because water is in accord with air through moistness, it gives moisture to the earth to temper the great dryness; therefore, the earth in the choleric man is gross and heavy and full of its nature, and the fire cannot consume him by heat, nor the air by moisture against dryness. Therefore, choleric men live longer than other men because they have good digestion through the heat of the fire, which is great....

As men that are born under Mars are choleric, through it, astronomers say that they love and have an appetite for the conditions of Mars. And for this reason, because the fire is more movable than any other element, the choleric man is more quickly angered than another, and has greater anger; but the anger does not last long, for fire consumes and the earth, through which the choleric man is dry, is quickly consumed through the great heat of the fire. They also say that the choleric man quickly gives his accord or refuses it, and quickly undertakes affairs and quickly neglects them, and is inconstant and ready to do an about-face. This nature comes to him through the great movement of fire, which Mars also multiplies in man with that movement of his own nature through the bile, in the same way that the Sun causes heat in fire in summer and by means of its light by day.

The man born under Mars is subtle and learns and understands quickly, but by nature he does not have a good memory and forgets as quickly as he understands and wishes. This happens through the imagination, which is too dry in the choleric man, for the great heat of the fire dries it out, and so the forms of the phantasy do not have a durable basis. ... And it is the same thing with the imagination as with the memory, that the imagination does not have the deliberation for imagining the figures and the dispositions of corporeal substances. And the same thing follows for the nature of the body, for the choleric man is more active than other men, but he is quickly worn out, for he has quickly consumed the constitution of cold in the earth and the moistness in the water through his great movement. ...

Also, a choleric man loves commerce of the constitution of fire more than other commerce....
... A choleric man also has a larger appetite for hot, dry meats than for moist, cold ones, and he loves yellow colors more than others, and long vestments, the chase, the sword and knife and also other things pertaining to the nature of fire. Also, the choleric man dreams more than another, but he has shorter dreams than others, and more quickly forgets them, and he naturally dreams according to the nature of Mars and fire.

Phlegmatic

Astronomers say that men born in the constellation of Venus have a natural instinct and appetite for the conditions of Venus and so are moderately phlegmatic because Venus does not have so intense a constitution through water as the Moon....

... The reason that the astronomers say that the Moon is good and evil is principally because it takes and collects in its sphere the influences that come below from above, as summer makes the fruit of the trees ripen. ... They also say that the Moon is evil because it is the cause of phlegm, which is cold and moist, and has evil constitution, through which it makes men too heavy and fat, and lazy and gives little ingenuity and movement, and makes them sleep too much, spit and cough, and it does not give them so good an appetite for eating, nor make them sense the odors and flavors of the meats so much as the other planets do.

APPENDIX D
NICHOLAS CULPEPER'S DESCRIPTIONS OF TEMPERAMENT
(from Chapter 59 of *Galen's Art of Physick*, pp. 52-57)*

Sanguine
A man or woman in whose body heat and moisture abounds, is said to be Sanguine of complexion. Such are usually of a middle stature, strong composed bodies, fleshy but not fat, great veins, smooth skins, hot and moist in feeling. Their body is hairy, if they be men they have soon beards, if they be women it were ridiculous to expect it. There is a redness intermingled with white in their cheeks. Their hair is usually of a blackish brown, yet sometimes flaxed. Their appetite is good, their digestion quick, their urine yellowish and thick, the excrements of their bowels reddish and firm, their pulse great and full. They dream usually of red things and merry conceits.

    As for their conditions, they are merry, cheerful creatures, bountiful, pitiful, merciful, courteous, bold, trusty, given much to the games of Venus, as though they had been an apprentice seven years to the trade. A little thing will make them weep, but so soon as 'tis over, no further grief sticks to their hearts.

Choleric
We call that man choleric in whose body heat and dryness abounds or is predominate. Such persons are usually short of stature, and not fat, it may be because the heat and dryness of their bodies consumes radical moisture, their skin rough and hot in feeling, and their bodies very hairy. The hair of their heads is yellowish, red or flaxen for the most part, and curls much, the colour of their face is tawny or sunburnt. They have some beards. They have little hazel eyes. Their concoction is very strong insomuch that they are able to digest more than they appetite. Their pulse is swift and strong, their urine yellow and thin. They are usually costive. They dream of fighting, quarrelling, fire and burning.

    As for Conditions they are naturally quick-witted, bold, no way shame-faced, furious, hasty, quarrelsome, fraudulent, eloquent, courageous, stout-hearted creatures, not given to sleep much, but much given to jesting, mocking and lying.

Melancholic
A melancholy person is one [in] whose body cold and dryness is predominate, and not such a one as is sad sometimes as the vulgar dream. They are usually slender and not very tall, of swarthy dusky colour, rough skin, cold and hard in feeling. They have very little hair on their bodies and are long without beards, and sometimes they are beardless with age. The hair of their heads is dusky brown usually, and

sometimes dusky flaxen. Their appetite is far better than their concoction usually, by reason the appetite is causes of a sour vapor sent up by the spleen, which is the seat of melancholy, to the stomach. Their urine is pale, their dung of a clavish colour and broken, their pulse slow, they dream of frightful things, black, darkish, and terrible businesses.

They are naturally covetous, self-lovers, cowards, afraid of their own shadows, fearful, careful, solitary, lumpish, unsociable, delighting to be alone, stubborn, ambitious, envious, of a deep cogitation, obstinate in opinion, mistrustful, suspicious, spiteful, squeamish, and yet slovenly. They retain anger long, and aim at no small things.

Phlegmatic
Such people in whom coldness with moisture abounds are called phlegmatick, yet are usually not very tall, but very fat. Some you shall find almost as thick as they are long, their veins and arteries are small, their bodies without hair, and they have but little beards. Their hair is usually flaxen or light brown, their face white and pale, their skin smooth, cold and moist in touching. Both appetite and digestion is very weak in them, their pulse little and low, their urine pale and thick, but the excrements of their bowels usually thin. They dream of great rains, water and drowning.

As for Conditions, they are very dull, heavy and slothful, like the scholar that was a great while a-learning a lesson, but when *once* he had it – he had quickly forgotten it. They are drowsy, sleepy, cowardly, forgetful creatures, as swift in motion as a snail, they travail (and that's but seldom) as though they intended to go 15 miles in 14 days. Yet they are shamefaced and sober.

* These descriptions may also be found in Graeme Tobyn, *Culpeper's Medicine*, pp. 52-56.

Appendix E
Poems on Temperament
(from the Regimen of Health, English version by John Harington, 1607)
(Quoted in Graeme Tobyn, *Culpeper's Medicine* pp. 52-6)

The Sanguine

Complexions cannot virtue breed or vice
Yet may they unto both give inclination.
The sanguine gamesome is and nothing nice,
Loves wine and women and all recreation,
Likes pleasant tales and news, plays, cards and dice,
Fit for all company and every fashion.
Though bold, not apt to take offence, not ireful
But bountiful and kind and looking cheerful.
Inclining to be fat and prone to laughter,
Loves mirth and music, cares not what comes after.

The Melancholic

The melancholy from the rest do vary,
Both sport and ease and company refusing.
Exceeding studious, ever solitary,
Inclining pensive still to be, and musing,
A secret hate to others apt to carry.
Most constant in his choice, tho' long a-choosing,
Extreme in love sometime, yet seldom lustful,
Suspicious in his nature and mistrustful.
A wary wit, a hand much given to sparing,
A heavy look, a spirit little daring.

The Choleric

Sharp choler is a humour most pernicious,
All violent and fierce and full of fire,
Of quick conceit and therewithall ambitious,
Their thoughts to greater fortunes still aspire.
Proud, bountiful enough, yet oft malicious,
A right bold speaker and as bold a liar.
On little cause to anger great inclin'd,
Much eating still, yet ever looking pin'd.
In younger years they use to grow apace,
In elder hairy on their breast and face.

The Phlegmatic

The phlegmatic are most of no great growth,
Inclining to be rather fat and square.
Given much unto their ease, to rest and sloth,
Content in knowledge to take little share,
To put themselves to any pain most loath.
So dead their spirits, so dull their senses are,
Still neither fitting, like to folk to dream,
Or else still spitting, to avoid the phlegm.
One quality doth yet these harms repair
That for the most part Phlegmatics are fair.

Appendix F
Culpeper's Compound Temperaments
From *Galen's Art of Physick*, Chapter 59, pp. 58-67

Choleric/Melancholic

It is a thing very difficult if not impossible to find a man in whom two Complexions are equally predominant, but one will more or less excel, therefore where Choler exceeds in chief, and next that Melancholy, that man I call Choleric-Melancholy.

They are higher of Stature than such as are simply Choleric, by reason their radical moisture is more prevalent, yet have they little lean Bodies, rough and hard Skin, meanly hairy, and but meanly neither, pretty temperate in feeling in respect of Heat, swarthy colour, their Hair of their Head is of a Chestnut colour or light brown, their digestion is meanly strong, their Pulse meanly strong, yet something slow, their Urine of a pale yellow and thin, their Excrements yellow and hard, they dream of falling from high places, Robberies, Murders, Hurts proceeding from fire, fighting or anger.

Such people by natural inclination are very quick Witted, excellent Students, yet will they begin many businesses ere they finish one, they are bold, furious, quarrelsome, something fraudulent, prodigal and eloquent. They are not so unconstant and scornful as Choleric men are, but more suspicious, and fretful, more solitary and studious after Curiosities, and retain their anger longer than Choleric men do.

Melancholic/Choleric

Such are usually tall of stature, yet are their Bodies somewhat slender and dry, their Skin rough, hard and cold in feeling, they have but very little Hair on their Bodies, and are long without Beards. They have also much superfluities at the Nose, the Face of a dark pale colour, their Hair usually of a blackish brown colour, their digestion weak and something less than their Appetite, their Pulse slow, their Urine subcitrine and, thin, their egestion sallow coloured and something thin; dreamings are of falling down from high places, vain idle and fearful things.

As for conditons they are very gentle and sober, willing to do good, admirable students, delighting to be alone, very shamefaced and bashful, somewhat fretful, constant to their Friends, and true in all their actions.

Melancholic/Sanguine

They are tall of stature, and have big, fleshy, firm, strong bodies. The colour of their Face of a darkish red, their Skin neither hard nor rough, and as little cold, but temperate in respect of softness and warmness. Their Bodies are not usually very hairy, yet have they soon Beards, their digestion is good and laudable, their Urine of a light Saffron colour, mean in substance, neither too thick nor too thin, the egestion or Excrements of the Belly reddish and soft, their dreams are pleasant, and many times happen truly to come to pass.

They are more liberal, bolder and merrier than Melancholy persons are, as also less cowardly, not so pensive nor solitary, neither are they troubled with such fearful conceits, but are gentle, sober, patient, trusty, affable, courteous, studious to do others good.

Sanguine/Melancholic

They are mean of Stature, but strong well compact Bodies, fleshy but not fat, big Veins and Arteries, smooth warm Skin, something hairy but not so hairy as Sanguine people have. Their Hair is either black or a very black brown, their Cheeks red, something clouded with duskiness, their Pulses great and full, the Urine yellow and mean in respect of thickness and thinness, their digestion good, the Excrements of their Bellies reddish and something thin, they usually dream of deep Pits and Wells and sometimes of flying in the Air.

Their Conditions are much like to the Conditions of a Sanguine Man, but that they are not altogether so merry nor so liberal, a spice of a Melancholy temper being inherent in them.

Sanguine/Phlegmatic

They are higher of Stature than Sanguine, with strong well set Bodies, not very fat, their Hair is flaxen or very light brown, their Face is of a paler red, than Sanguine peoples is, neither are their Bodies so hairy. Their Pulse is Moderate, their Appetite good, their Digestion indifferent; their Urine subcitrine and mean in substance, their egestion white in some places and red in others, they dream of flying in the Air, Rain and Waters.

As for Conditions they are less liberal and not so much addicted to the Sports of Venus as Sanguine are, neither are their Spirits so bold, nor their Bodies so hairy.

Phlegmatic/Sanguine

Phlegmatic-Sanguine people are but mean of stature, somewhat gross and fat of Body, smooth soft Skin, and somewhat cold in touching. They have but few hairs upon their Bodies and are long without Beards, their hair is light yellow, light brown or flaxen, no ways curling, their colour whitely, with some very small redness, if any; their digestion is somewhat weak and less than their Appetites, their Pulse small and low, their Urine somewhat thick and palish, they sometimes dream of falling down from some high place into the water.

Their Conditions are so-so, between Phlegmatic and Sanguine, neither very liberal nor very covetous, neither very idle nor much imployed, neither very merry not very sad; rather fearful of the two than valiant.

Phlegmatic/Choleric

Such are tall of stature but not too big, nor yet so fat as Phlegmatic, their Bodies are something hairy and they pretty soon have Beards, they have usually Hair of a Chestnut colour, not curling, and soft, their Faces of a tawny red, full of Freckles, their Appetite and Digestion is indifferent, as being pretty well met; a moderate and pretty full Pulse, their Urine subcitrine and mean in respect of thickness, the Excrements of their Belly a pale yellow and thick. They usually dream of swimming in the Water, Snow and Rain.

They are not such drowsy, lazy, sleepy Creatures as Phlegmatic folks are, but are nimbler, bolder, and kinder, merrier and quicker witted.

Choleric/Phlegmatic
Such are mean of stature, but stout lusty strong Bodies, strong Bones, well set Creatures, neither fat nor lean, but in the respect they keep the Golden Mean, they have lusty great Bones, their Skin is hairy and moderate to feeling in respect of heat and moisture, their Hair is yellowish or sandy flaxen, and their Face of a tawnyish yellow colour, their Digestion is good, their Pulse swift, their Urine thin and of the colour of Saffron, their egestion yellow and hard. They dream of fighting, Lightning and Rain, hot Baths and hot Waters.

Their Conditions are not much different from those of Choleric men, only the Vices of Choler is moderated by Phlegm, therefore a Choleric-Phlegmatic man is nothing so vicious as one purely Choleric; neither doth any Humour set a stop to the unbridled passions of Choler, so as Phlegm doth, because 'tis so contrary to it, judge the like by the rest.

Appendix G:
Roy Wilkinson's Temperament Charts

(From *The Temperaments in Education* by Roy Wilkinson, pp. 38-41. Reprinted by kind permission of the Rudolf Steiner College Press, 9200 Fair Oaks Boulevard, Fair Oaks, CA 95628 USA.)

How to Recognize the Temperaments

	CHOLERIC	SANGUINE	PHLEGMATIC	MELANCHOLIC
Physical appearance	Short, stocky, bull necked, upright	Slender, elegant, well-balanced	Big, fleshy, rotund	Large, bony, heavy-limbed with bowed head
Walk	Firm, digging heels in ground	Light, tripping on the toes	Rolling, ambling (steam-roller)	Slow with drooping, sliding gait
Eyes	Energetic, active	Dancing, lively	Sleepy, often half-closed	Tragic, mournful
Gestures	Short, abrupt	Graceful, lively	Slow, deliberate	Drooping
Manner of speaking	Sharp, emphatic, deliberate, to the point	Eloquent, with flowery language	Ponderous, logical, clear	Hesitating, halting, not competing sentences
Relationships	Friendly as long as recognized leader	Friendly to all, changeable, fickle	Friendly but reserved, impassive	Poor, has sympathy only with fellow sufferers
Habits	Must jolly everyone else along	Is flexible, has no fixed habits	Likes routine, has set habits	Likes solitary occupations
Food	Enjoys spicy foods, well-prepared	Nibbles, likes nicely prepared things	Eats good square meals of anything	Is finicky. Likes sweet things
Dress	Likes something individual and outstanding	Likes anything new and colorful	Has a conservative taste	Chooses drab clothes, is difficult to please
Powers of observation	Observes what is of interest but forgets	Notices everything and forgets everything	Observes and remembers exactly when sufficiently awake	Observes little but remembers it
Memory	Poor	Like a sieve	Good concerning the world	Good concerning self
Interests	The world, self and the future	The immediate present	The present without getting involved	Self and the past
Attitudes	Commanding, aggressive, eventually understanding	Kind, understanding, sympathetic	Discerning, objective	Egoistical, vindictive, self-sacrificing in cases of suffering
Disposition	Boasting, enthusiastic, generous, intolerant, impatient, gambling	Changeable, superficial, unreliable, kind, impatient, friendly	Faithful, stable, methodical, lethargic, self-contented, trustworthy, motherly	Self-absorbed, easily depressed, fearful, moody, tyrannical, helpful, artistic
Paintings and drawings (childrens')	Volcanoes, precipices with self overcoming obstacles, strong colors	Lots of bright colors, movement and detail	Bland, uninteresting, unfinished in appearance	Strong harmonious colors; attempts too much detail

Reactions of Children to various situations according to Temperament

	CHOLERIC	SANGUINE	PHLEGMATIC	MELANCHOLIC
Fall in the playground	Finds the reason outside himself. Blames somebody. Proud of his injuries.	Asks, "Did I fall?" Cries for a moment and forgets.	Is a Stoic. Gets up and continues unperturbed.	Endures unbearable suffering. The world is at an end. It was intentionally caused to hurt me.
Cancelled outing	Masters the situation by calling a meeting of protest	Enjoys the novelty and thinks of alternatives	Indifferent. Will not forget but is not vindictive	Knew all the time it would be cancelled. It was done on purpose to hurt.
New Teacher	Possible rival. Must introduce new teacher to class. Will either help or hinder	Somebody new. Enjoys the situation.	Realizes after several weeks that there is a new teacher and stops calling him by the name of the old one.	New enemy. Was just getting used to the old one. More suffering
A task to complete	Rushes at it and gets it done	Finds it easy and interesting but gives up easily when novelty wears off	Considers, contemplates, plans and has difficulty in finishing in limited time	Another burden in life to bear

The Golden Rules for treating Children according to Temperament

	CHOLERIC	SANGUINE	PHLEGMATIC	MELANCHOLIC
To stimulate activity	Issue a challenge	Ask a personal favor	Use shock tactics. Speak directly and to the point	Explain how others will suffer if non-compliant
If admonition is necessary	Recall the misdeed later and discuss	Have a friendly word immediately	Take immediate action	Point out at once the later consequences
General	Give stories or descriptions where rashness becomes dangerous or ridiculous. Give plenty of different things to do which present a challenge	Give lively stories and exciting descriptions with endless pictures and variations. Give plenty of different things to do	Give indifferent stories in an indifferent way. Give a set task and the advice to get on with it	Give stories or descriptions of sad events to show how the human spirit eventually triumphs. Enter into the sad moods and ask assistance for someone less capable
Teacher's attitude	Be firm, strong and to the point	Show friendly interest. Be firm	Show a calm strength	Show sympathy

Appendix H
Birthcharts of the Children used in the Waldorf Study

166 Temperament: Astrology's Forgotten Key

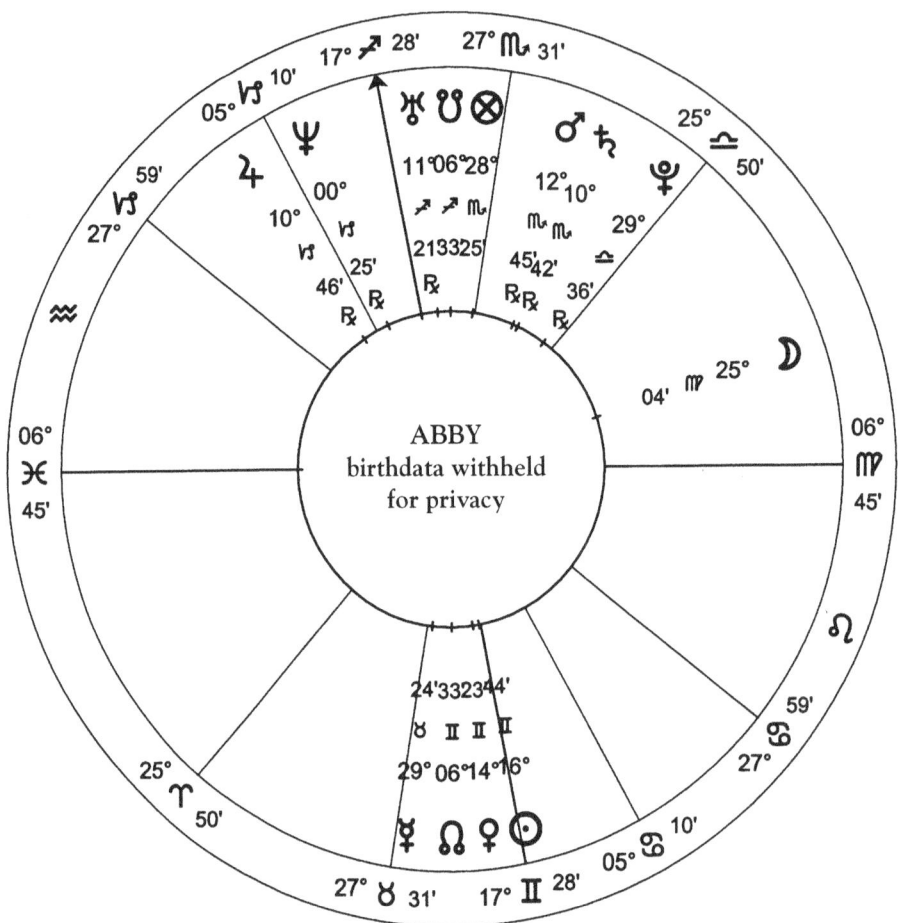

Appendices

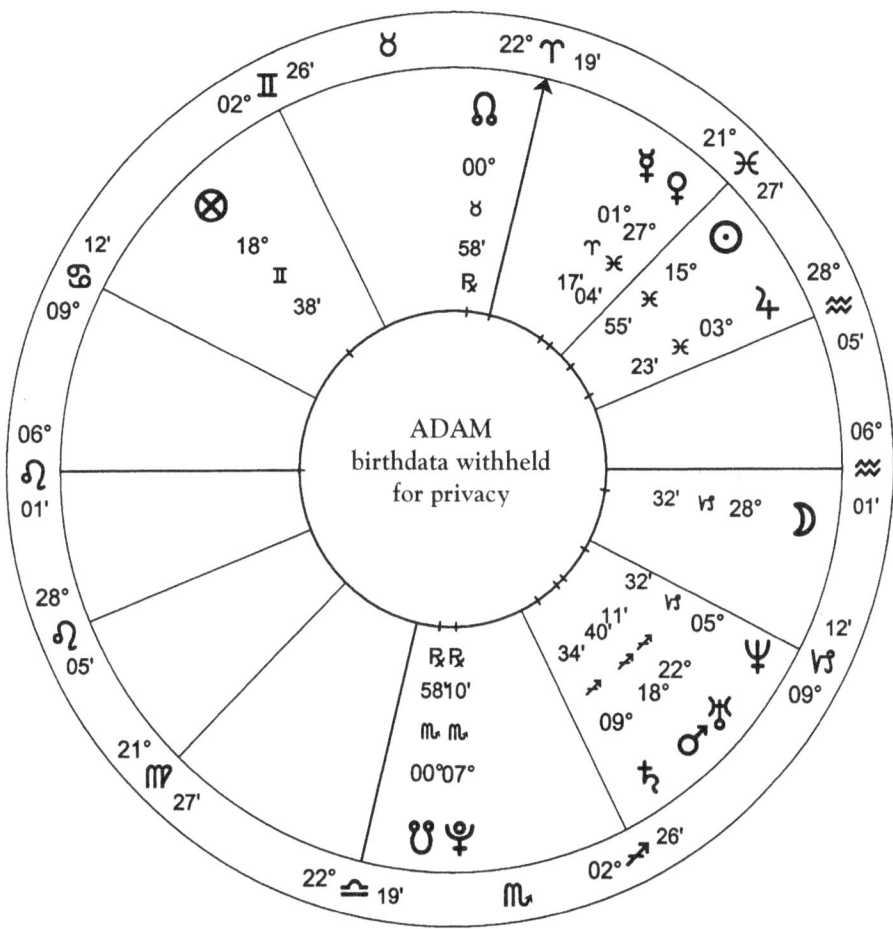

168 *Temperament: Astrology's Forgotten Key*

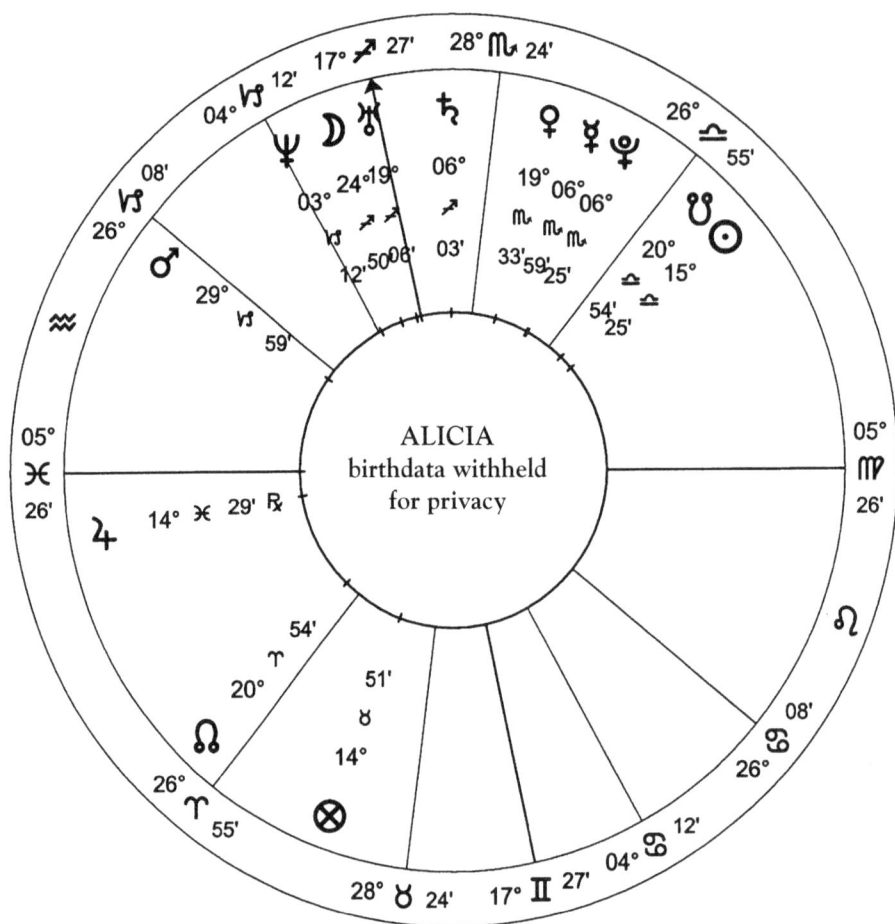

Appendices 169

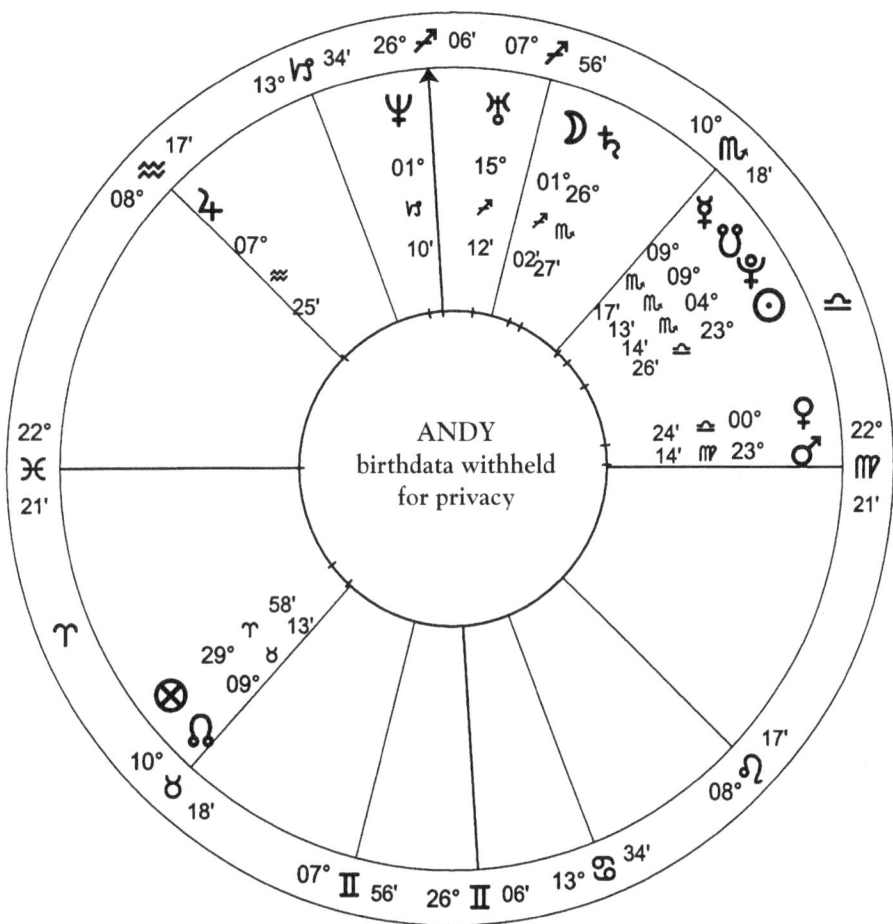

170 Temperament: Astrology's Forgotten Key

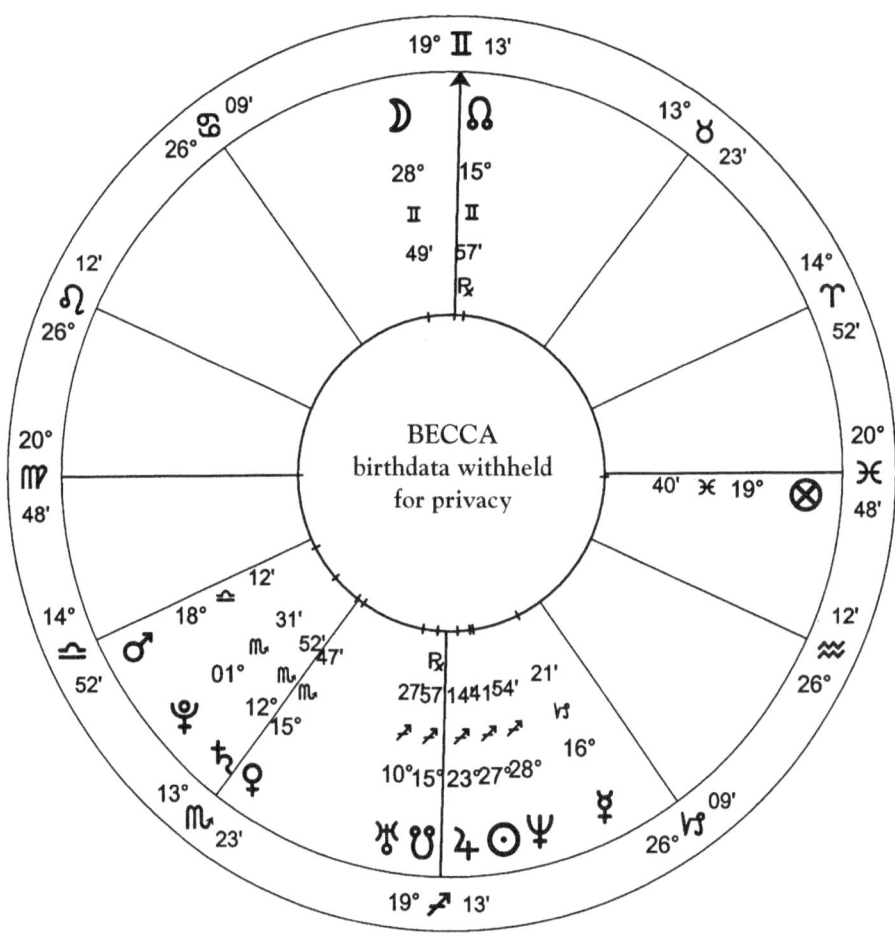

Appendices 171

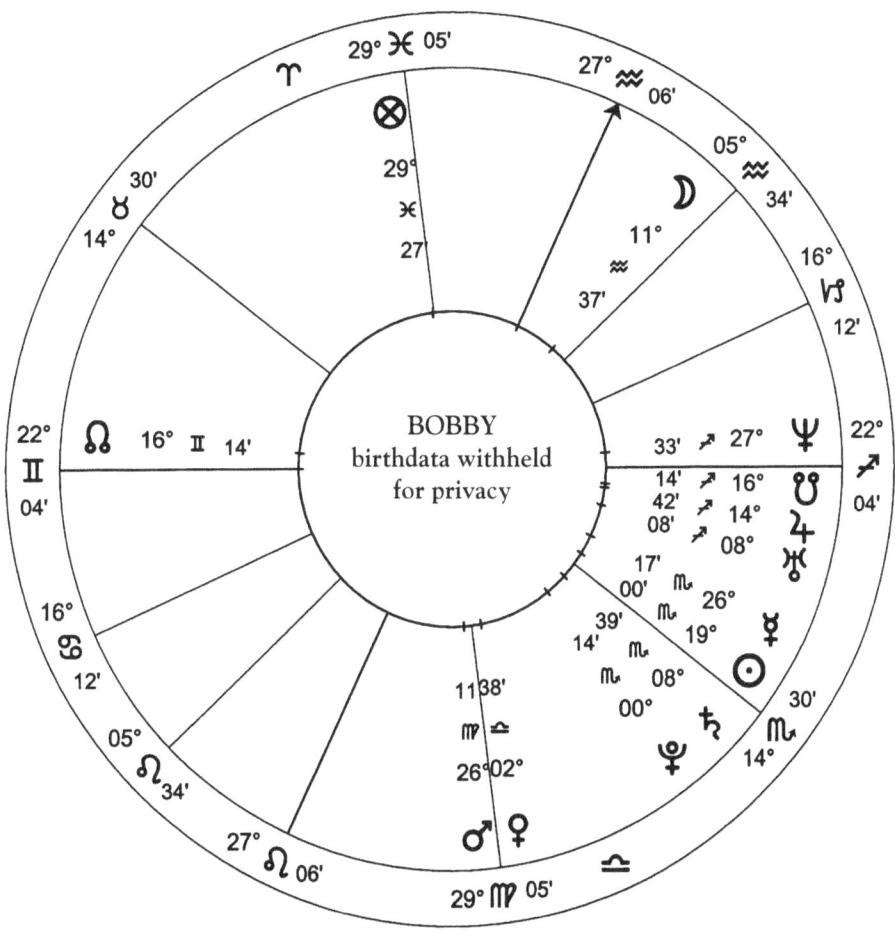

Hs	Alm.
1	☿
2	☽
3	☉
4	☉
5	☿
6	♂
7	♃
8	♂ ♄
9	♄
10	♄
11	♃
12	☽

Day of ♀ Hour of ☉
2nd Hour of Night
Last Hr ♂ −44 mins
Next Hr ♀ +26 mins

DIGNITY/ALMUTEN SCORES
Almuten of Chart (Ibn Ezra)

Planet	♂	♀	♃	♄	☿	☽	☉
Score	29	29	23	20	15	14	10

NEAREST LUNAR PHASES

1st Q	Oct 13 1983	2:42 pm	19° ♑ 54
Full	Oct 21 1983	4:53 pm	27° ♈ 56
3rd Q	Oct 28 1983	10:36 pm	05° ♌ 08
New	Nov 4 1983	5:21 pm	11° ♏ 56
1st Q	Nov 12 1983	10:49 am	19° ♒ 41

ESSENTIAL DIGNITIES

Pt	Ruler	Exalt	Trip	Term	Face	Detri	Fall	Score
☽	♄	—	☿	☿	☿	☉	—	+0 p
☉	♂	—	♂	♀	☉ +	♀	☽	+1
☿	♂ m	—	♂	☿ +	♀	☽	—	+2
♀	♀ +	♄	☿	♄	☽	♂	☉	+5
♂	☿ m	☿	☽	♂ +	☽	♀	—	+2
♃	♃ +	☋	♃ +	♃	☽	☿	☊	+8
♄	♂	—	♂	♃	♂	☽	♀	+0 p
♅	♂	—	♂	♀	♂	☿	☊	—
♆	♃	☋	♃	♂	♄	☿	☊	—
♇	♂	—	♂	♂	♀	☽	☊	—
☊	☿	☊	☿	♀	♂	♃	☋	—
☋	♃	☋	♃	☿	☽	☿	☊	—
As	☿	☊	☿	♄	☉	♃	☋	—
Mc	♄	—	☿	♂	☽	☉	—	—
⊗	♃	♀	♂	♄	♂	☿	—	—

172 *Temperament: Astrology's Forgotten Key*

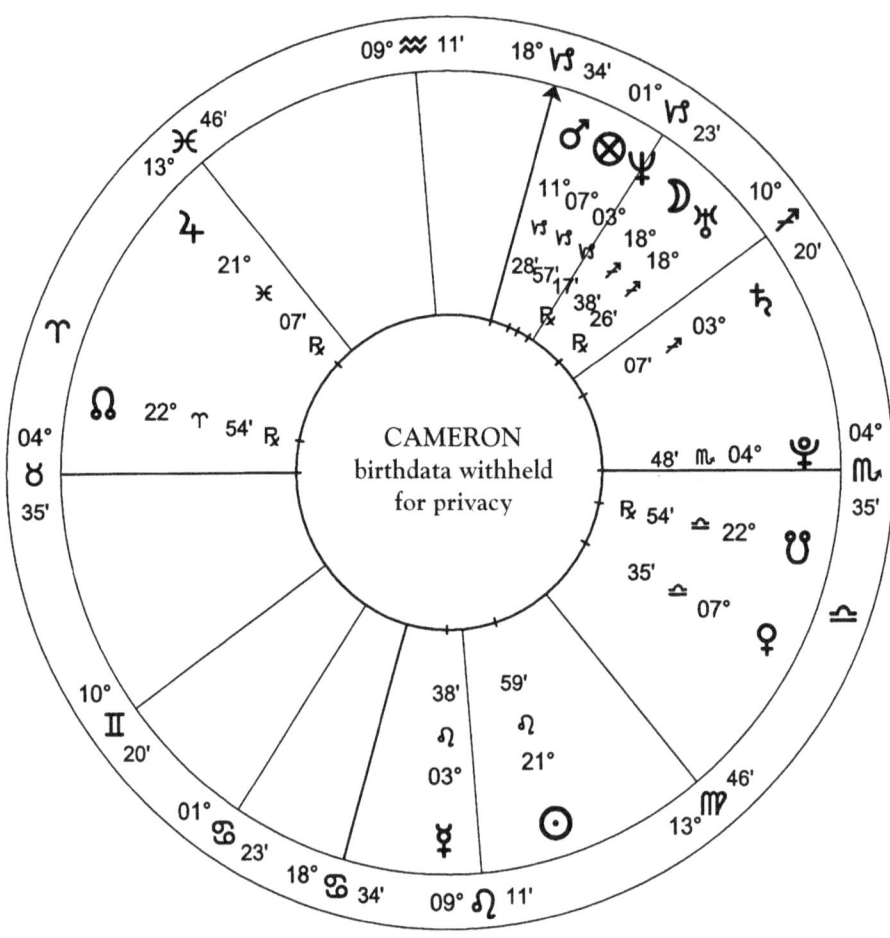

Appendices 173

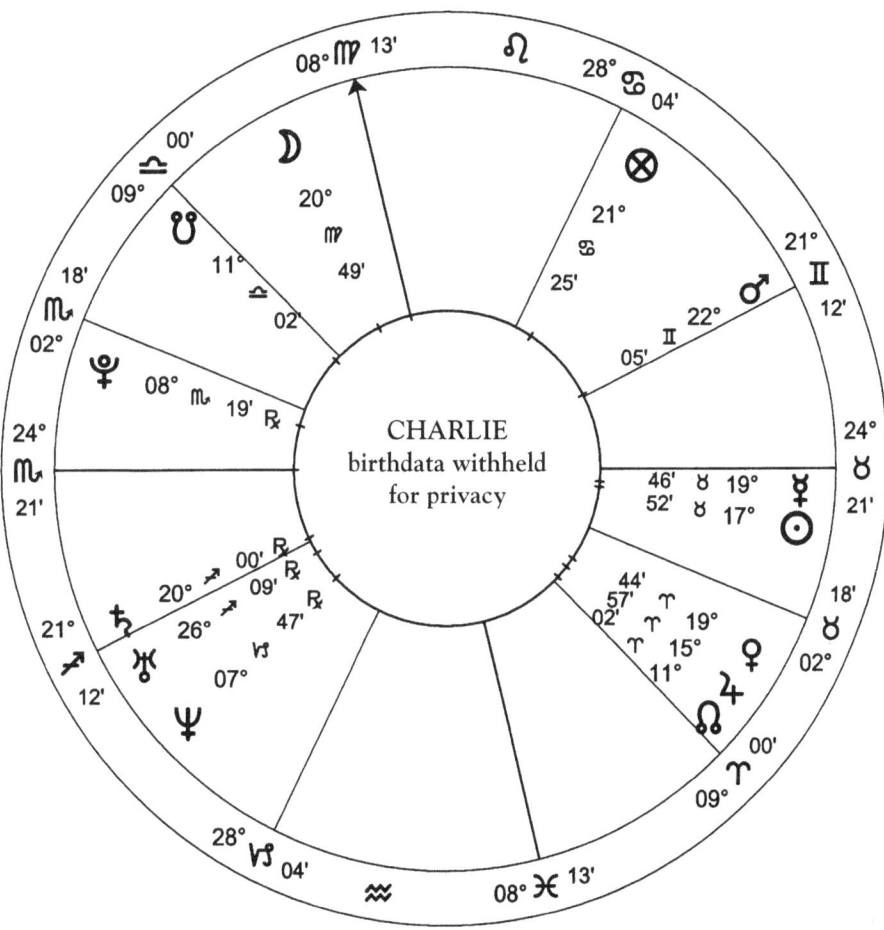

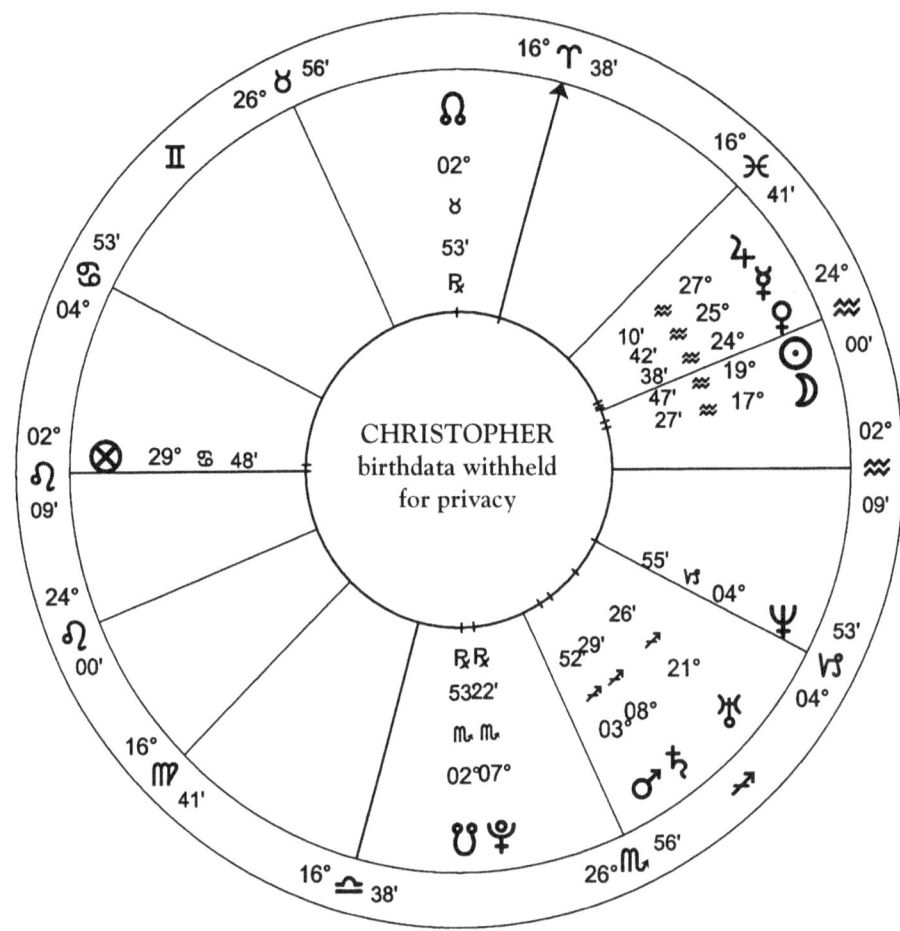

Appendices 175

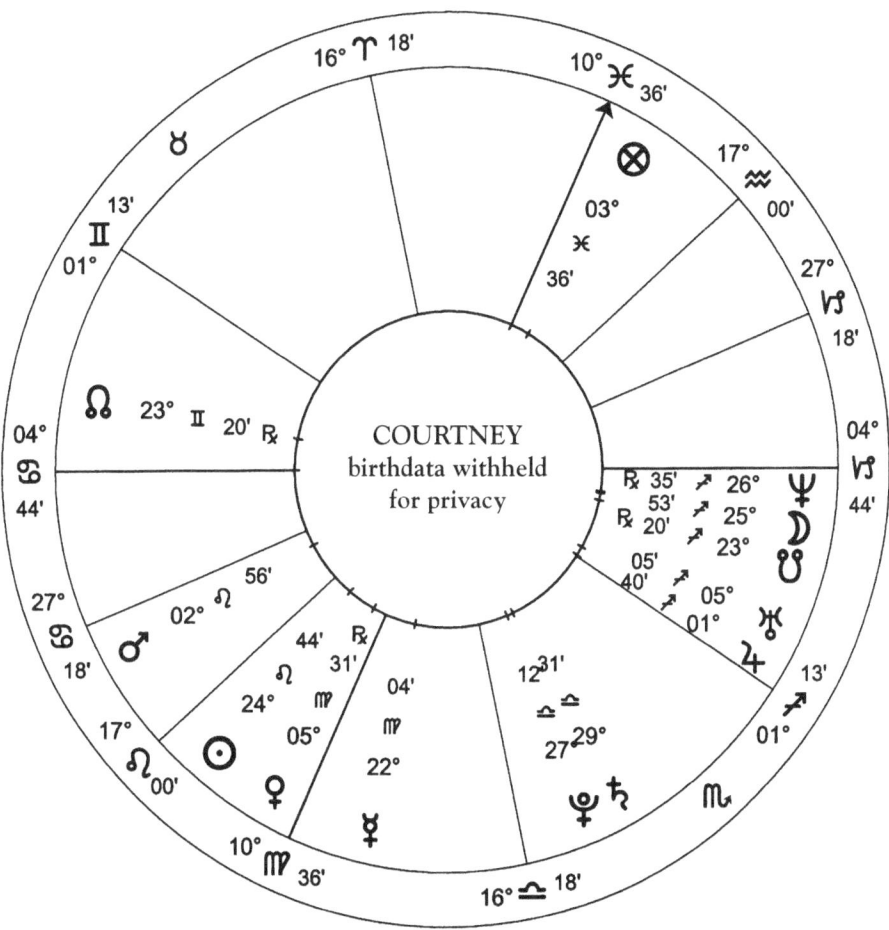

176 Temperament: Astrology's Forgotten Key

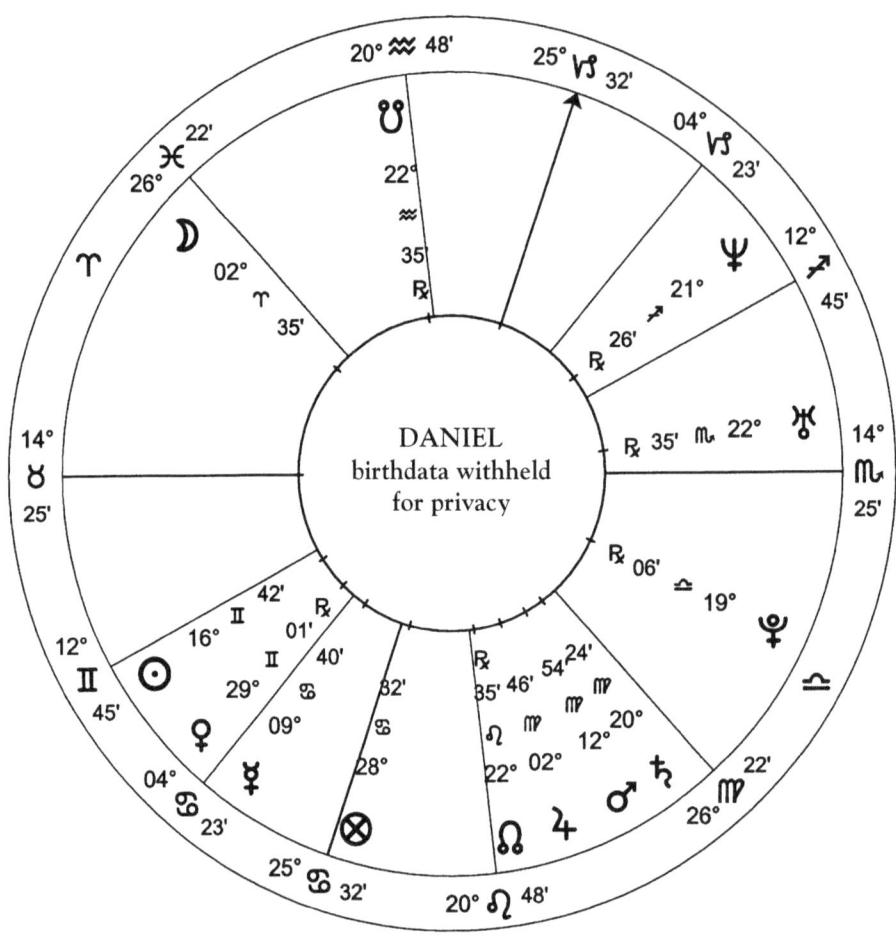

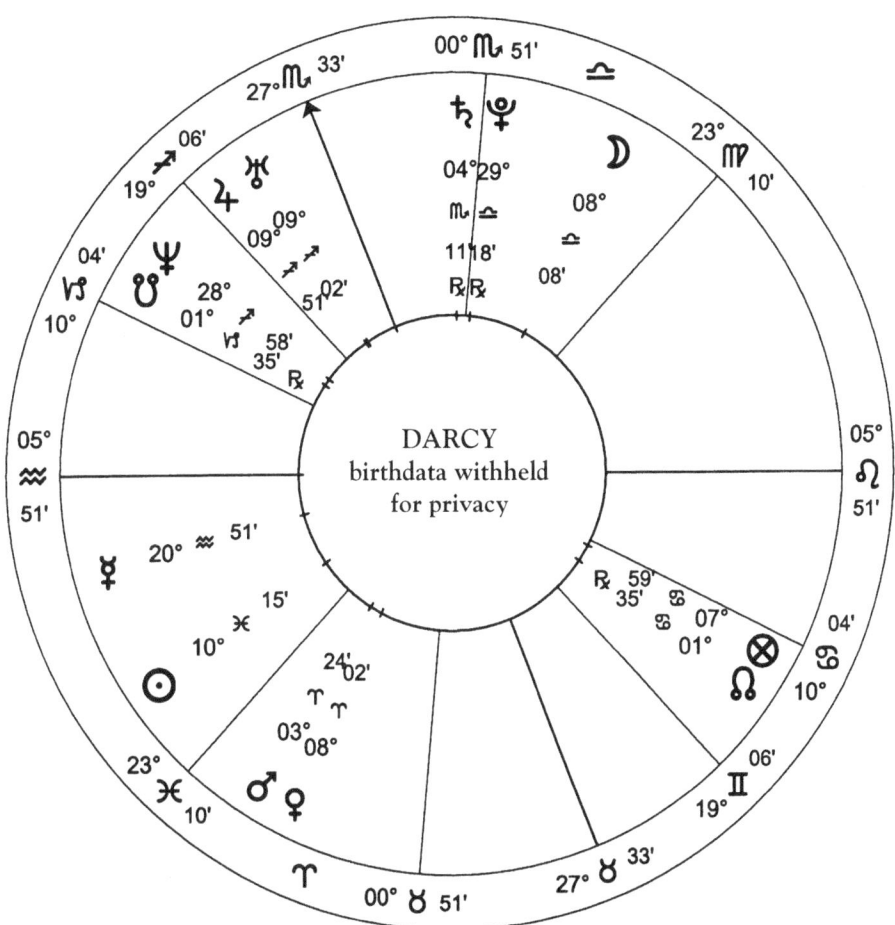

178 *Temperament: Astrology's Forgotten Key*

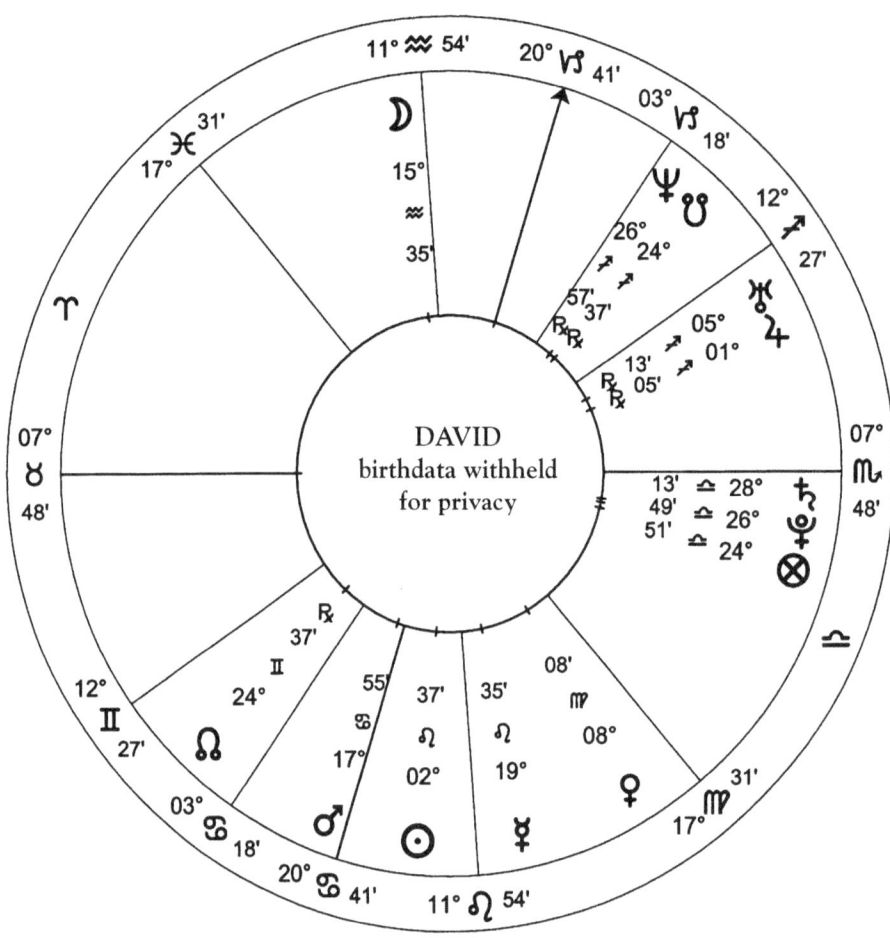

Appendices 179

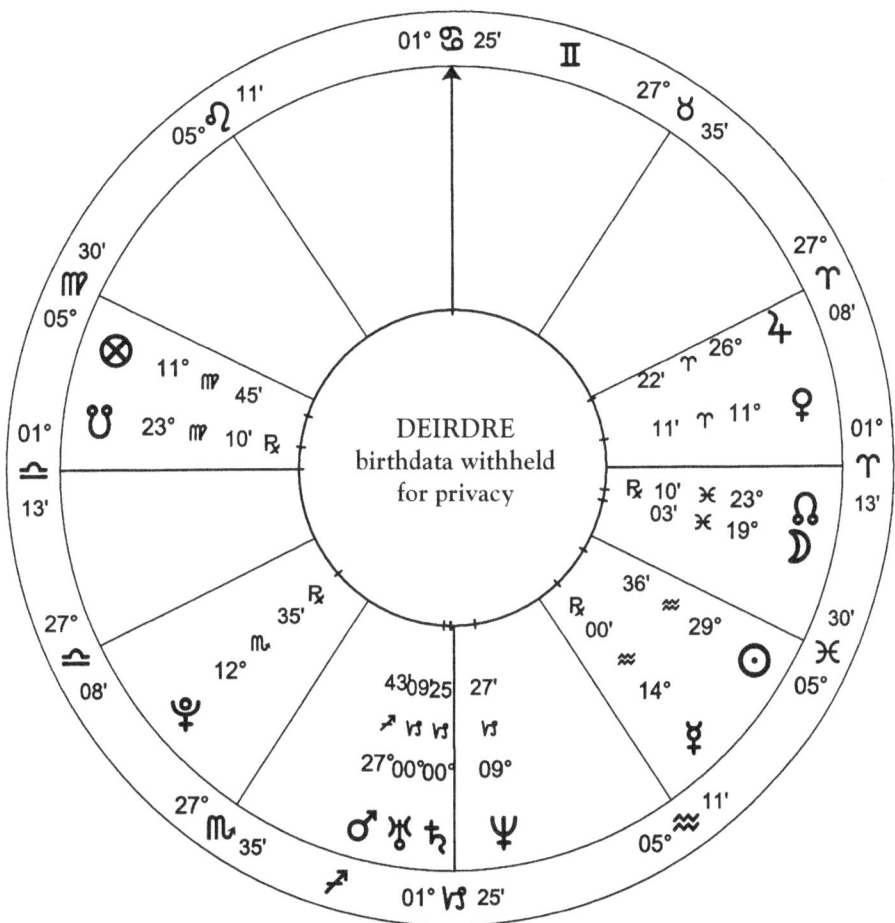

180 *Temperament: Astrology's Forgotten Key*

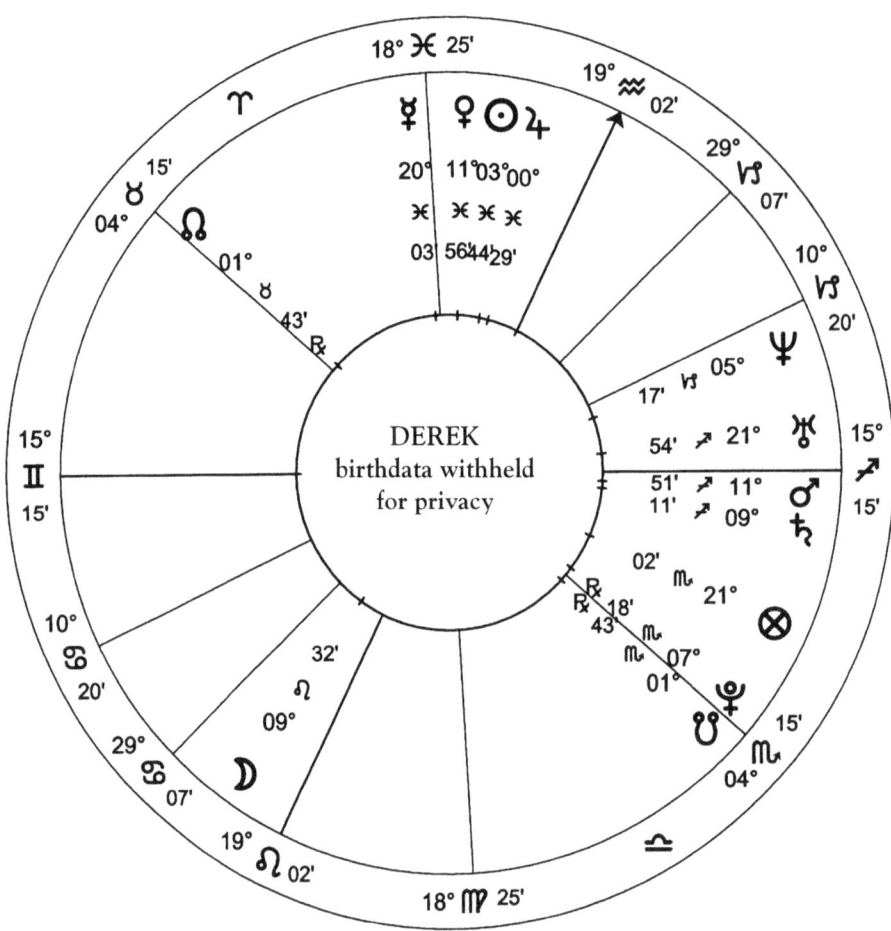

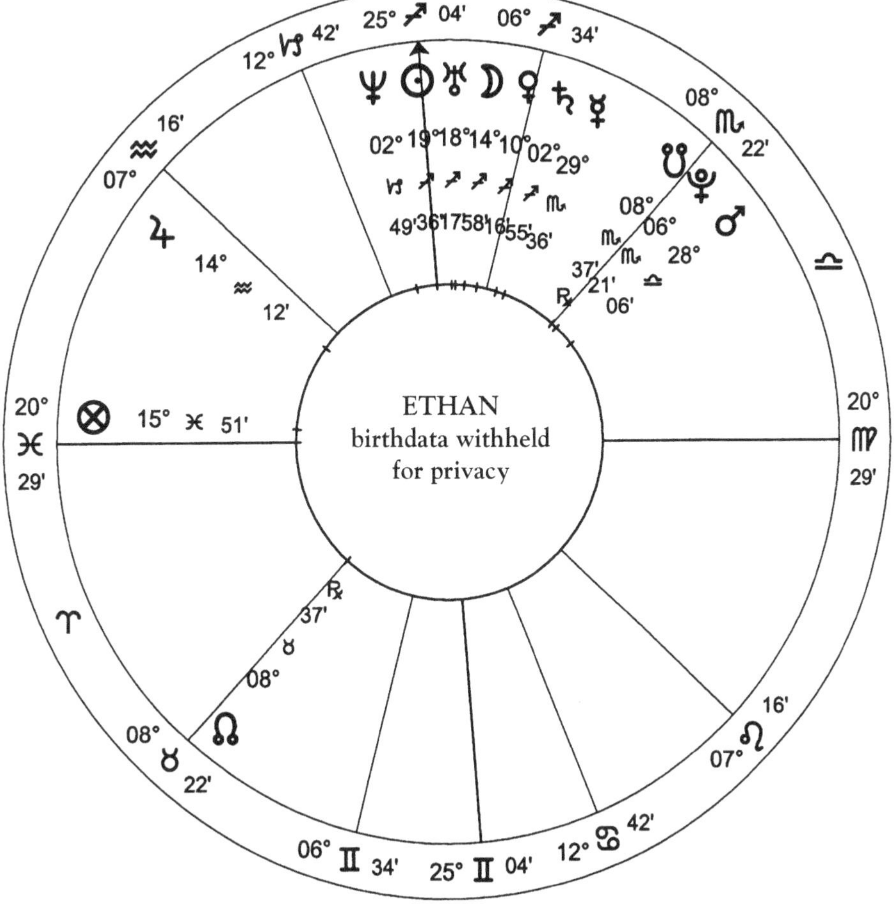

Hs	Alm.
1	♂
2	♀
3	☿
4	☿
5	♃
6	☉
7	☿
8	♂
9	♃
10	♃
11	♂ ♄
12	♄

Day of ☿ Hour of ♀
7th Hour of Day
Last Hr ☉ −24 mins
Next Hr ☿ +21 mins

DIGNITY/ALMUTEN SCORES							
Almuten of Chart (Ibn Ezra)							
Planet	♃	♀	☿	♂	☉	♄	☽
Score	35	27	23	19	17	13	13

NEAREST LUNAR PHASES				
New	Nov 12 1985	9:20 am	20° ♏ 09	☄
1st Q	Nov 19 1985	4:03 am	26° ♒ 59	
Full	Nov 27 1985	7:41 am	05° ♊ 13	
3rd Q	Dec 5 1985	4:01 am	13° ♍ 10	
New	Dec 11 1985	7:54 pm	19° ♐ 56	

ESSENTIAL DIGNITIES								
Pt	Ruler	Exalt	Trip	Term	Face	Detri	Fall	Score
☽	♃	☋	☉	☿	☽ +	☿	☊	+1
☉	♃	☋	☉ +	♄	☽	☿	☊	+3
☿	♂	--	♂	♄	♀	♀	☽	+0 p
♀	♃	☋	☉	♀ +	☽	☿	☊	+2
♂	♀	♄	♄	♂ +	♃	♂ −	☉	−3
♃	♄ m	--	♄	♀	☿	☉	--	+0 p
♄	♃ m	☋	☉	♃	☿	☿	☊	+0 p
♅	♃	☋	☉	☿	☽	☿	☊	--
♆	♄	♂	♀	♀	♃	☽	♃	--
♇	♂	--	♂	♃	♂	♀	☽	--
☊	♀	☽	♀	☿	☿	♂	--	--
☋	♂	--	♂	♃	♂	♀	☽	--
As	♃	♀	♂	♂	♂	☿	☿	--
Mc	♃	☋	☉	♂	♄	☿	☊	--
⊗	♃	♀	♂	☿	♃	☿	☿	--

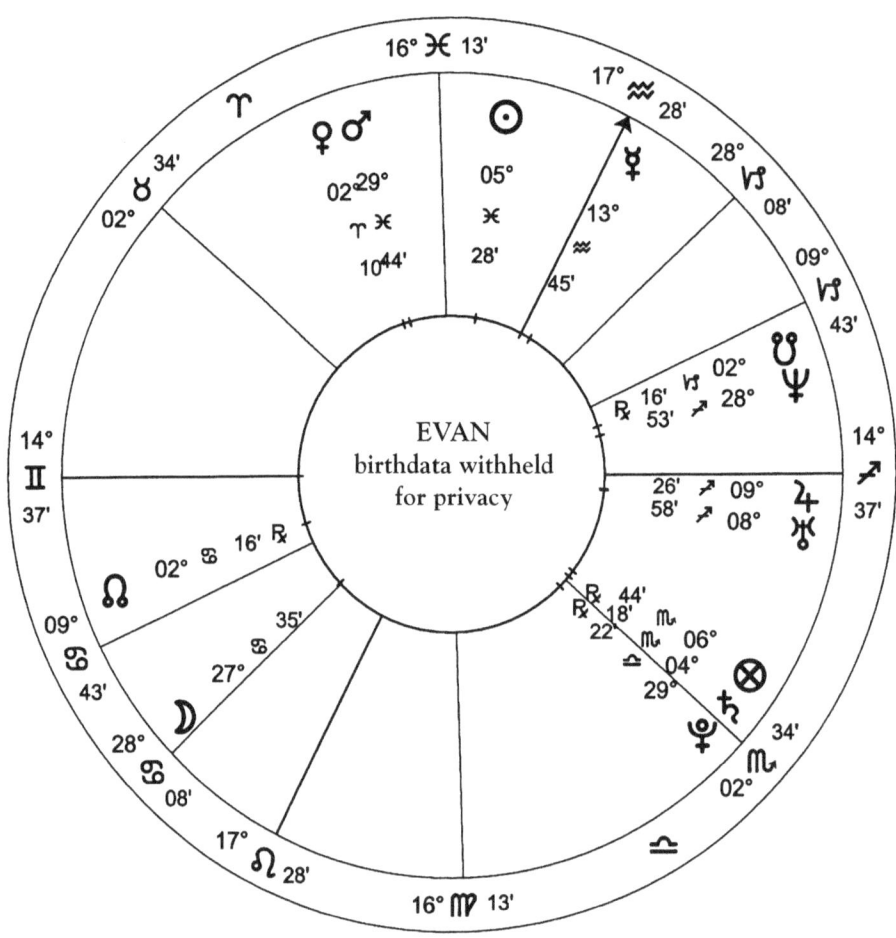

Appendices 183

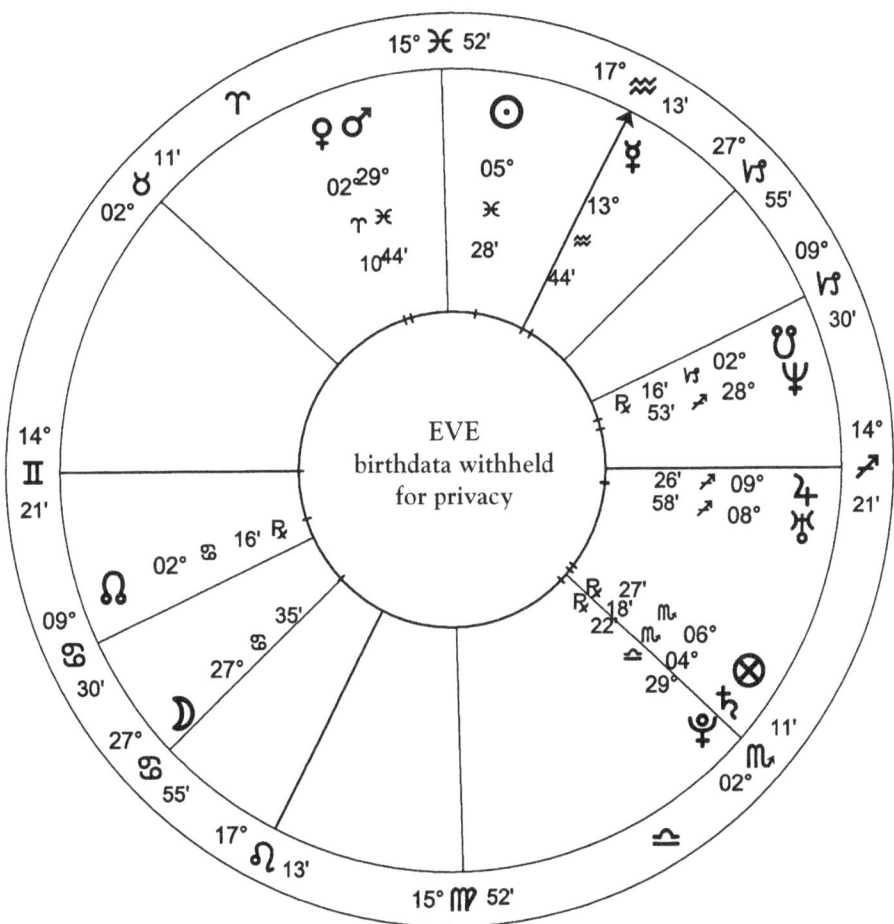

184 Temperament: Astrology's Forgotten Key

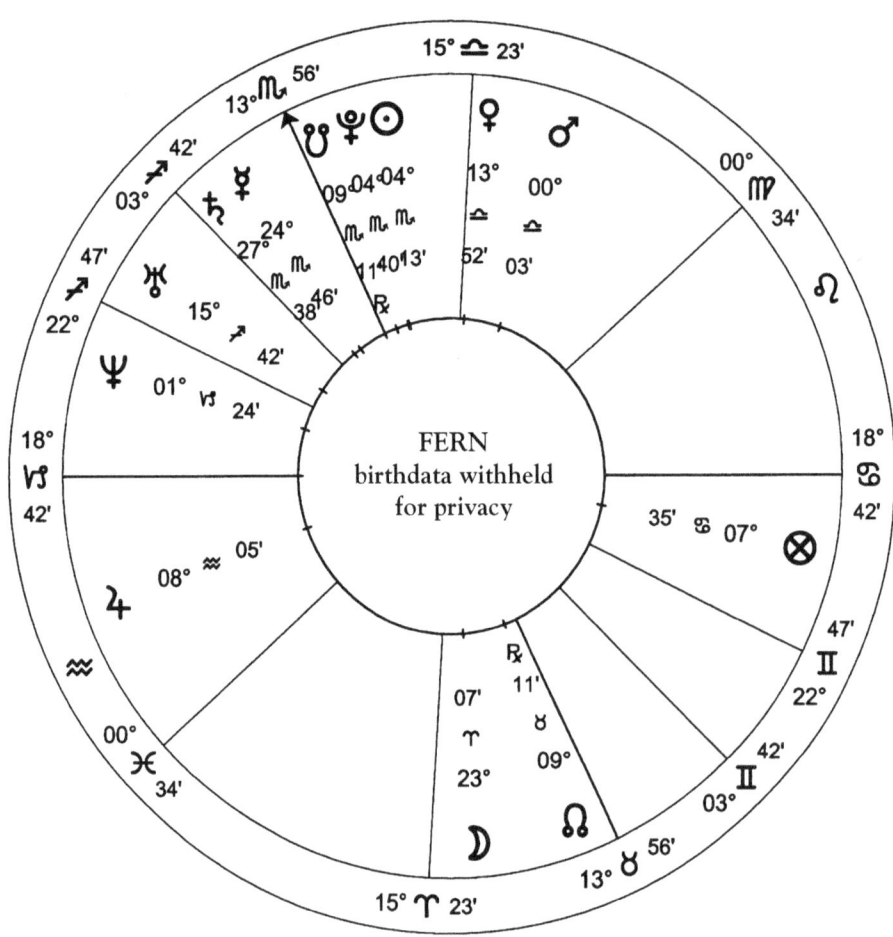

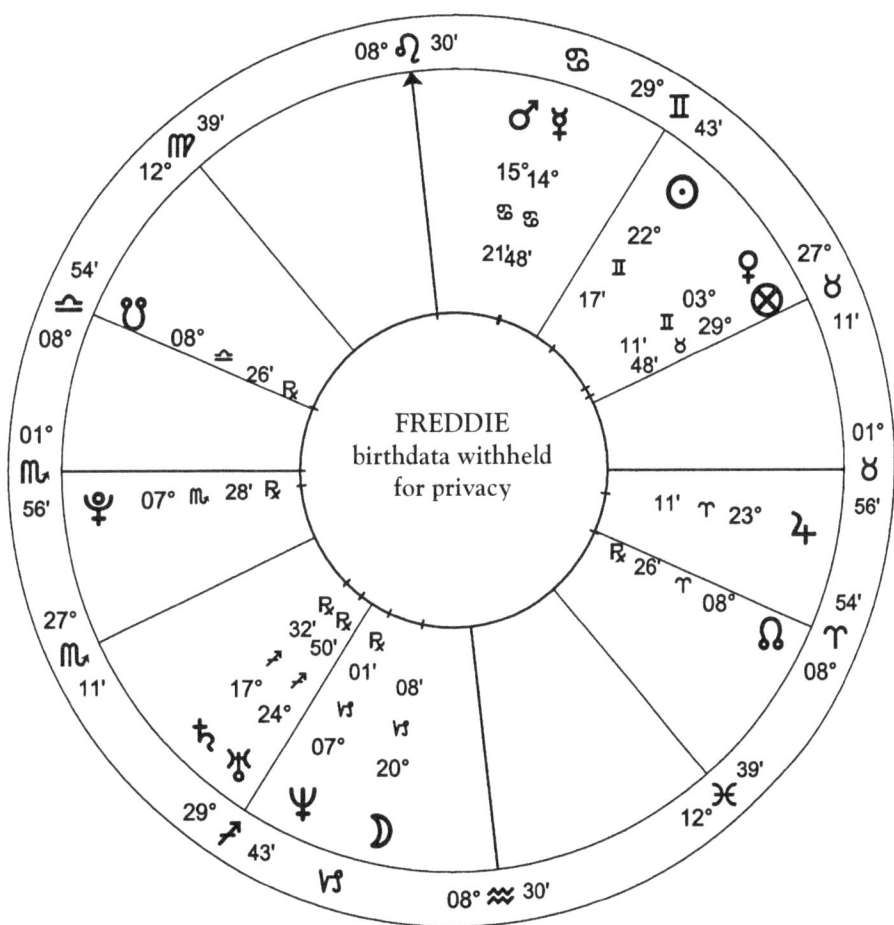

Hs	Alm.
1	♂
2	♂
3	♃
4	♄
5	♃
6	☉
7	♀
8	♀
9	☿
10	☉
11	☿
12	♀ ♄

Day of ♄ Hour of ♃
9th Hour of Day
Last Hr ♄ −47 mins
Next Hr ♂ +28 mins

DIGNITY/ALMUTEN SCORES
Almuten of Chart (Ibn Ezra)

Planet	♂	♄	♀	♃	☽	☿	☉
Score	30	26	20	18	16	15	9

NEAREST LUNAR PHASES

3rd Q	May 20 1987	0:02 am	28° ♒ 38
New	May 27 1987	11:13 am	05° ♊ 49
1st Q	Jun 4 1987	2:52 pm	13° ♍ 38
Full	Jun 11 1987	4:48 pm	20° ♐ 24
3rd Q	Jun 18 1987	7:02 am	26° ♓ 42

ESSENTIAL DIGNITIES

Pt	Ruler	Exalt	Trip	Term	Face	Detri	Fall	Score
☽	♄	♂	♀	♂	☉	☽ −	♃	−5 p
☉	☿	♌ m	♄ m	♄	☉ +	♃	♅	+1
☿	♀	☊	♃	☿ +	☿ +	♃	♂	+3
♀	♀	♄	♄	♃ m	♃	♂		+0 p
♂	☽	♃	♂ +	☿	☿	♄	♂ −	−1
♃	♂	☉	☉	♂	♀ m	♀		+0 p
♄	♃	♎	☉ m	☽	☿	☉	☊	+0 p
♅	♃	☊	☉	♄	♄	☿	☊	--
♆	♄	♂	♀	♃	♂	♀	☽	--
☊	♀	☽ m	♀	♀	☉	♂	♃	--
As	♂	--	♄	♀	♀	♀	☽	--
Mc	☉	--	☉	☿	♄	♄		--
⊗	♀	☽	♀	♂	♄	♂		--

186   *Temperament: Astrology's Forgotten Key*

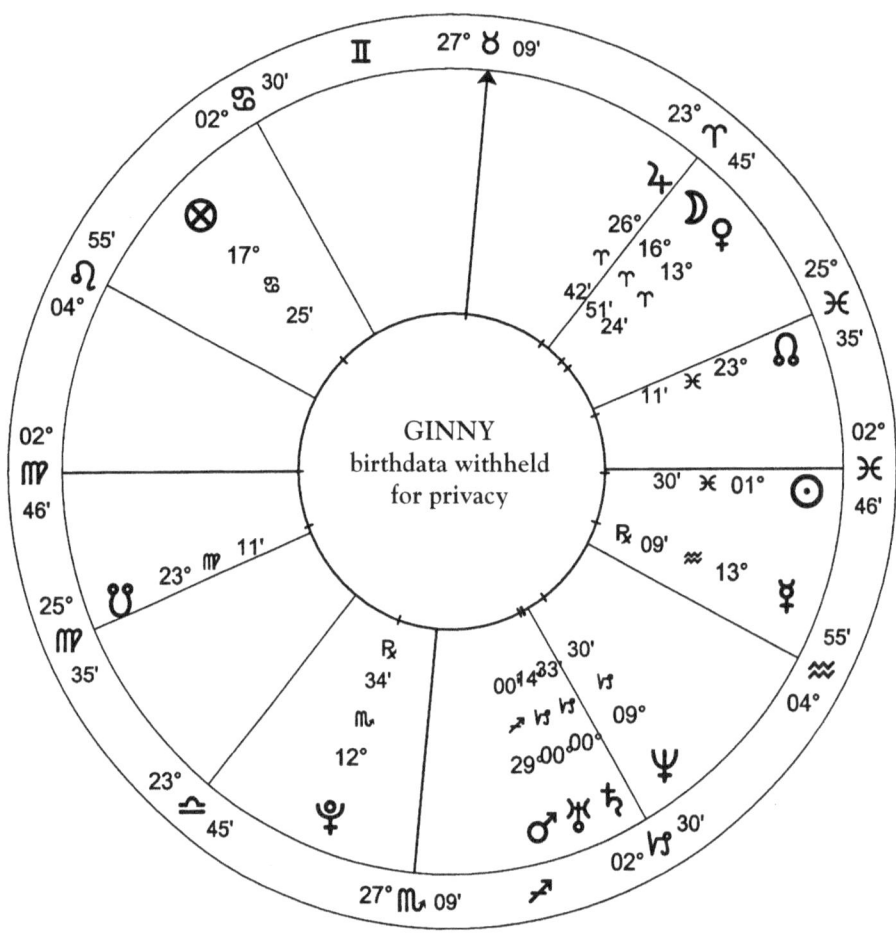

Appendices 187

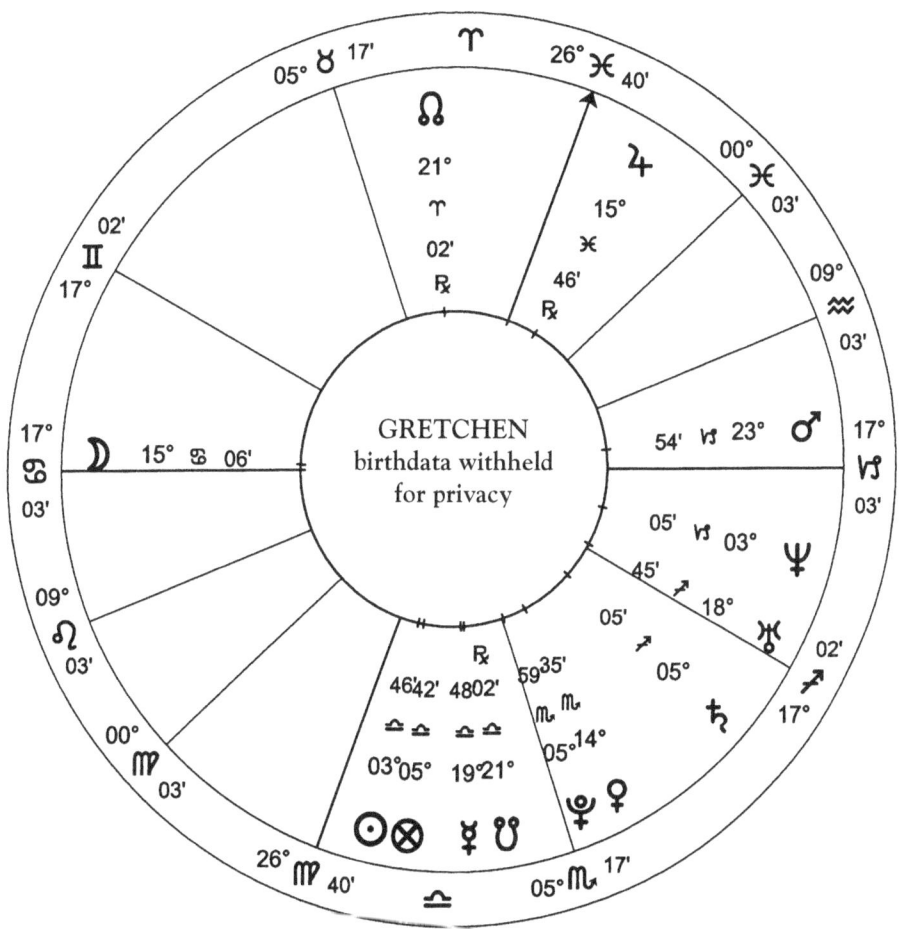

188 *Temperament: Astrology's Forgotten Key*

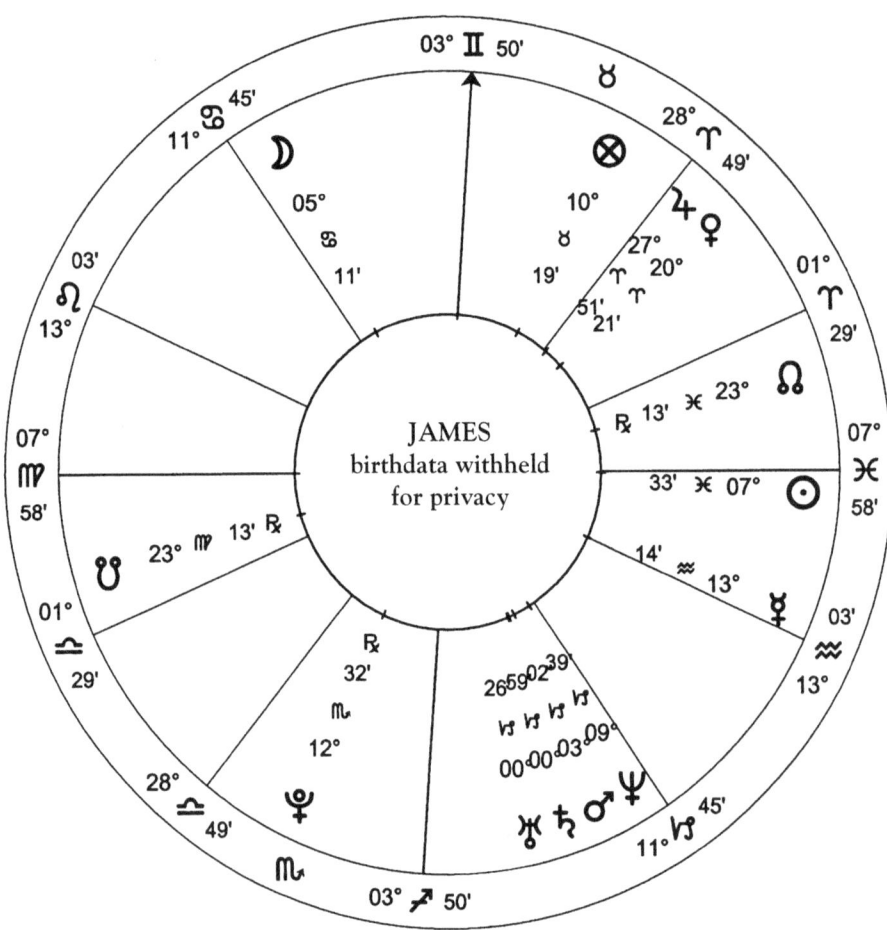

Appendices 189

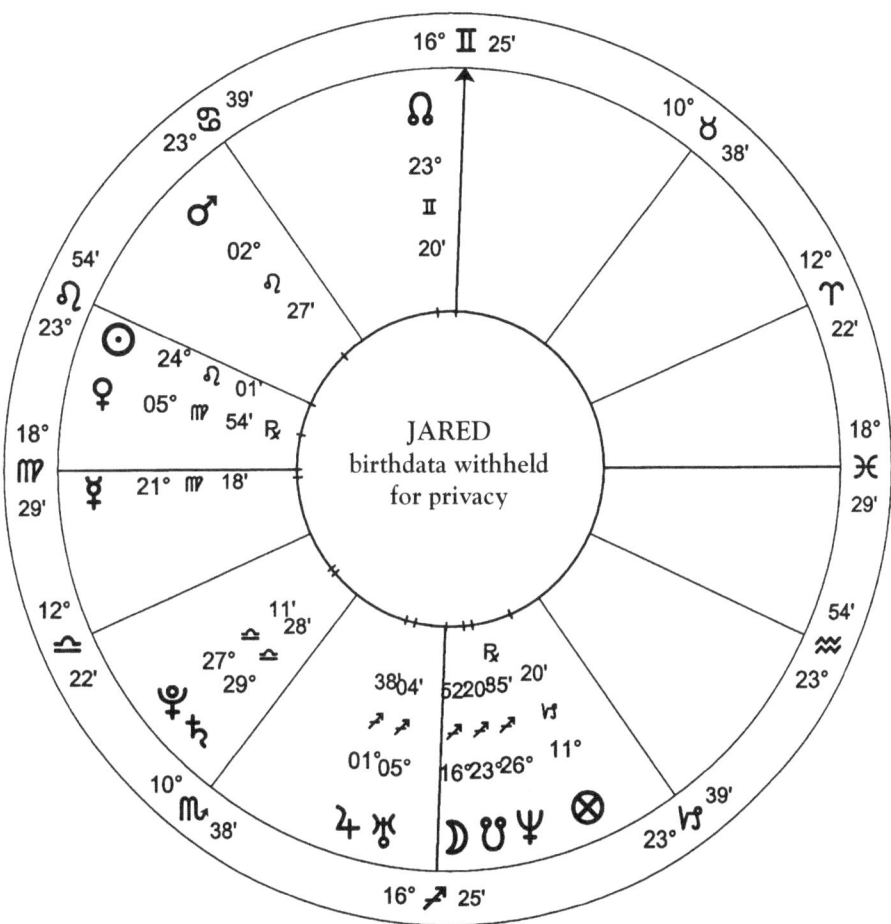

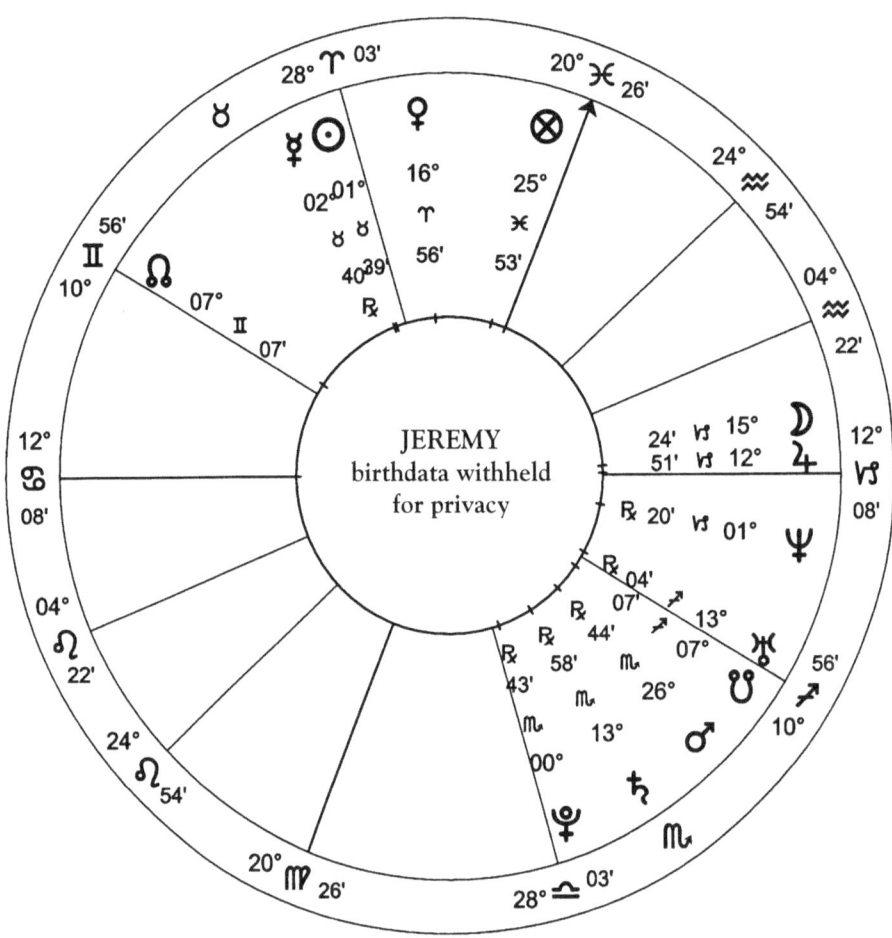

Appendices 191

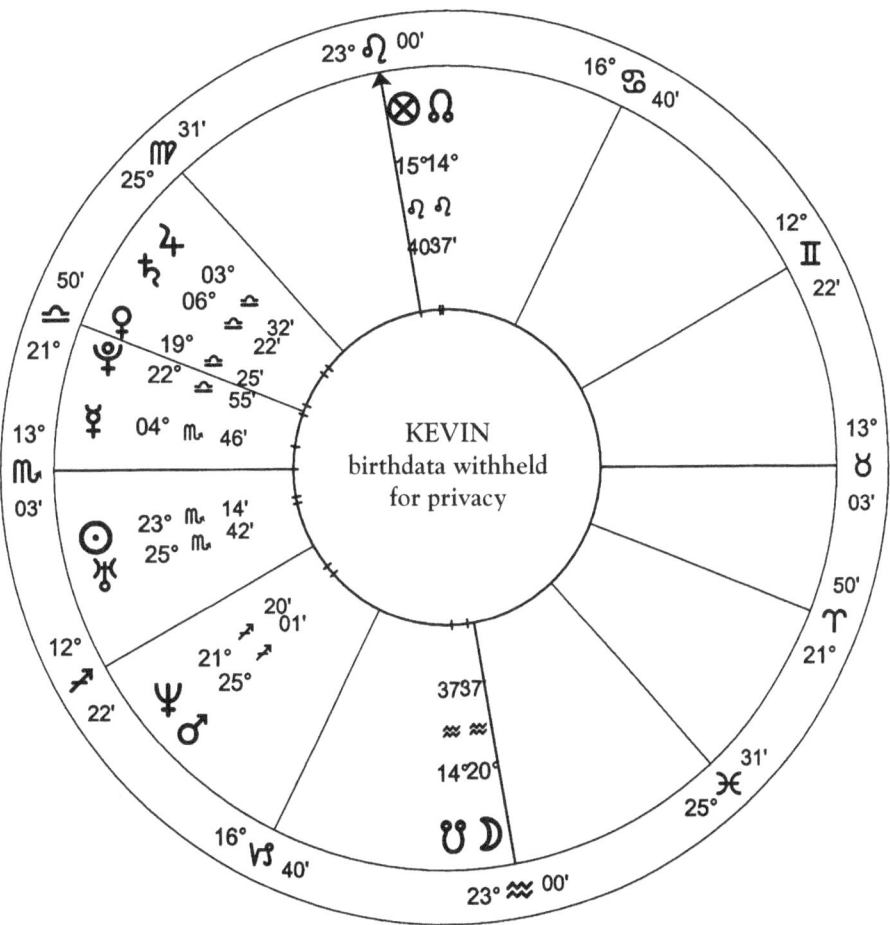

192 Temperament: Astrology's Forgotten Key

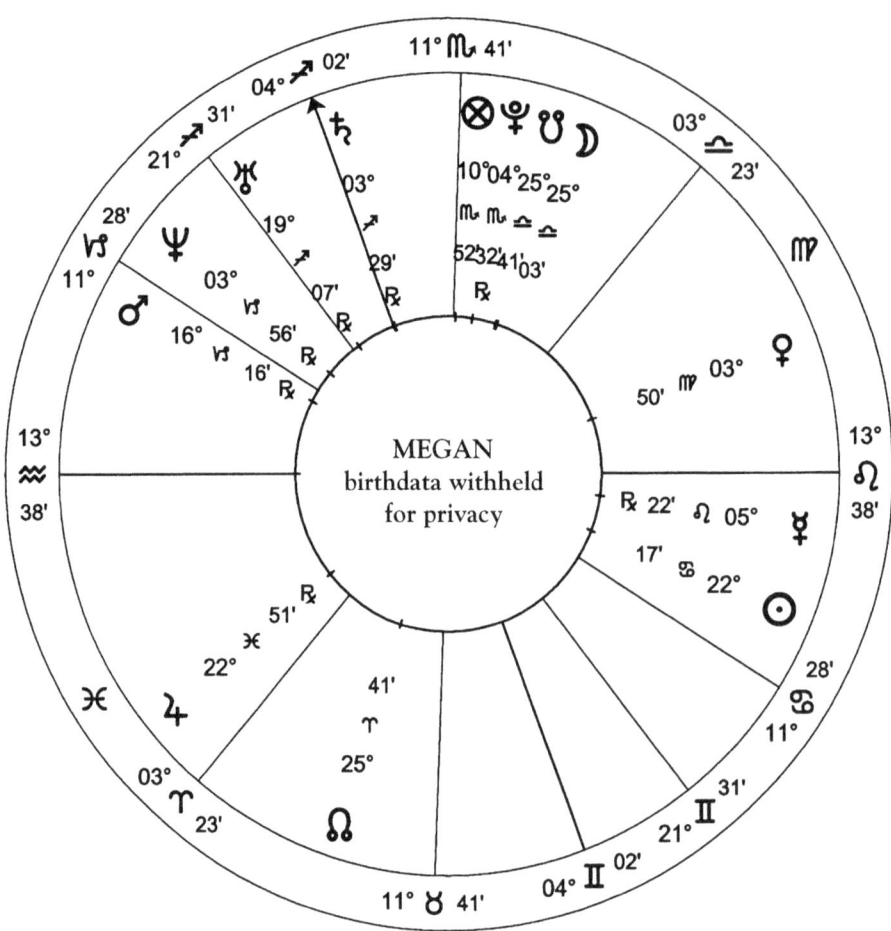

Appendices 193

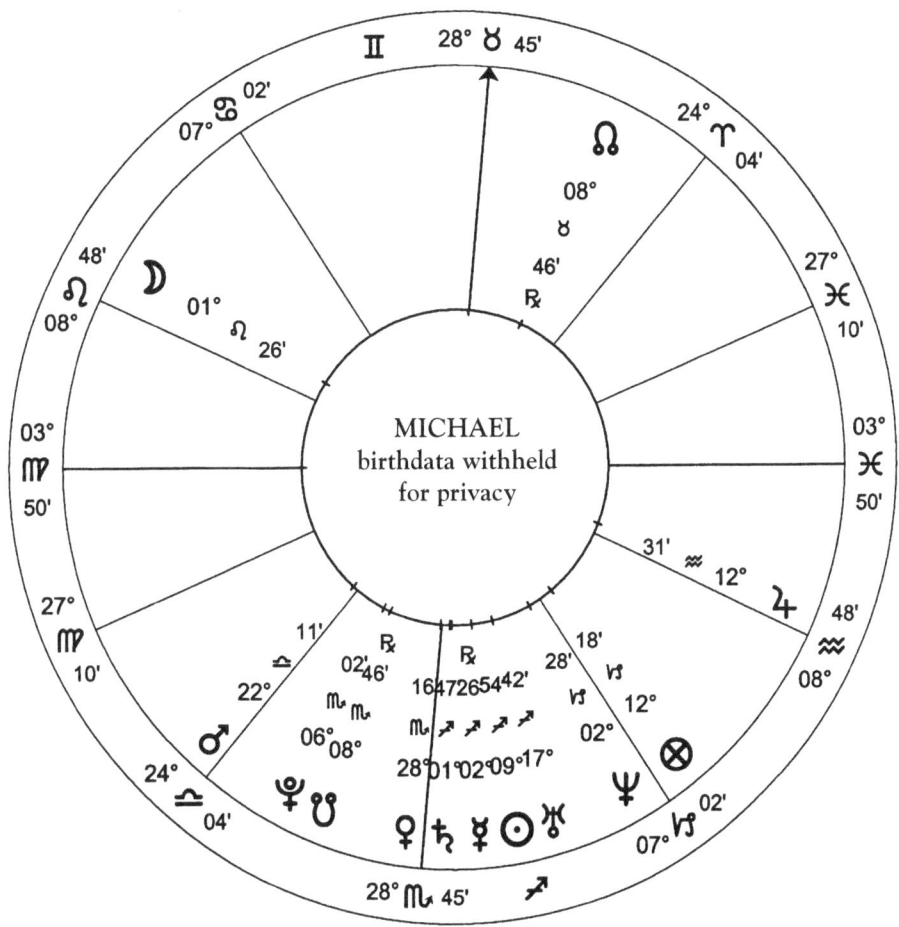

Hs	Alm.
1	☿
2	☿
3	♀
4	♂
5	♄
6	☿ ♄
7	♀
8	♃
9	♂
10	☽
11	♃
12	☉

Day of ☉ Hour of ☽
6th Hour of Night
Last Hr ☿ −27 mins
Next Hr ♄ +47 mins

DIGNITY/ALMUTEN SCORES						
Almuten of Chart (Ibn Ezra)						
Planet	☿	☉	♄	♃	☽	♀	♂
Score	31	28	24	22	20	15	14

NEAREST LUNAR PHASES				
3rd Q	Nov 5 1985	3:06 pm	13° ♌ 21	
New	Nov 12 1985	9:20 am	20° ♏ 09	♂
1st Q	Nov 19 1985	4:03 am	26° ♒ 59	
Full	Nov 27 1985	7:41 am	05° ♊ 13	
3rd Q	Dec 5 1985	4:01 am	13° ♍ 10	

ESSENTIAL DIGNITIES								
Pt	Ruler	Exalt	Trip	Term	Face	Detri	Fall	Score
☽	☉	---	♃	♄	♄	♄	---	+0 p
☉	♃	☋	♃	♀	☿	☿	☊	+0 p
☿	♃	☋	♃ m	♃	☿ +	☿ −	☊	−4
♀	♂ m	---	♂	♄	♀ +	♀ −	☽	−4
♂	♀ m	♄	☿	☿	☿	♂ −	☉	−5 p
♃	♄ m	---	☿ m	♃	☿	☉	---	+0 p
♄	♃ m	☋	♃	♃	☿	☿	☊	+0 p
♆	♄	☋	♃	☿	☽	☽	♃	---
♇	♂	☋	☽	♂	♂	♀	☽	---
☊	♀	☽	☽	☿	♂	♂	---	---
☋	♂	---	♂	♃	♂	♀	☽	---
As	☿	☿	☽	☿	☉	♃	♀	---
Mc	♀	☽	☽	♂	♄	♂	---	---
⊗	♄	♂	☽	♃	♂	☽	♃	---

194 *Temperament: Astrology's Forgotten Key*

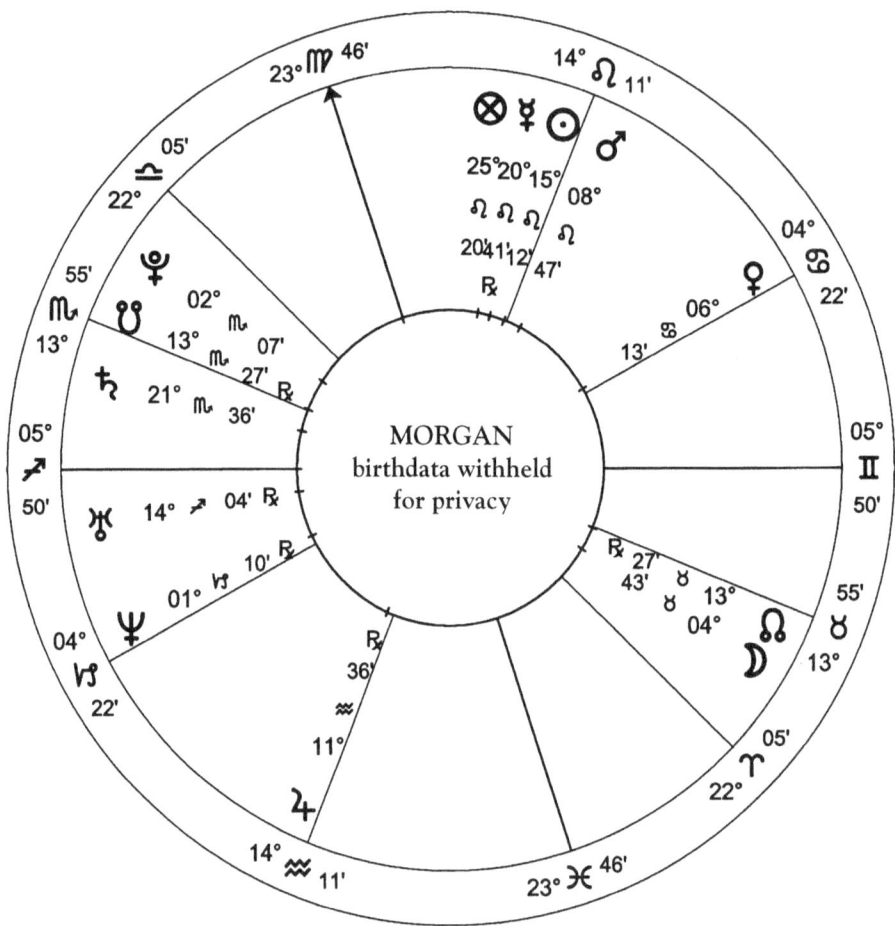

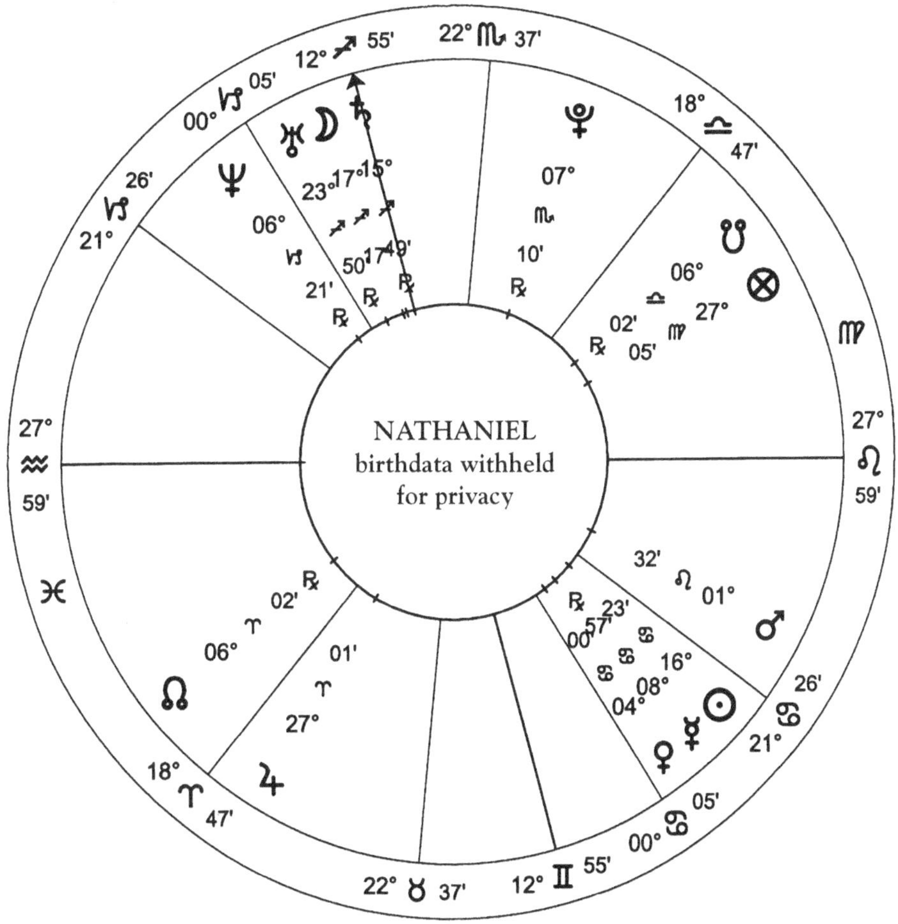

Hs	Alm.
1	♄
2	☉♂
3	☽
4	☿
5	☽
6	☽
7	☉
8	♀ ♄
9	♂
10	♃
11	♄
12	♂

Day of ☿ Hour of ☿
3rd Hour of Night
Last Hr ♀ −36 mins
Next Hr ☽ +9 mins

DIGNITY/ALMUTEN SCORES							
Almuten of Chart (Ibn Ezra)							
Planet	☿	☽	♃	♄	♀	♂	☉
Score	38	32	25	24	17	14	10

NEAREST LUNAR PHASES			
Full	Jun 11 1987	4:48 pm	20° ♐ 24
3rd Q	Jun 18 1987	7:02 am	26° ♓ 42
New	Jun 26 1987	1:36 am	04° ♋ 07
1st Q	Jul 4 1987	4:34 am	11° ♎ 52
Full	Jul 10 1987	11:32 pm	18° ♑ 20

ESSENTIAL DIGNITIES

Pt	Ruler	Exalt	Trip	Term	Face	Detri	Fall	Score
☽	♃	☋	♃	☿	☽ +	☿	☊	+1
☉	☽	♃ m	♂	☿	☿	♄	♂	+0 p
☿	☽	♃	♂	♃	♀	♄	♂	+0 p
♀	☽	♃	♂	♂	♀ +	♄	♂	+1
♂	☉	--	♃	♄	♄	♄	--	+0 p
♃	♂	☉ m	♃ +	♄	♀	♀	♄	+3
♄	♃	☋ m	♃	☿	☽	☿	☊	+0 p
♅	♃	☋	♃	♄	♄	☿	☊	--
♆	♄	♂	☽	☿	♃	☽	♃	--
♇	♂	--	♂	♃	♂	♀	☽	--
☊	♂	☉	♃	♀	♂	♀	♄	--
☋	♀	♄ m	☿	♀	☽	♂	☉	--
As	♄	--	☿	♂	☽	☉	--	--
Mc	♃	☋	♃	♀	☽	☿	☊	--
⊗	☿	☿	☽	♂	☿	♃	♀	--

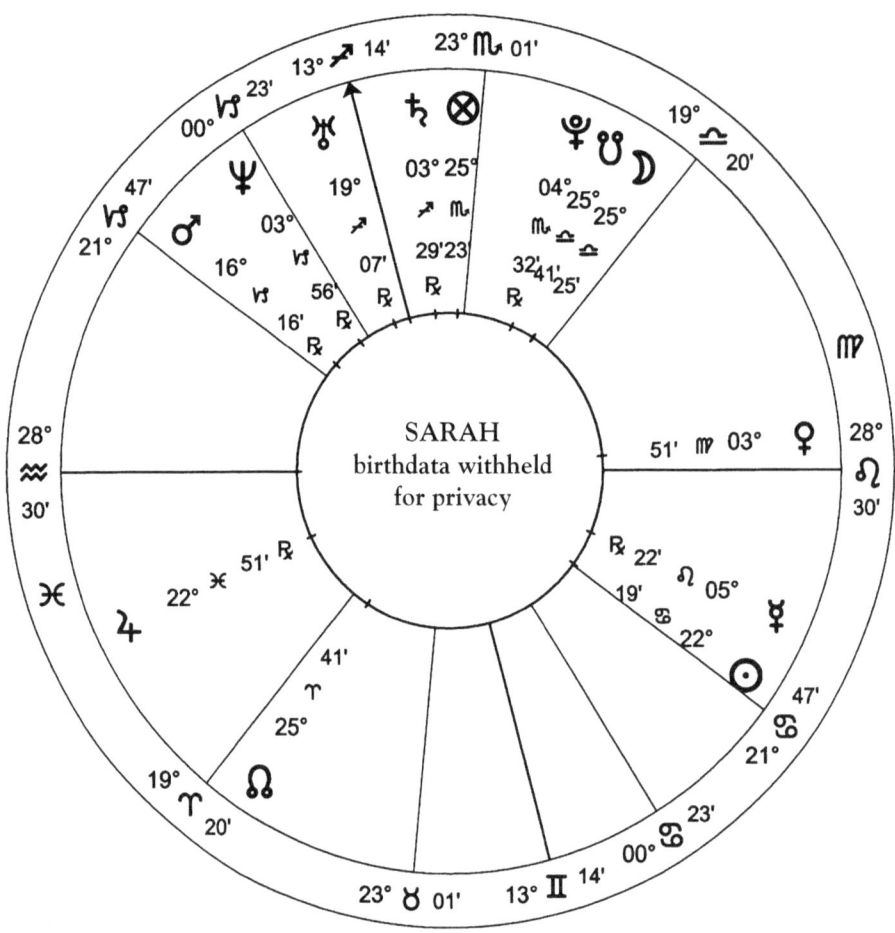

Appendices 197

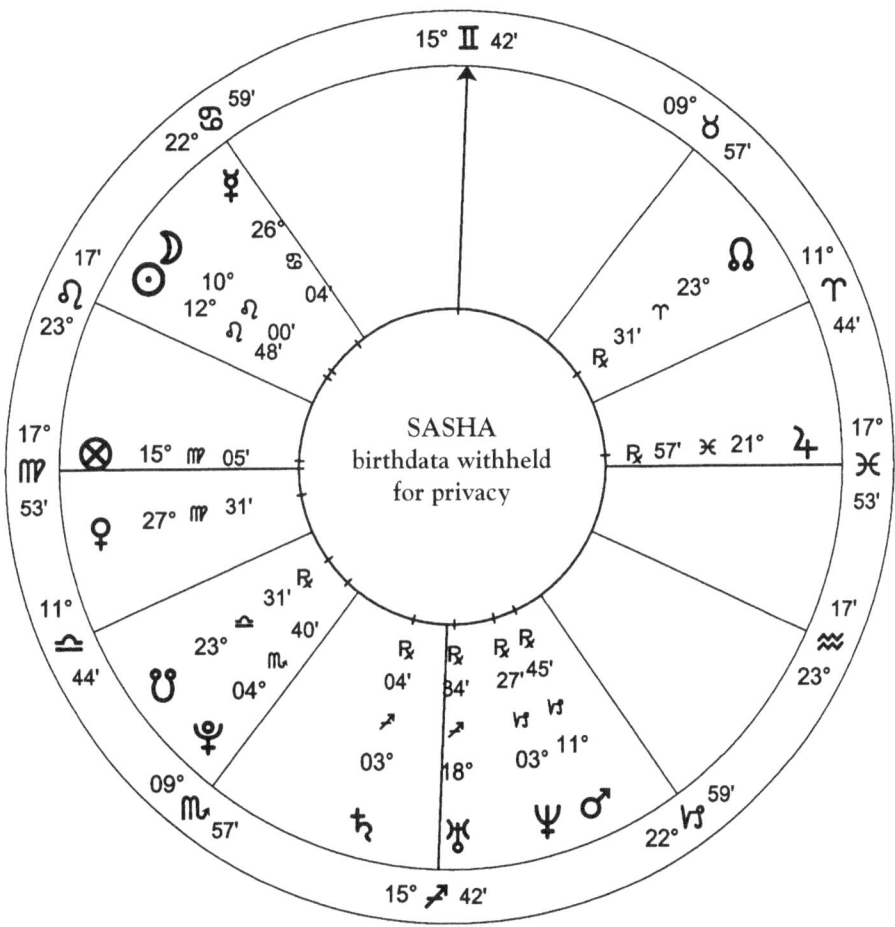

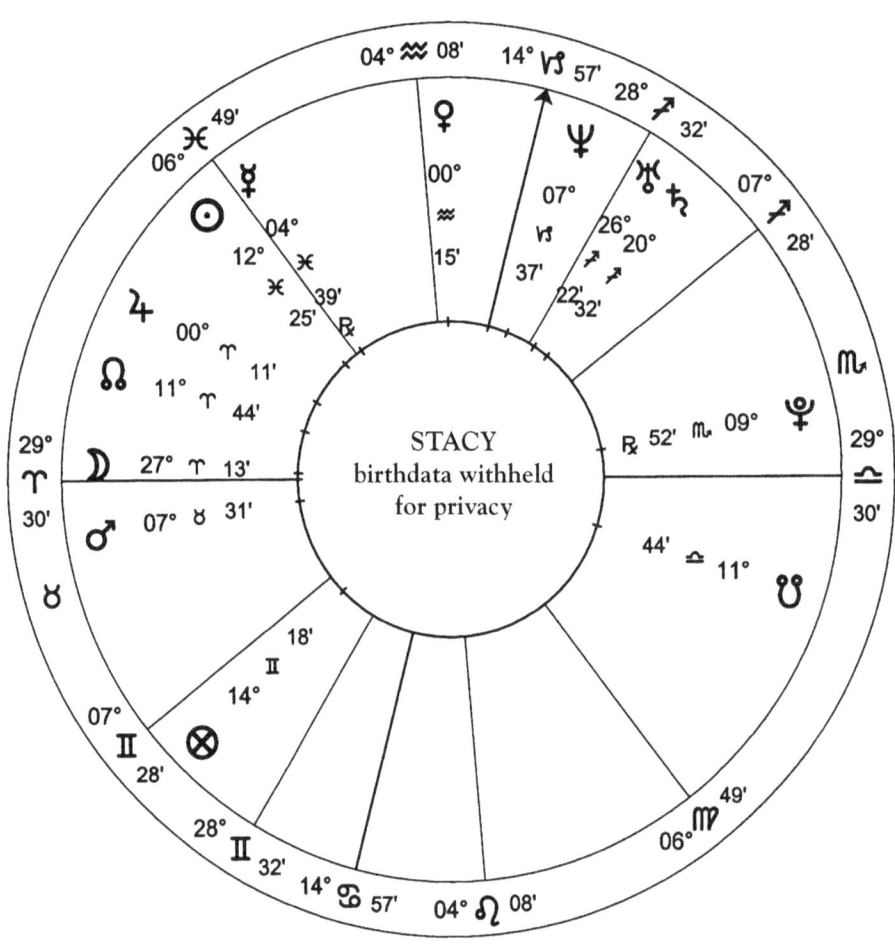

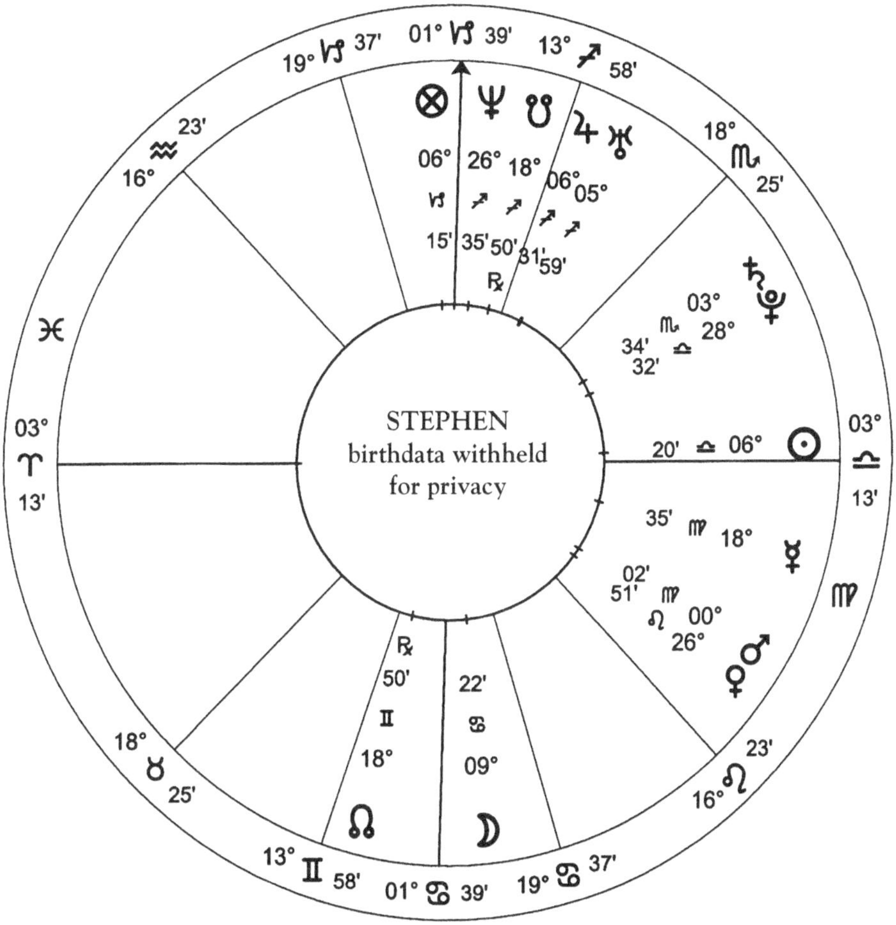

Hs	Alm.
1	☉
2	♀
3	☿
4	☽
5	☽
6	☉
7	♄
8	♂
9	♃
10	♀ ♄
11	♂
12	♄

Day of ♃ Hour of ☿
12th Hour of Day
Last Hr ♀ −52 mins
Next Hr ☽ +7 mins

DIGNITY/ALMUTEN SCORES							
Almuten of Chart (Ibn Ezra)							
Planet	♃	♄	☽	♀	♂	☉	☿
Score	29	27	24	22	21	17	14

NEAREST LUNAR PHASES			
New	Sep 6 1983	7:34 pm	13° ♍ 55
1st Q	Sep 13 1983	7:23 pm	20° ♐ 43
Full	Sep 21 1983	11:36 pm	28° ♓ 42
3rd Q	Sep 29 1983	1:05 pm	06° ♋ 06
New	Oct 6 1983	4:15 am	12° ♎ 38

ESSENTIAL DIGNITIES								
Pt	Ruler	Exalt	Trip	Term	Face	Detri	Fall	Score
☽	☽ +	♃	♂	♃	♀	♄	♂	+5
☉	♀ m	♄	♄	♀	☽	♂	☉ −	−4 p
☿	☿ +	☿ +	♀	♄	♀	♃	♀	+9
♀	☉ m	--	☉	♂	♂	♄	--	+0 p
♂	☿	☿	♀	☿	☉	♃	♀	+0 p
♃	♃ +	☋	☉	♃ +	☿	☿	☊	+7
♄	♂	--	♂	♂	♂	♀	☽	+0 p
♅	♃	☋	☉	♃	☿	☿	☊	--
♆	♃	☋	☉	♂	♄	☿	☊	--
♇	♀	♄	♄	♂	♃	♂	☉	--
☊	☿	☊	♄	♀	♂	♃	☋	--
☋	♃	☋	☉	☿	☽	☿	☊	--
As	♂	☉	☉	♃	♂	♀	♄	--
Mc	♄	♂	♀	♀	♃	☽	♃	--
⊗	♄	♂	♀	☿	♃	☽	♃	--

200 Temperament: Astrology's Forgotten Key

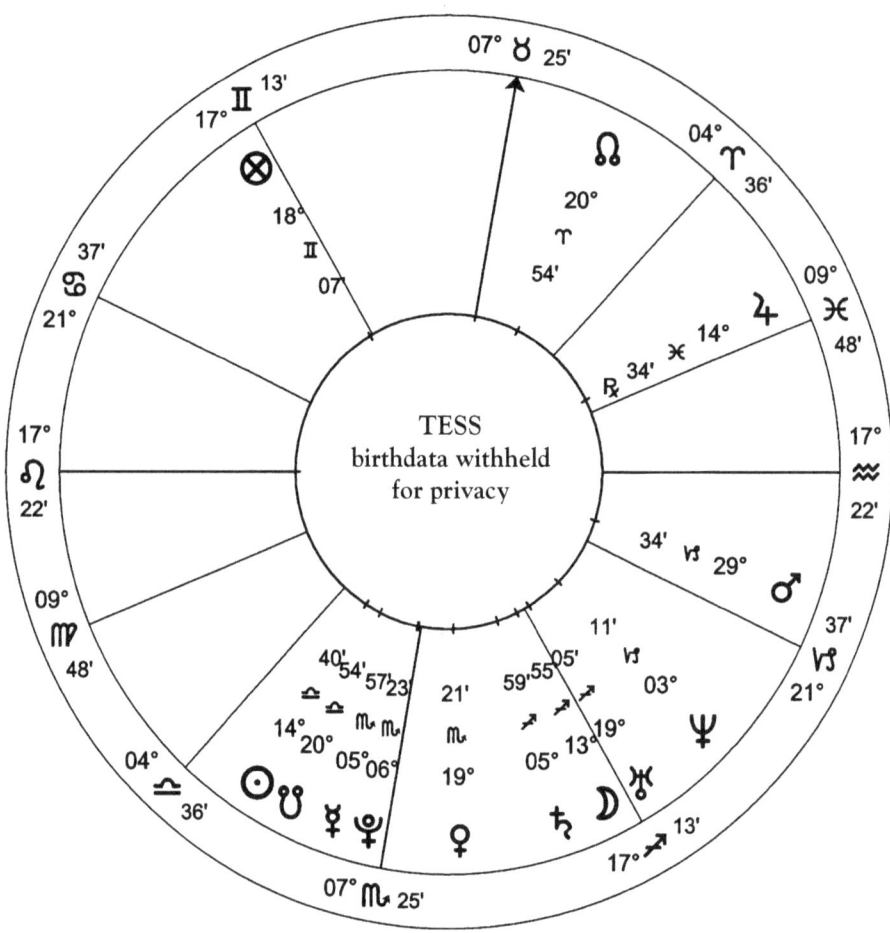

Appendix I

Names, Temperaments and Temperament Factors

NAME (ALIAS)	TEMPERA-MENT	☉ SIGN	ASC SIGN	☽ SIGN	ASC RULER	ASC ALMUTEN	☽ RULER	☽ PHASE	LORD OF GEN.	SEASON
Abby	chol./sang.	♊	♓	♍	♃ in ♑	♀ in ♊	☿ in ♉	1st Q	☿ in ♉	spring
Adam	mel./sang. chol./phleg.	♓	♌	♑	☉ in ♓	☉ in ♓	♄ in ♐	last Q	♂ in ♐, ☉ in ♓	winter
Alicia	mel./phleg.	♎	♓	♐	♃ in ♓	♀ in ♏	♃ in ♓	new	♃ in ♓	autumn
Andy	mel./chol.	♎	♓	♐	♃ in ♒	♂ in ♍	♃ in ♒	new	♃ in ♒	autumn
Becca	sang./chol./mel.?	♐	♍	♊	☿ in ♑	☿ in ♑	☿ in ♑	full	☿ in ♑	autumn
Bobby	phleg./sang.	♏	♊	♒	☿ in ♏	☿ in ♏	♄ in ♏	new	♂ in ♍, ♀ in ♎	autumn
Cameron	mel./chol.	♌	♉	♐	♀ in ♎	♀ in ♎, ☽ in ♐	♃ in ♓	1st Q	♃ in ♓	summer
Charlie	chol./mel.	♉	♏	♍	♂ in ♊	♂ in ♊	☿ in ♉	1st Q	☽ in ♍	spring
Christopher	chol./sang./mel.	♒	♌	♒	☉ in ♒	☉ in ♒	♄ in ♐	last Q	♄ in ♐	winter
Courtney	sang./chol./phleg.	♌	♋	♐	☽ in ♐	☽ in ♐, ♂ in ♌	♃ in ♐	1st Q	♃ in ♐	summer
Daniel	mel.	♊	♉	♈	♀ in ♊	☽ in ♈	♂ in ♍	last Q	♀ in ♊	spring
Darcy	sang.	♓	♒	♎	♄ in ♏	♄ in ♏	♀ in ♈	full	♀ in ♈	winter
David	sang./chol.	♌	♉	♒	♀ in ♍	☽ in ♒, ♀ in ♍	♄ in ♎	full	♃ in ♐	summer
Deirdre	phleg.	♒	♎	♓	♀ in ♈	♄ in ♑	♃ in ♈	new	♄ in ♑	winter
Derek	mel.	♓	♊	♌	☿ in ♓	☿ in ♓	☉ in ♓	1st Q	♀ in ♓	winter
Ethan	mel./sang.	♐	♓	♐	♃ in ♒	♂ in ♎	♃ in ♒	last Q	♃ in ♒	autumn
Evan	chol./phleg./mel.?	♓	♊	♋	☿ in ♒	☿ in ♒	☽ in ♋	1st Q	♃ in ♐	winter
Eve	phleg./chol./mel.?	♓	♊	♋	☿ in ♒	☿ in ♒	☽ in ♋	1st Q	♃ in ♐	winter
Fern	mel.	♏	♑	♈	♄ in ♏	♄ in ♏, ♂ in ♎	♂ in ♎	1st Q	♂ in ♎	autumn
Freddie	sang./chol.	♊	♏	♑	♂ in ♋	♂ in ♋	♄ in ♐	full	♂ in ♋	spring
Ginny	mel./sang.?	♓	♍	♈	☿ in ♒	☿ in ♒	♂ in ♐	new	♄ in ♑	winter
Gretchen	phleg.	♎	♋	♋	☽ in ♋	☽ in ♋	☽ in ♋	last Q	♀ in ♏	autumn
James	phleg.	♓	♍	♋	☿ in ♒	☿ in ♒	☽ in ♋	1st Q	♀ in ♈	winter
Jared	mel./phleg.	♌	♍	♐	☿ in ♍	☿ in ♍	♃ in ♐	1st Q	☿ in ♍	summer
Jeremy	sang./phleg.	♉	♋	♑	☽ in ♑	♃ in ♑	♄ in ♏	full	♀ in ♈	spring
Kevin	phleg.	♏	♏	♒	♂ in ♐	♂ in ♐	♄ in ♎	new	♂ in ♐	autumn
Megan	sang./chol.	♋	♒	♎	♄ in ♐	♄ in ♐	♀ in ♍	1st Q	♃ in ♓, ☽ in ♎	summer
Michael	mel./phleg.	♐	♍	♌	☿ in ♐	☿ in ♐	☉ in ♐	full	☿ in ♐	autumn
Morgan	chol./sang.	♌	♐	♉	♃ in ♒	♃ in ♒	♀ in ♋	full	☉ in ♌	summer
Nathaniel	mel./chol./phleg.	♋	♒	♐	♄ in ♐	♄ in ♐	♃ in ♈	1st Q	☿ in ♋	summer
Sarah	sang./mel.	♋	♒	♎	♄ in ♐	♄ in ♐	♀ in ♍	1st Q	☽ in ♎	summer
Sasha	mel./chol.	♌	♍	♌	☿ in ♋	☿ in ♋	☉ ♌	last Q	♀ in ♍	summer
Stacy	sang.	♓	♈	♈	♂ in ♉	☉ in ♓	♂ in ♉	new	♂ in ♉	winter
Stephen	phleg./sang.	♎	♈	♋	♂ in ♍	☉ in ♎	☽ in ♋	last Q	♃ in ♐	autumn
Tess	mel.	♎	♌	♐	☉ in ♎	☉ in ♎	♃ in ♐	new	♄ in ♐	autumn

Glossary

almuten — planet which has the most counts of dignity in a particular degree of the zodiac.

diurnal — of a chart, one with the Sun above the horizon. Of planets, the Sun, Jupiter and Saturn.

hyleg — term used in medieval astrology for the 'giver of life,' a planet said to have influence on life expectancy. The Greek term for hyleg (which comes from Arabic) is *apheta*.

lord of the geniture — a planet said to be the 'ruler' of the chart, sometimes called the 'Almuten of the Chart.' Different astrologers had different methods for finding it. Some examples: for Firmicus, it is the ruler of the sign following the natal Moon position. For Ibn Ezra, it is the planet with the most essential (using the 5-point system) and accidental dignity (using a point system created by Ibn Ezra) in the positions of the Sun, Moon, Ascendant, Part of Fortune and Prenatal Syzygy. For Schoener, it is the planet with the most essential dignity in the positions of the Sun, Moon, Ascendant, Part of Fortune and Prenatal Syzygy. For Lilly, it is the planet with the most essential and accidental dignity, and also well-placed in the chart.

nocturnal — of a chart, one with the Sun below the horizon. Of planets, the Moon, Venus and Mars.

occidental — of a planet, rising after the Sun in the morning. A planet occidental to the Sun will have a higher zodiacal longitude, e.g. if Jupiter is at 20 Pisces and the Sun at 5 Pisces, Jupiter is occidental.

oriental — of a planet, rising before the Sun in the morning. A planet oriental to the Sun will have a lower zodiacal longitude, e.g. if Mercury is at 16 Taurus and the Sun is at 24 Taurus, Mercury is oriental.

partile(ly) — when planets make an aspect by exact degree, e.g. Sun at 24 Leo and Mars at 24 Scorpio are in partile square. The partile condition remains in effect throughout the whole degree, whether the planets are applying or separating.

prenatal syzygy — the new or full moon before a birth. The word syzygy comes from Greek roots meaning 'a yoking together.' These 'yokings' would occur both at the new moon (conjunction) and the full moon (opposition). The prenatal syzygy is often one of the zodiacal degrees used in computing the almuten of the chart.

BIBLIOGRAPHY

Primary Sources

Abu Mashar, trans. Charles Burnett. *The Abbreviation to the Introduction to Astrology*. Reston, Va.: ARHAT, 1997.

Al Biruni, trans. R. Ramsay Wright. *The Book of Instruction in the Elements of the Art of Astrology*. London: Luzac and Co., 1934.

Anonymous of 379, trans. Robert Schmidt. *Treatise on the Bright Fixed Stars*. Berkeley Springs, W. Va.: The Golden Hind Press, 1993.

Antiochus of Athens, trans. Robert Schmidt. *The Thesaurus*. Berkeley Springs, W. Va.: The Golden Hind Press, 1993.

Aristotle, trans. E.S. Forster, D.J. Furley. *Aristotle III, On Sophistical Refutations; On Coming-to-be and Passing Away; On the Cosmos*. Loeb Classical Library. Cambridge, Mass.: Harvard University Press, 1955, 1992.

_____, trans. W. S. Hett, H. Rackham. *Aristotle XVI, Problems Books XXII-XXXVIII; Rhetorica ad Alexandrum*. Loeb Classical Library. Cambridge, Mass.: Harvard University Press, 1937, 2001.

Beatles, The. *Abbey Road*, 1969.

Bonatti, Guido, trans. Robert Zoller. *Liber Astronomiae, Part I*. Berkeley Springs, W. Va.: The Golden Hind Press, 1994.

_____, trans. Robert Zoller. *Liber Astronomiae, Part 2*. Berkeley Springs, W. Va.: The Golden Hind Press, 1994.

_____, trans. Robert Hand. *Liber Astronomiae, Part 3*. Berkeley Springs, W. Va.: The Golden Hind Press, 1995.

_____, *Liber Astronomiae*, Book 9. Erhard Ratdolt, 1491.

Burton, Robert, ed. Floyd Dell and Paul Jordan-Smith. *The Anatomy of Melancholy*. New York: Tudor Publishing Company, 1927.

Chaucer, Geoffrey. *The Canterbury Tales: Prologue; The Knight's Tale*. [accessed 1 March 2004] http://www.litrix.com/canterby/cante001.htm#1 http://www.litrix.com/canterby/cante002.htm

_____, trans. Vincent F. Hopper. *Chaucer's Canterbury Tales (Selected), An Interlinear Translation*. Woodbury, N.Y.: Barron's Educational Series, Inc., 1948, 1970.

Cleese, John. Biography online [accessed April 29, 2004] at http://www.pythonline.com/plugs/cleese/index.shtml.

Coley, Henry. *Key to the Whole Art of Astrology*. 1676. Ballantrae Reprint.

Culpeper, Nicholas. *Culpeper's Complete Herbal*. Ware, Herts.: Wordsworth Editions Ltd., 1995.

_____, *Galen's Art of Physick*. London: Peter Cole, 1652.

Ficino, Marsilio, various translators. *Meditations on the Soul, Selected Letters of Marsilio Ficino*. Rochester, Vermont: Inner Traditions International, 1997.

_____, ed. and trans. Carol V. Kaske and John R. Clark. *Three Books on Life*. Tempe, Ariz.: Medieval and Renaissance Texts and Studies in conjunction with the Renaissance Society of America, 1998.

Frank, Anne, trans. B.M. Mooyaart-Doubleday. *The Diary of a Young Girl*. New York: Pocket Books, 1967.

Gadbury, John. *The Doctrine of Nativities*, 1658. Ballantrae Reprint.

Galen, Claudius. *Galeni De temperamentis (Γαλενοῦ περὶ κράσεων) Libri III*, ed. George Helmreich. Stuttgart: B.G. Teubner, 1969.

_____, trans. W.J. Lewis with the assistance of J.A. Beach and S. Rubio-Fernandez. *On the Elements According to Hippocrates*. Ancient Medicine/Medicina Antiqua Website [accessed 1 March 2004]: http://www.medicinaantiqua.org.uk/tr_GalElem.html.

_____, trans. W.J. Lewis with the assistance of J.A. Beach. *On Hippocrates' On the Nature of Man*. Ancient Medicine/Medicina Antiqua Website [accessed 1 March 2004]: http://www.medicinaantiqua.org.uk/tr_GNatHom.html.

_____, trans. Arthur John Brock. *On the Natural Faculties*. Loeb Classical Library. Cambridge, Mass.: Harvard University Press, 1916, 1991.

Garcaeus, trans. Robert Hand. *Astrologiae Methodus in qua secundum doctrinum Ptolemaei...*. Unpublished translation of "On the Temperament Type," 1574.

Harrison, George. Quote taken from the "Beatles on Abbey Road" website [accessed April 29, 2004], at http://webhome.idirect.com/~faab/AbbeyRoad/george2.htm.

Hephaistio of Thebes, trans. Robert H. Schmidt. *Apotelesmatics, Book II*. Cumberland, Md.: The Golden Hind Press, 1998.

Hippocrates, trans. W.H.S. Jones. *Hippocrates IV*. Loeb Classical Library. Cambridge, Mass.:Harvard University Press, 1931, 1998.

Jones, Marc Edmund. *Lecture-Lessons, Hermetic Astrology I-XXIV*. Privately typed lessons, 1933.

Jonson, Ben. *Every Man in his Humour*. Project Gutenberg Release [accessed 30 Dec 2004] at http://digital.library.upenn.edu/webbin/gutbook/lookup?num=3694.

―――, *Cynthia's Revels*. Project Gutenberg Release [accessed 30 Dec 2004] at http://www.gutenberg.org/catalog/world/readfile?fk_files=5176&pageno=49.

Jung, Carl G., trans. H.G. Baynes. *Psychological Types*, vol. 6, collected works of C.G. Jung. Bollingen Series XX. Princeton, N.J.:Princeton University Press, 1971.

Kant, Immanuel, trans. Victor Lyle Dowdell, ed. Hans H. Rudnick. *Anthropology from a Pragmatic Point of View (Anthropologie in pragmatischer Hinsicht)*. Carbondale & Edwardsville, Ill.:Southern Illinois University Press, 1978.

Lilly, William. *Christian Astrology*. Facsimile edition. Exeter:Regulus Publishing Co., Ltd., 1985.

Lull, Ramon, trans. Kris Shapar. *Treatise on Astronomy*. Berkeley Springs, W. Va.:The Golden Hind Press, 1994.

Lull, Ramon, trans. Kristina M. Shapar. *Treatise on Astronomy, Books II – V*. Berkeley Springs, W. Va.:The Golden Hind Press, 1994.

Manilius, Marcus, trans. G.P. Goold. *Astronomica*. Loeb Classical Library. Cambridge, Mass.:Harvard University Press, 1977, 1997.

Marlowe, Christopher. "Tamburlaine the Great." 1587.

Masha'allah, trans. Robert Hand. *Book of Nativities*. Berkeley Springs, W. Va.:The Golden Hind Press, 1994.

Maternus, Julius Firmicus, trans. Jean Rhys Bram. *Matheseos Libri VIII "Astrological Treatise in Eight Books."* Park Ridge, New Jersey: Noyes Press, 1975 (reprinted by Ascella Publications, 1995).

de Montulmo, Antonius, trans. Robert Hand. *On the Judgment of Nativities, Parts 1 and 2*. Berkeley Springs, W. Va.:The Golden Hind Press, 1995.

Paracelsus, trans. and ed. Nicholas Goodrick-Clarke. *Paracelsus, Essential Readings*. Berkeley, Ca.:North Atlantic Books, 1999.

Partridge, John. *Mikropanastron, or an Astrological Vade Mecum…*, 1679. Issaquah, Wash.:Just Us and Associates, 1995.

Paulus Alexandrinus and Olympiodorus, trans. Dorian Gieseler Greenbaum. *Late Classical Astrology: Paulus Alexandrinus and Olympiodorus, with the Scholia from Later Commentators*. Reston, Va.:ARHAT, 2001.

Plato, trans. R.G. Bury. *Plato IX: Timaeus, Critias, Cleitophon, Menexenus and Epistles*. Loeb Classical Library. Cambridge, Mass.:Harvard University Press, 1929, 1989.

Ptolemy, Claudius, trans. F.E. Robbins. *Tetrabiblos*. Loeb Classical Library. Cambridge, Mass.:Harvard University Press, 1940, 1994.

―――, trans. Robert H. Schmidt. *Tetrabiblos, Books I, III*. Berkeley Springs, W. Va.: 1994, 1996.

Rhetorius, "On the Nature and Virtue of the Planets," in *Catalogus Codicum Astrologorum Graecorum VII*, pp. 213-224. Brussels, 1898-1953.

Rudhyar, Dane. *An Astrological Study of Psychological Complexes*. Berkeley, Calif.: Shambhala Publications, 1976.

Schoener, Johannes, trans. Robert Hand. *Opusculum Astrologicum*. Berkeley Springs, W. Va.: The Golden Hind Press, 1994.

_____, trans. Robert Hand. *On the Judgment of Nativities*. Book I. Reston, Va.: ARHAT, 2001.

Simon, Paul. Quoted on The Art Garfunkel Website [accessed April 29, 2004], at http://www.artgarfunkel.com/chrono/1970-1974.htm.

Steiner, Rudolf, trans. Brian Kelly. "The Four Temperaments," in *Anthroposophy in Everyday Life*. Hudson, N.Y.: Anthroposophic Press, 1995.

_____, trans. Helen Fox. *Discussions with Teachers*. Hudson, N.Y.: Anthroposophic Press, 1997.

Valens, Vettius, trans. Robert H. Schmidt. *The Anthology, Book I*. Berkeley Springs, W. Va.: The Golden Hind Press, 1993.

_____, trans. Robert Schmidt. *The Anthology, Book IV*. Berkeley Springs, W. Va.: The Golden Hind Press, 1996.

Secondary Sources

Anschütz, Marieke, trans. Tony Langham and Plym Peters. *Children and Their Temperaments*. Edinburgh: Floris Books, 1995.

Barnes, Jonathan. *Early Greek Philosophy*. London: Penguin Books, 1987.

Berg, A. Scott. Interview with Elizabeth Farnsworth on "PBS Newshour with Jim Lehrer," April 23, 1999 [accessed April 29, 2004] at http://www.pbs.org/newshour/bb/entertainment/jan-june99/pulitzer_4-23.html.

Billman, Larry. Biography of Fred Astaire [accessed April 29, 2004] at http://www.fredastaire.net/biography/broadway.htm and http://www.fredastaire.net/biography/rko.htm.

Brady, Bernadette. *Brady's Book of Fixed Stars*. York Beach, Me.: Samuel Weiser, 1998.

Brazelton, T. Berry. *Infants and Mothers: Differences in Development*. New York: Dell Publishing Co., revised edition, 1989.

Bryant, Steve. Biography of John Cleese [accessed April 29, 2004] at http://www.museum.tv/archives/etv/C/htmlC/cleesejohn/cleesejohn.htm.

Burnet, John. *Early Greek Philosophy*. Cleveland, O.: Meridian Books, the World Publishing Company, 1961.

Childs, Gilbert. *Balancing Your Temperament*. London:Sophia Books, 1999.

_____, *Understand Your Temperament!*. London:Sophia Books, 1995, 1998.

Crane, Joseph. *A Practical Guide to Traditional Astrology*. Orleans, Mass.:ARHAT, 1997.

Druitt, Ann. "The Temperaments," in Davy, Gudrun and Voors, Bons, *Lifeways:Working with family questions*. Stroud:Hawthorn Press, 1983.

Eyheramonno, Joelle, biography of Antoine de Saint-Exupéry [accessed April 29, 2004] at http://www.members.lycos.nl/tlp/antoine.htm.

Fodor, Beverly. *A Model of Carl Jung's Psychological Functions in Relation to the Annual Cycle*. Dahlgren, Va.:self-published, 1993.

Frawley, John. *The Real Astrology Applied*. London:Apprentice Books, 2002.

_____, "The Pilot of the Soul," lecture presented at the conference of the International Society for Astrological Research, October 10, 2003.

Greene, Liz. *Relating*. York Beach, Me.:Samuel Weiser, 1978.

Guthrie, Kenneth Sylvan, ed. David Fideler. *The Pythagorean Sourcebook and Library*. Grand Rapids, Mich.:Phanes Press, 1987, 1988.

Holden, James Herschel. *A History of Horoscopic Astrology*. Tempe, Ariz.:AFA, 1996.

Kaplan, Justin, ed. *Bartlett's Familiar Quotations*, 16th edition. Boston: Little, Brown & Company, 1992.

Keirsey Web Site [accessed 1 March 2004]: http://www.keirsey.com.

Kingsley, Peter. *Ancient Philosophy, History and Magic: Empedocles and the Pythagorean Tradition*. Oxford:Oxford University Press, 1995.

Klibansky, Raymond, Panofsky, Erwin and Saxl, Fritz. *Saturn and Melancholy*. New York: Basic Books, 1964.

Lehman, J. Lee. *Classical Astrology for Modern Living*. Atglen, Pa.:Whitford Press, 1996.

Lloyd, G.E.R. *Greek Science After Aristotle*. New York:W.W. Norton, 1973.

Pottenger, Mark, ed. *Astrological Research Methods Volume 1: an ISAR Anthology*. Los Angeles:ISAR, 1995.

Ranfranz, Patrick. Biography of Charles Lindbergh [accessed April 29, 2004] at http://www.charleslindbergh.com/history/index.asp.

Sambursky, S. *Physics of the Stoics*. Princeton, N.J.:Princeton University Press, 1959, 1987.

The Traditional Medicine Network online, at http://www.traditionalmedicine.net.au/canonavi.htm [accessed 4 July 2004].

Tobyn, Graeme. *Culpeper's Medicine: A Practice of Western Holistic Medicine*. Rockport, Me.:Element Books, 1997.

Wilkinson, Roy. *The Temperaments in Education*. Fair Oaks, Ca.:Rudolf Steiner College Press, 1977, 1994.

INDEX

A

Abu Mashar, 24-5, 27, 147
Adelard of Bath, 25
Aidoneus (Hades), 7
Al Biruni, 25-6, 147
Albinoni, Tomaso, 97
Albubater, 39
Albumasar. *See* Abu Mashar
Alchabitius, 27-8
Alcmaeon of Croton, 7-8
Alcott, Louisa May, 122
Alexander the Great, 10
Ali, Muhammad, 113
Allen, Woody, 118-20
    as example of sanguine/melancholic temperament, 118, 120
    birthchart of, 119
almuten, 28, 30, 36-7, 40-1, 59, 62-70, 72, 78-9, 84, 87, 89, 114, 129, 133-5, 137-8, 141, 201-2
Alzheimer, Alois, 97
Anaximander, 6
Anaximenes, 6
Anouilh, Jean, 106
Anschütz, Marieke, 55
Anthroposophy, 51-3
Antiochus of Athens, 22
Aphrodite (planet Venus), 18. *See also* Venus
Aristotle, 3, 5-7, 9-16, 18, 21, 28-30, 47, 52, 133
    and theory of elements, 10-13
    De Anima, 30
    On Coming-to-be and Passing-away, 10-13
    Aristotle (Corpus)
    Problems XXX,1, 13
Armstrong-Jones, Anthony, 114, 125
Asclepius, 14
Aspects to temperament significators, 37, 41, 62, 69, 75, 83-4, 87, 141-4, 146
Aspects to significators of manners, 133-4, 145
Astaire, Adele, 111
Astaire, Fred, 111-13
    as example of sanguine/choleric temperament, 111, 113
    birthchart of, 112

Atkins, Chet, 101
Averrhoes, 32
Avicen, 32. *See also* Avicenna
Avicenna (Ibn Sina), 25

B

Bakker, Jim, 127
Ball, Lucille, 108
Barnes, Jonathan, 5n-7n, 10n
Barrymore, Drew, 127
Bates, Marilyn, 48
Beatles, The, 101, 103, 137
Beethoven, Ludwig von, 97, 100
Beltane
    as air point, 3
Belushi, John, 127
Berg, A. Scott, 116
Bergman, Ingrid, 94
Berlioz, Hector, 103
Bernstein, Leonard, 114
black bile, 2, 4, 8-9, 13, 15-16, 18, 24, 26, 39, 49, 55, 88. *See also* melancholer. *See also* humors
Black, Shirley Temple, 113
Blair, Cherie, 94-5
Blair, Tony, 95-6
    as example of sanguine temperament, 95
    birthchart of, 96
Blake, William, 130
blood, 2, 4, 8-9, 15-18, 24, 26, 43, 49, 51, 55, 88, 139. *See also* humors
Bocelli, Andrea, 106
body
    and temperament, 19-20, 30-1, 36, 40, 43-4, 51-3, 133, 141-3
    applying elements and/or qualities to, 7-8, 10, 16-17, 20, 25-6
    composition of and disease in Plato, 10
Bonatti, Guido, 25-9, 79, 148
    and *Liber Astronomiae*, 26
Borgia, Cesare, 123
Brady, Bernadette, 79-80, 84
Brahms, Johannes, 94

Branagh, Kenneth, 128-9
   as example of melancholic/phlegmatic temperament, 129
  birthchart of, 128
Brazelton, T. Berry, 1n
Briggs, Katharine, 48
Britten, Benjamin, 130
Brooks, Garth, 125
Burnet, John, 5-7
Burnett, Frances Hodgson, 100
Burton, Robert, 39-40, 150, 152-3
   and *Anatomy of Melancholy*, 39, 150-2
   birthchart of, 153
Bush, George W., 92-5
   as example of choleric temperament, 93-4
   birthchart of, 92
Bush, Laura, 130

C

Camus, Albert, 122
Cardanus (Jerome Cardan), 39
Caruso, Enrico, 130
Cash, Johnny, 103
Cavalcanti, Giovanni (friend of Ficino), 33
Cavett, Dick, 100
Cezanne, Paul, 103
Character
  definition of, 1
Charles, Prince of Wales, 106
Chase, Chevy, 120
Chaucer, Geoffrey, 31-3, 37
Cheney, Dick, 129
Childs, Gilbert, 52, 54-5
cholē. *See* yellow bile
choler, 2, 38, 71, 76, 82, 86, 93, 104, 108, 114, 155, 159-60, 162. *See also* yellow bile
choleric, 1-2, 5, 9, 21, 24-5, 27, 29, 36, 39-40, 42-3, 48, 52-3, 59-60, 65n, 67- 71, 74, 83, 86, 88-9, 91, 93-5, 103, 105-6, 108-9, 111, 113-4, 116, 118, 123, 132, 137-8, 154-5, 157, 163-4. *See also* temperament, choleric *and* humors, choleric
Christie, Agatha, 120-2
   as example of melancholic/sanguine temperament, 120, 122
   birthchart of, 121
Cleese, John, 106-8
   as example of melancholic/choleric temperament, 106, 108
  birthchart of, 107
Clift, Montgomery, 100
Clinton, Chelsea, 118
Clooney, Rosemary, 125
Coley, Henry, 42-3, 75, 85, 146
Collins, Judy, 111
Commodus, 14
Connery, Sean, 100
Connors, Jimmy, 113
Copernicus, Nicolaus, 108
Crane, Joseph, 47
Crichton, Michael, 108
Cronin, A.J., 118
Crosby, David, 106
Culpeper, Nicholas, 40-2, 91, 100, 149, 157-60

D

da Vinci, Leonardo, 123-5
   as example of sanguine/phlegmatic temperament, 123, 125
  birthchart of, 124
Daltry, Roger, 125
Damon, Matt, 100
Dante Alighieri, 26
Darwin, Charles
  as extravert thinker, 45
Dayan, Moshe, 122
de Beauvoir, Simone, 118
Debussy, Claude, 100, 114
Deiscorides (Dioscorides), 32
DeNiro, Robert, 118
Dershowitz, Alan, 111
Dion, Celine, 111
Disney, Walt, 122
Domingo, Placido, 130
Dorotheus of Sidon, 23
Dostoevsky, Feodor, 97
Douglas, Lord Alfred, 97

E

Eastman, Linda, 137
Eco, Umberto, 114
Eddy, Mary Baker, 111

Edwards, John (politician), 125
elements (fire, earth, air, water), Introduction, 2-3, 5-12, 14-18, 21-6, 28, 42, 47, 52, 60, 73, 83, 87-8, 139
    and Empedocles, 7
    and humors, 4-5, 8, 23-5, 55, 88
    and planets, 4, 23-4, 27, 88
    and seasons, 4, 22, 88
    and Stoic association with qualities, 14
    and zodiac signs, 21, 26-7, 88
    Aristotelian view of, 3, 10-13
    correlated to Jungian functions, 47
    Galenic view of, 14-17
    generated by qualities, 3, 10, 16, 28
    Hippocrates' view of, 8
    Manilius' view of, 21
    stoicheion, 7, 9
Elizabeth I of England, 100
Elizabeth II, Queen of England, 108, 114
Empedocles, 1, 5, 7-10, 14, 21
Esculapius, 32. *See also* Asclepius

F

Falstaff
    and sanguine temperament, 38, 86, 127
Farrow, Mia, 118, 130
Fauré, Gabriel, 125
Ficino, Marsilio, 20, 33-5, 39-40, 122
    and melancholy, 33
    birthchart of, 34
Firmicus Maternus, Julius, 22, 34
First house planets and temperament, 37, 40-1, 63-4, 75, 83-4, 87, 141-4, 146
Fisher, Carrie, 100
Fitzgerald, F. Scott, 122
Fitzgerald, Zelda, 114
fixed stars, 20, 28, 30, 36-7, 41, 65, 75, 84, 135, 141-2, 144, 146
Flack, Roberta, 125
Fodor, Beverly, 57
Fonda, Jane, 122
Frank, Anne, 109-11
    as example of choleric/sanguine temperament, 109, 111
    birthchart of, 110
Fraser, Lady Antonia, 103
Frawley, John, 73n, 85, 134
Frost, David, 106

G

Gadbury, John, 40, 42-3, 94, 204
Galen, Claudius, 1-2, 7, 9-10, 14-18, 20, 32, 42, 91, 139, 157, 160
    and influence of Aristotle, 16
    and influence of Hippocrates, 15-17
    De temperamentis, 14-15
    and humors as psychological, 17
    Hippocrates' On the Nature of Man, 16
    On Hippocrates' On the Nature of Man, 17
    On the Elements According to Hippocrates, 15
    On the Natural Faculties, 15
Garbo, Greta, 101
Garcaeus (Johann Gartze), 36-7, 39-40, 58, 63, 65, 75, 79, 81, 84-5, 133, 143, 148, 152
Garfunkel, Art, 98, 100
Gates, Bill, 46
Gauquelin, Michel, 57, 106
Gauquelins, The, 57
Gauricus, Lucas, 40
Getty, J. Paul, 129
Gibson, Mel, 127
Gifford, Kathie Lee, 113
Glass, Philip, 3
Goethe, Johann, 50
Gone With the Wind, 132
Goodrick-Clarke, Nicholas, 35n
Graf, Steffi, 97
Grant, Cary, 97
Greene, Liz, 47
Grey, Joel, 113

H

Hades (Greek God), 7
haima. *See* blood
Haldeman, H.R., 129
Hamlet
    and melancholy, 38
Hand, Robert, 2, 4n, 19n, 23n, 27n-30n, 36n-7n, 77, 81, 133n, 141-3
harmonia, 6

Harrison, George, 101-3, 137
    as example of phlegmatic temperament, 101, 103
    birthchart of, 102
Harry Potter, 132
Hemingway, Ernest, 108
Hephaistio of Thebes, 22
Hera, 7
Heraclitus, 6, 21
Hermes (planet Mercury), 19-20, 62, 141. *See also* Mercury
Hippocrates, 1, 7-9, 13-18, 32, 139
    Aphorisms, 9
    Humours, 9
    On Ancient Medicine, 8
    The Nature of Man, 8, 15
Hoffman, Dustin, 108
Holly, Buddy, 101
Horne, Lena, 94
humors (choler/yellow bile, melancholer/black bile, blood, phlegm), 2, 4, 8-9, 14-18, 22-7, 32, 36, 49, 79, 82-3, 88
    and balance for health, 2, 8, 38
    and elements, 4-5, 8, 23-5, 55, 88
    and planets, 24-5, 27
    and psychological traits, 9, 17
    and qualities, 8, 15-16, 24, 26-7, 36
    and seasons, 8-9, 17, 52
    and zodiac signs, 24-7, 49
    choleric, 2, 4, 9, 24-9, 36, 49
    Galenic view of, 14-17
    Hippocrates' view of, 8-9
    melancholic, 9, 24, 26-7, 36, 49
    phlegmatic, 9, 24, 26-7, 36, 49
    sanguine, 9, 24-7, 36, 49
Hyleg, 30-1, 40, 142

I

Ibn Ezra, Abraham, 59, 66, 84, 138
Ibn Sina. *See* Avicenna
Imbolc (Candlemas)
    as water point, 3
Ives, Burl, 127

J

Jacobi, Derek, 100
Joel, Billy, 125
John Damascene, 32
John Paul II, Pope, 97
Jones, Marc Edmund, 8, 20, 44, 48-9
Jonson, Ben, 38
Joplin, Scott, 94
Junctinus, 39
Jung, Carl Gustav, Introduction, 5, 44-8, 50, 54, 56-7, 73
    birthchart of, 45
Jupiter (planet), 18-19, 23-4, 27, 33, 62-4, 66n-7, 71n, 77-9, 85, 88, 135, 138, 146-9, 154, 156
    and qualities, 19, 24, 27, 37, 62, 66n, 77-8, 88, 147-9
    and sanguine temperament, 27, 88, 154
    diurnal planet, 202

K

Kant Immanuel, 3, 43-5, 97, 130
    as introvert thinker, 45
Kaske, Carol & Clark, John R., 33n, 35n
Keirsey Temperament Sorter, 48
Keirsey, David, 48, 56
Kennedy, Ethel, 113
King, Martin Luther, 130
King, Stephen, 118
Kingsley, Peter, 7n
Klibansky, Raymond, 13
Krishnamurti, Jiddu, 51
Kronos (planet Saturn), 22, 62. *See also* Saturn

L

Lammas
    as fire point, 3
Lane, Nathan, 103
Lange, Jessica, 111
Lear, Edward, 120
Lee, Jane, 57
Leek, Sybil, 103
LeGuin, Ursula, 122
Lehman, Lee, 73n
Lehrer, Jim, 116n
Leigh, Vivien, 120
Lennon, John, 101, 103, 106, 137
Leovitius, 39, 152
Levine, James, 118

Lewis, Jerry, 103
Lilly, William, 1, 21, 29, 40-3, 58-9, 64-7, 74-6, 79, 81-5, 87, 89-90, 133-5, 138-9, 144, 149
   Christian Astrology, 40-1, 74, 89-90, 144, 149
Limbaugh, Rush, 125-7
   as example of phlegmatic/sanguine temperament, 125, 127
   birthchart of, 126
Lindbergh, Anne Morrow, 116
Lindbergh, Charles, 116-18
   as example of phlegmatic/choleric temperament, 116, 118
   birthchart of, 117
Lindhout, 40
Llewellyn, Roddy, 114
Lloyd-Webber, Andrew, 94
Locklear, Heather, 106
Lord of the Geniture, 22, 34, 37, 40, 59, 64-6, 68, 75-6, 84-5, 134, 138, 144, 146, 152
Lord of the Rings, The, 132
Louis XII of France, 123
Lull, Ramon, 28-9, 82, 154

M

Machiavelli, Niccolo, 91
Maharishi Mahesh Yogi, 103
Mallowan, Max, 122
Manilius, Marcus, 21
manners, 26, 36, 40-1, 75, 84, 90, 133-8, 145-6
Marcus Aurelius (emperor), 14
Margaret, Princess of England, 114-15
   as example of choleric/phlegmatic temperament, 114
   birthchart of, 115
Marlowe, Christopher, 139
Mars (planet), 19, 23-4, 29, 33, 35-6, 40, 59, 62-4, 66n, 68-9, 71n, 76-9, 88, 114, 146-9, 152, 155
   and choleric temperament, 29, 88, 155
   and elements, 24, 27, 88
   and humors, 24, 27, 88
   and qualities, 19, 23-4, 27, 37, 63-4, 77-8, 147-9
   nocturnal planet, 202
Masha'allah, 23-4
McCartney, Paul, 101, 135-9
   birthchart of, 136
   delineation of his manners, 136-8

McGregor, Ewan, 97
Medici, Cosimo de, 33
melaina cholē. *See* black bile
melancholer, 2
melancholic, 2, 5, 9, 13, 17, 21, 24-5, 27, 31, 33, 36, 40, 42-3, 48-9, 52-4, 57-60, 63, 65, 68-71, 74, 83, 85, 88-9, 98, 100, 104, 106, 108-9, 114, 118, 122, 129-30, 132, 163-4. *See also* temperament, melancholic *and* humors, melancholic
melancholy, 13, 27, 32-3, 38-40, 42, 70, 74, 82, 86, 98, 104, 108, 111, 137, 151, 154, 157, 159
   in Aristotelian *Problems XXX, 1*, 13
Menuhin, Yehudi, 100
Mercury (planet), 20, 23-4, 28, 30, 33, 35-6, 39- 41, 62-3, 66, 68-70, 71n, 77-80, 87-9, 133-8, 142-3, 145-9, 152
   and elements, 28, 88
   and manners, 145
   and qualities, 19, 23, 28, 63, 66, 68-9, 77-8, 87-9
   and quality of soul, 141-3
   as co-significator of manners with Venus, 137
   ruling rational soul, 20, 23, 30, 133-4
   microcosm and macrocosm, 8, 35
Milken, Michael, 94
Minnelli, Liza, 103
Mitchell, Joni, 103
Montessori, Maria, 114
Montulmo, Antonius de, 29-31, 36, 58, 62, 65, 75, 79, 133-4, 139, 141, 148
   and *On the Judgment of Nativities*, 29
Monty Python's Flying Circus, 106
Moon
   and phlegmatic humor and/or temperament, 27, 69-70, 88, 156
   and qualities, 19, 25, 27, 37, 69, 77-8, 88, 147-9
   as component in temperament and/or quality of soul, 21, 36-7, 40, 43, 59, 65-7, 72, 74-6, 85-9, 133, 141-6
   nocturnal luminary, 31, 202
   ruling sensitive soul, 20, 30-1, 133, 137
   ruling the body, 20, 30-1, 133
Moon Phase
   as component of temperament, 36, 59, 66, 75, 80-3, 87-9, 135
Munch, Charles, 129
Myers, Isabel Briggs, 48

Myers-Briggs Type Indicator, 48, 56-7

N

Navratilova, Martina, 94
Nestis, 7
Newman, Paul, 129
Newton-John, Olivia, 129
Nijinski, Vaslav, 127
Norman, Jessye, 118
Nostradamus, 118

O

O'Hair, Madalyn Murray, 97
O'Brien, Conan, 120
oikodespotēs, 20, 84, 141. *See also* almuten
Olivier, Sir Laurence, 120
Olympiodorus, 14, 22, 81
Ono, Yoko, 137
Origan, 40

P

Palin, Michael, 103
Panofsky, Erwin, 13
Paracelsus, 35-6, 39
Parker-Bowles, Camilla, 114
Partridge, John, 42-3, 58, 64-5, 73, 75-6, 85, 127, 146
Paulus Alexandrinus, 22, 81
Pavarotti, Luciano, 94
Peale, Norman Vincent, 94
Peanuts (comic strip), 132
Peck, Gregory, 97
Pergamum, 14
Peron, Eva, 111
personality
    and manners, 84, 90, 133-4, 136
    as distinct from temperament, 1, 48, 71, 75
    definition of, 1
Peters, Bernadette, 118
Phaedrus (Platonic dialogue), 134
Phillips, Zara, 113
Phillipson, Garry, 74, 85-7, 106, 108
phlegm, 4, 8-9, 15-18, 24, 26-7, 76, 82, 88, 156, 159. *See also* humors
phlegma. See phlegm

phlegmatic, 1-2, 5, 9, 21, 24-5, 27, 36, 40-3, 48-9, 52-4, 59-60, 69-71, 74, 80, 83, 86, 88-9, 91, 101, 103, 109, 114, 116, 123, 127, 129-30, 132, 156, 159, 163-4. *See also* temperament, phlegmatic *and* humors, phlegmatic
phusis, 2, 5, 16
    definition of, 5
Picasso, Pablo, 106
Pinter, Harold, 100
planets
    correlated to temperament, 4
    phases (oriental and occidental), and temperament, 20, 37, 62-4, 67-8, 75-7, 87-9, 135, 137, 147-9
Plato, 7, 9-10, 14, 134
Plutarch, 6
pneuma
    as first principle, 6
Poitier, Sidney, 127
Pontanus, Jovianus, 39, 152
Poulenc, Francis, 103
Presley, Elvis, 127
Ptolemy, Claudius, 1, 9-10, 14, 18-23, 25, 29-30, 36, 40, 58-9, 62, 65-6, 73, 75-6, 79, 81-4, 133-4, 137, 139, 141, 147
    and quality of soul, 20, 133, 141
    and temperament, 19-20, 30, 133, 141
    Tetrabiblos, 19-20, 141
Pythagoras, 6-8

Q

qualities (hot, cold, wet, dry),
    Introduction, 1-23, 25-6, 28, 36-7, 40, 44, 47, 52, 59, 60, 62, 64, 69-71, 74-83, 85-8, 109, 133-4, 141, 143-4, 146
    active and passive, 10, 14
    and balance for health, 7, 18
    and moon phases, 19, 37, 81-2
    and planets, 19, 24, 27, 37, 147-9
    and seasons, 8, 18-19, 37
    and zodiac signs, 18, 24-7, 37
    Aristotelian view of, 3, 10-13
    correlated to Jungian functions, 47-8
    Galenic view of, 14
    general description of, 2
    Hippocrates' view of, 8

Lull's view of, 28-9
Manilius' view of, 21
Ptolemy's view of, 18-19
Quality of Soul, 20, 22, 29-30, 36, 133-4, 141-3

R

Ranzovius, 40
Redgrave, Vanessa, 108
Regiomontanus, 29
Rhazes, 32
Rhetorius, 23
Rilke, Rainer Maria, 120
Rodden, Lois, 50n, 95n, 103n, 120n, 125n, 129n
Rommel, Erwin, 100
Rudhyar, Dane, 77
Rumsfeld, Donald, 111
Ryan, Meg, 108

S

Saint-Exupéry, Antoine de, 104-6
    as example of choleric/melancholic temperament, 104, 106
    birthchart of, 105
Samhain
    as earth point, 3
sanguine, 2, 5, 9, 21, 24-5, 27, 31, 36, 40, 42-3, 48, 52-4, 57-60, 67-71, 74, 82-3, 85-9, 93, 95, 97-8, 109, 111, 113, 118, 122-3, 127, 132, 135, 137-8, 154, 159, 163-4. *See also* temperament, sanguine *and* humors, sanguine
sanguis. *See* blood
Sarandon, Susan, 100
Saturn (planet), 13, 19, 22-4, 27, 33-6, 39-40, 42, 62-4, 66n, 68-71n, 74, 76-9, 84, 88-9, 113, 130, 134, 146-9, 151-2, 154-5
    and humors, 24, 27, 88
    and melancholic temperament, 27, 33, 42, 70, 88, 151, 154-5
    and qualities, 19, 22-4, 27, 62-4, 77-8, 88-9, 147-9
    diurnal planet, 202
Saxl, Fritz, 13
Schmidt, Robert, 18n, 20n-22n, 81
Schoener, Johannes, 4, 29, 36, 39, 58, 63, 65, 75, 79, 84-5, 133-4, 139, 142, 148
Schopenhauer, Arthur, 130-1
    as example of phlegmatic/melancholic temperament, 130
    birthchart of, 131
seasons, 3-5, 8-9, 17-19, 22, 52, 79-80, 82, 88, 106, 139
    and stages of life, 9, 88
Sforza, Ludovico, 123
Shakespeare, William, Introduction, 37-8
Shankar, Ravi, 103
Shapar, Kristina, 29n, 154
Sharif, Omar, 97
Shatner, William, 120
Shepherd, Cybill, 125
Signoret, Simone, 122
Simmons, Gene, 106
Simmons, Richard, 97
Simon, Paul (singer), 98-100
    as example of melancholic temperament, 98, 100
    birthchart of, 99
Simpsons, The (cartoon show), 132
Sinatra, Frank Jr., 103
Sondheim, Stephen, 122
soul
    parts of the, 30, 39, 133, 141-2
    rational, 20, 30, 39, 133, 138, 141
    sensitive, 20, 30, 39, 133, 138, 141
    vegetative, 30-1, 39, 133, 142
Spears, Britney, 97
Springsteen, Bruce, 120
Stallone, Sylvester, 111
Starr, Ringo, 101, 114, 137
Steiner, Rudolf, Introduction, 44, 50-4, 56-7, 139, 163
    birthchart of, 50
Stewart, Martha, 94
Stoics, 13-14, 18, 47
Stojko, Elvis, 103
Streisand, Barbra, 94
Strindberg, August, 129
Sun
    and qualities, 19, 27, 66n, 77-80, 147-9
    as component of temperament, 43, 59, 65, 75, 79-80, 88, 143-4, 146
    correlated to seasons and qualities, 37, 80
    luminary of diurnal sect, 202

T

tastes
  of planets, 23
  of zodiac signs, 24, 26
temperament
  and *krasis*, 6, 13, 20
  and manners, 40-1, 133-8, 144-5
    example of, 135-8
  and stages of life, 53, 88
  and use in astrological practice, 18-22, 25-31, 34-7, 39-43, 73-90, 141-4, 146, 201
  choleric, 1-2, 5, 21, 36, 39-43, 49, 52-5, 67-71, 88, 91, 93, 155, 157, 159, 163-4
    descriptions of, 5, 41, 49, 52-3, 55, 91-4, 155, 157, 163-4
    in literature, 39, 159
    examples of, 67-8, 92-4
    notable cholerics, 94
  components of, 2, 5, 13, 16, 20, 28, 30-1, 37, 40, 43, 48-9, 51-3, 59, 65-7, 75-89, 141-4, 146, 201
  compound, 44, 60, 65, 69-71, 103-31
    choleric/melancholic, 42, 103-4, 160
      example, 104-6
      notable choleric/melancholics, 106
    choleric/phlegmatic, 42, 113-14, 162
      example, 114-16
      notable choleric/phlegmatics, 114
    choleric/sanguine, 108
      example, 109-11
      notable choleric/sanguines, 111
      in Culpeper, 42, 160-2
    melancholic/choleric, 42, 103, 106, 160
      example, 106-8
      notable melancholic/cholerics, 108
    melancholic/phlegmatic, 127, 129
      example, 128-9
      notable melancholic/phlegmatics, 129
    melancholic/sanguine, 42, 118, 120, 160-1
      example, 120-2
      notable melancholic/sanguines, 122
    phlegmatic/choleric, 42, 113, 116, 161-2
      example, 116-18
      notable phlegmatic/cholerics, 118
    phlegmatic/melancholic, 127, 129-30
      example, 130-1
      notable phlegmatic/melancholics, 130
    phlegmatic/sanguine, 42, 122, 125, 161
      example, 125-7
      notable phlegmatic/sanguines, 127
    sanguine/choleric, 108, 111
      example, 111-13
      notable sanguine/cholerics, 113
    sanguine/melancholic, 42, 118, 161
      example, 118-20
      notable sanguine/melancholics, 120
    sanguine/phlegmatic, 42, 122-3, 161
      example, 123-5
      notable sanguine/phlegmatics, 125
  definitions of, 1-2, 43, 51
  discussions of in Waldorf Study, 60-71
  melancholic, 2, 5, 21, 25, 31-3, 36, 38-43, 49, 52-5, 60, 65, 68-9, 88, 95, 97-8, 154, 157-9, 163-4
    descriptions of, 5, 41-3, 49, 53, 55, 97-8, 154, 157-8, 163-4
    examples of, 60-5, 68-9, 98-100
    in literature, 31, 38, 159
    notable melancholics, 100
  phlegmatic, 1-2, 5, 21, 25, 36, 40-3, 49, 52-5, 69, 88, 98, 100-3, 154, 157-9, 163-4
    descriptions of, 5, 41-3, 49, 53, 55, 100-1, 154, 157-8, 163-4
    examples of, 69, 101-3
    in literature, 31, 38, 159
    notable phlegmatics, 103
  sanguine, 2, 5, 21, 25, 31, 36, 40-2, 49, 52-5, 67-9, 88-9, 94-7, 154, 157, 159, 163-4
    descriptions of, 5, 41, 49, 53, 55, 94-5, 154, 157, 163-4
    examples of, 67-9, 95-7
    in literature, 31, 159
    notable sanguines, 97
  volatile (M.E. Jones), 49
Thales, 5-6, 21
Theophrastus, 7, 13
Theosophy, 51
Timaeus (historian), 7
Timaeus (Platonic dialogue), 9
Tobyn, Graeme, 41-2, 73n, 91n, 149, 158-9
Tomlin, Lily, 114

Townsend, Peter, 114
Transcendental Meditation, 103
Travolta, John, 130
Trump, Donald, 94
Turin, Shroud of, 125

U

Unani medicine system, 25

V

Valens, Vettius, 21-2
Venus (planet), 18-19, 23-5, 27, 33, 62-3, 66, 68, 70-1n, 77-80, 84, 87-9, 134-5, 137-9, 146-9, 156-7, 161
   and elements, 24, 26
   and humors, 24-6, 156
   and intrinsic quality, 66, 77-8, 87-9, 147-9
   and qualities, 19, 23, 25-7, 37
   as co-significator of manners with Mercury, 137
   nocturnal planet, 202
von Trapp, Maria, 125

W

Wagner, Richard, 91
Waldorf education, Introduction, 51, 56
Waldorf Study, The, 57-8, 60, 73-4, 80, 85-7, 89
Walters, Barbara, 120
Weaver, Sigourney, 129
Whitman, Walt, 111
Wilkinson, Roy, 56, 163
Williams, Venus, 97
Winnie the Pooh, 132
Wizard of Oz, The, 132

X

Xenophanes of Colophon, 6

Y

Yeats, William Butler, 120
yellow bile, 2, 4, 8, 15-16, 18, 24, 26, 55, 88. *See also* choler. *See also* humors

Z

Zeno of Citium, 14
Zeus, 7
Zeus (planet Jupiter), 18. *See also* Jupiter
Zoller, Robert, 27n, 80n

www.ingramcontent.com/pod-product-compliance
Lightning Source LLC
Chambersburg PA
CBHW081350230426
43667CB00017B/2781